SPIRITUAL AWAKENING

3 books in 1: Your complete guide to healing yourself through Chakras for Beginners, Third Eye for Beginners and Reiki for Beginners

EMILY ODDO

Contents

CHAKRAS FOR BEGINNERS

AWAKEN YOUR SPIRITUAL POWER BY BALANCING AND HEALING THE 7 CHAKRAS WITH SELF-HEALING TECHNIQUES

Introduction

WHAT ARE CHAKRAS?

What are chakras? This is a question that may have many different answers depending on who you ask. The word chakra comes from the Pali word *cakka* which means "wheel". As early as 2500 BCE, we have evidence of the wheel symbol used by the Indus Valley civilization to signify the sun, light, and knowledge. Traditionally, chakras have been an important part of three of the great ancient Indian religions, Hinduism, Buddhism, and Jainism. We may never know when the ancients first discovered the concept of chakras as energy centers, but we can trace their earliest mention back to medieval Hindu and Tantric Buddhist texts.

Buddhism

The eighth-century Buddhist texts, the Hevajra Tantra and the Caryagiti, both mention four centers of powerful inner energy stored in the core of the body. These are the first mentions we know of chakras as a center of power in the body. The words *cakka* (wheel), *pitha* (mound), and *padma* (lotus) are used interchangeably to describe these energy centers in the texts.

One of the core beliefs of Buddhism is the Dharmachakra. The Dharmachakra tells the story of Gautama Buddha's journey to enlightenment by preaching his message. Buddha supposedly set in motion the "wheel of dharma", and by doing so, he started bringing great change to the world.

The usage of a wheel metaphor and symbol stems from the Hindu myth of the *chakravartin* (wheel-turner). The chakravartin is the ideal king—a leader in possession of many great tools, including a wheel with which he can move his empire effortlessly in any direction. Although this is not exactly the chakra we know and want to learn about in this book, it's important to understand the origin of this ancient term.

The chakras in our bodies are powerful driving forces. With enough discipline and practice, we can use them to get closer to enlightenment. We can become our *own* chakravartin, driving ourselves toward success, happiness, and knowledge.

A wheel turning symbolizes the cycle of life in Buddhism. These constant cycles of birth and death, health and sickness, and suffering and happiness are defining features of Buddhist doctrine. Similarly, and possibly because of this symbolism, the chakras in our bodies are visualized as spinning wheels of energy.

Hinduism

In Tantric Hinduism, the *Kubjikamata* and *Kaulajnananirnaya* are the first texts we know of which include chakras as bodily energy sources. These texts, which were written between the first and fifth centuries CE, took the Buddhist concept of four chakras and built on it significantly, adding thousands of minor chakras and increasing the amount of primary chakras up to seven.

In the first millennium CE, following Hinduism's expansion of the chakra concept, Hindu scholars and religious leaders started to explore and document chakras more comprehensively. Over the coming centuries, a clear central belief was built around the energy points. According to Hinduism, human life exists in two parallel planes of existence: the physical (*sthula sarira*) and the emotional or psychological, which is also called the subtle (*sukshma sarira*).

The subtle is made up from energy that drives our emotions, intelligent thought, and conscious being. The physical, on the other hand, is made up from the physical body and world we inhabit. The physical and subtle influence and affect each other mutually. The subtle body can be described as paths of energy called *nadi*, which are connected to centers of power that are our chakras.

The Chakras and Their Properties

THE CHAKRAS

Root Chakra

The root chakra is also known as the Muladhara, which is Sanskrit for "root and basis of existence". This is the first of the seven chakras that we will be covering in this chapter. The root chakra is located at the base of the spine and the pelvic floor. Inactive Kundalini is said to be found residing in this chakra. Kundalini is power from the divine feminine, the mother goddess. This power resides inside each person. By unblocking and opening each chakra, this power will rise until it reaches our crown chakra. Once Kundalini has reached the crown chakra, we will experience enlightenment.

Think of this first chakra as the roots of a great tree. This tree grows tall and wide with plenty of fruit-laden branches. The Muladhara provides us with a solid base, an intimate connection to the earth and the ground around us, and the stability needed for us to grow. This chakra also has a strong connection to the things we need to ground ourselves. Our basic human needs of food, water, shelter, and feelings of love and safety are the most important grounding elements in our lives. Once these needs have been satisfied, we are much more likely to be content and comfortable. This chakra can also associate itself with the need to be fearless and face our worries.

The earth element is heavily associated with this chakra and also the color red, which symbolizes soil, rock, and clay, the building blocks of our world. This chakra is symbolized by a red lotus with four petals and a yellow square at its center. On each petal is a Sanskrit syllable which represents the four aspects of consciousness associated with this chakra. These syllables are vaṃ (joy), ṣaṃ (control), saṃ (concentration), and śaṃ (pleasure). The center syllable of this chakra is laṃ (Pride). The god Indra, deity of heaven, rain, and war, is most associated with this chakra. His western equivalents can be seen as Zeus, Jupiter, and Thor.

* * *

Sacral Chakra

The sacral chakra is also known as the Svadhisthana, Sanskrit for "where the self is established". It is the second of the seven chakras. We'll find this one at the base of the sexual organs. The sacral chakra is the source of sexual desire, and it is believed that this may be the hardest chakra to unblock for those wishing to raise their Kundalini through it. Think of this energy point as the lowest branches of the great tree. These branches take time to develop and are the first to bear fruit. This chakra takes much meditation and discipline to balance, but once it is done, the rewards are plentiful.

This second chakra provides us with our sexual energy, pleasure, sensuality, and sense of intimacy. The Svadhisthana is the first place our Kundalini will travel toward once awakened. This is the source of our love and fertility, two of the core aspects of the mother goddess. This chakra has a strong connection to many emotional aspects of our relationships with other people and is responsible for our ability to give and receive love, intimacy, and sexual energy. One who masters meditation on it can obtain mental clarity, a strengthened natural charisma, and increased confidence.

The element of water is representative of this chakra with its healing, flowing, and life-giving properties. The color associated with this chakra is orange, which symbolizes joy, activity, and energy. The Svadhisthana is naturally a chakra of great physical activity and vigor. Orange serves to visualize the energy of the sun and world around us, which helps to feed the energy in this chakra.

It is symbolized by a six-petaled orange lotus with a silver crescent moon sitting horizontally in the bottom-center. Each petal contains the Sanskrit syllables representing six aspects of consciousness that are related to this chakra and must be overcome. These syllables are baṃ (possessiveness), maṃ (destructiveness), bhaṃ (pitilessness), laṃ (suspicion), yaṃ (delusion), and raṃ (disdain). The center syllable of this chakra is vaṃ (joy).

Two gods are most associated with this chakra, including the creator of the universe Brahma and the god of knowledge Saraswati. Brahma can be likened to the Abrahamic monotheistic God, Yahweh or Allah. Brahma is viewed as the great creator and father, which explains his link to this chakra that is involved so heavily in reproduction. On the other hand, Saraswati is more closely related to Apollo the Greek and Roman god of music and knowledge. Along with being a center for sexual energy, this chakra is also a hub for creativity and personal knowledge. Saraswati represents the creative energy and inner knowledge one can release through meditation on the sacral chakra.

Solar Plexus Chakra

Our third chakra is the solar plexus, or Manipura, chakra. Manipura translates to "resplendent gem". This center of power is located just above the navel in the complicated network of nerves that makes up the solar plexus. The Manipura chakra is responsible for our dynamism, power of will, inner strength, and sense of achievement. This chakra is believed to be the source of all "prana" that we produce. Prana is the all-permeating essential lifeforce of the world that powers our body.

While the root chakra makes up the roots of a great tree and the sacral chakra makes up the fruit-bearing branches, the solar plexus chakra is the xylem or pith. The xylem in every tree are the soft core cells which are responsible for transporting nutrients around the tree and providing it with the energy needed to grow. This chakra is heavily associated with energy and forces of change. It is said to drive our metabolism and influence the powers of transformation that come naturally to us. It radiates into our other chakras as well and enhances the emotions connected to them.

An opened Manipura will enhance the love felt in the Anahata chakra above it, increase the sensuality felt in the Svadhisthana below it, and empower the strength down in the Muladhara chakra, among other things. In essence, it acts as the source of all positivity which drives the positive aspects of every chakra. By meditating on the Manipura, one positively improves all aspects of their being.

The Manipura chakra is most associated with the element of fire. This energetic and transformative element perfectly signifies the aspects most important to the Manipura. This chakra is visualized as a red downward triangle surrounded by a yellow circle, with ten darker-colored petals along its edges. Yellow is the color most associated with this chakra and the inner flame which it radiates throughout the body.

Contained within the petals are ten syllables that represent the ten aspects of this chakra which must be overcome in order to proceed. These syllables are phaṁ (sadness), ḍaṁ (narrowmindedness), naṁ (delusion), paṁ (foolishness), ḍhaṁ (greed), ṇaṁ (jealousy), taṁ (treachery), daṁ (fear), dhaṁ (disgust), and thaṁ (shame).

The two deities most associated with this chakra are Vishnu the god of protection and Lakshmi the god of prosperity. Vishnu is one of the three most powerful gods in Hinduism, alongside Brahma and Shiva. His primary role is that of a protector and god of change. Some similar gods to Vishnu from different regions are Tyr, the norse god of justice and protection, and Horus, the Egyptian god of the sky and protection. Lakshmi is one of the three most powerful female goddesses in Hinduism, along with Saraswati and Parvati. She represents wealth, beauty, and health and is considered the mother goddess of Hinduism. Her western equivalent could be seen as Hera, the queen of the greek pantheon.

* * *

Heart Chakra

The fourth chakra on our journey to enlightenment is the heart chakra, or Anahata. Anahata is Sanskrit for "unhurt, unstruck, and unbeaten". This name stems from the Vedic idea of Anahata Nad, which means the unstruck sound, or the sound which emanates from the celestial realm. Although called the heart chakra, the Anahata is actually in the center of our chest, just behind our heart. The heart chakra is responsible for our ability to make decisions of a higher nature.

Every chakra below the Anahata is bound by the rules of karma and fate. The bottom three chakras are dictated by earthly desires and emotions. On the other hand, the heart chakra is dictated by one's higher consciousness. With an open Anahata, we can make decisions on a spiritual level rather than at the level of a lower human. Just like with the heartwood of a tree which protects the plant from decay and rot, the heart chakra protects us from spiritual decay and falling victim to our base desires.

The heart chakra is most associated with love, compassion, balance, and inner peace. It is believed that this chakra acts as the middle ground between our spiritual and physical selves. It helps to integrate and accommodate for our base desires and our spiritual needs. Inner peace can be achieved once one opens the Anahata chakra and balances their desires and needs from both a spiritual and physical standpoint. This chakra acts as a mediator between our two aspects of self and allows us to follow our heart and make decisions for the betterment of our higher self.

The Anahata is closely linked to the element of air, and like the wind, the love from this chakra flows through and around everything it comes into contact with. This chakra is visualized as a lotus flower with twelve petals. In the center of this flower are two intersecting triangles that form a six-pointed star. This symbol represents the union of woman and man, as well as the union of body and spirit. The color of this chakra and its symbols is green. The reason that green is the color of this chakra is that it is the color most associated with safety, abundance, and health. These qualities are equally important for our physical and spiritual selves.

In the twelve petals around the edge of the lotus lay twelve syllables that are representative of the twelve divine qualities of the heart. These syllables include kam (bliss), kham (peace), gam (harmony), gham (love), ngam (understanding), cham (empathy), chham (clarity), jam (purity), jham (unity), nyam (compassion), tam (kindness), and tham (forgiveness). These twelve divine qualities have twelve counterparts that one must discard and overcome in order to fully open their Anahata. They are asha (desire), cinta (worry), cesta (struggle), mamta (possessiveness), dhamba (vanity), viveka (discrimination), vikalata (depression), ahamkara (pride), lolata (selfishness), kapatata (hypocrisy), vitarka (indecision), and anutapa (guilt).

Lastly, this chakra is heavily linked to the deity Vayu, the god of air and wind. Vayu is also seen as the god in control of breathing, therefore he is often considered the giver of life. His western counterpart is Amun, the Egyptian god of creation and wind.

* * *

Throat Chakra

The throat chakra is our fifth chakra and is also known as the Vishuddha chakra. The word Vishuddha translates to "especially pure". This name stems from the fact that the purity and openness of this energy point is incredibly important for all aspects of our life. This is the first of the three spiritual chakras, meaning that this chakra has more power over our spiritual forms than our physical forms. Although it is known as the throat chakra, it is actually based in the region of our larynx. The Vishuddha chakra is responsible for our ability to take words, thoughts, and ideas and turn them into reality. This chakra is the home of our creativity and the willpower needed to make thoughts a reality.

For example, someone with a blocked throat chakra may complain about their job all day but never have the willpower to make a change. Those who open their throat chakra have the ability to make the changes they want in life. Humans are unique in needing to open this chakra for themselves. If we observe plants and animals, we can see that they never think twice about doing what they believe is best for them. Trees always grow toward the light at the top of the canopy, and animals always do whatever they must to survive. Humans are the only creatures that need to work toward having that willpower to turn their desires into reality.

The throat chakra is most commonly associated with expression, creativity, our connection to other realms, purpose, and the ability to learn from mistakes. It is believed that this chakra is the source of our independence. Only we control our lives and this chakra, when open, affords us the knowledge, wisdom, and willpower to do that. In connection with the third eye chakra, this is where we discover our purpose in life. Just as the heart chakra before this allows us to follow our heart and make decisions for our higher self, this chakra gives us the tools and power to follow through with those decisions.

The Vishuddha chakra is most commonly associated with the elements of space and sound. Space provides us with the room to grow and expand on a psychological level, and sound is needed for us to speak our minds and hear new lessons. This chakra is visualized as a white lotus flower with sixteen violet petals. Violet and blue are the primary colors for this energy point. Within this lotus is a blue downward-facing triangle and within that triangle is a circle. Inside the lotus below the triangle is an upward-facing half-moon. The sixteen petals around the lotus contain syllables that represent the sixteen siddhis (powers) that one can attain through meditation. Included in these sixteen powers are abilities such as immunity to hunger and thirst, perfect balance and health, out-of-body experiences, and influencing others.

This chakra is linked to the deity Shiva, specifically his form of panchavaktra with five heads and four arms. An ancient Hindu story recalls how in a struggle between the gods and a great serpent, the world was put at risk by the poison the beast spewed from its fangs. Desperate to save the world, the gods gathered all the poison into a bowl, but they couldn't figure out how to dispose of it. Lord Shiva, ever gracious, decided that he would risk his life and drink the poison. He emptied the bowl, but instead of drinking the poison down his throat, he held it there in the Vishuddha chakra and purified it into water. In this way, he saved the world from certain destruction.

Shiva is a unique deity with many aspects that make it hard to compare him with deities from other pantheons. The closest comparison we may get is Osiris from the Egyptian pantheon; they both share very polarizing roles in being protectors and guardians of man while being very violent deities.

Third Eye Chakra

The third eye chakra is the sixth and second-last chakra that will feature in this chapter. This chakra is also known as Ajna which translates to "perception" and "command". This name comes from the fact that this chakra is believed to be the force which guides us in life. It houses our intuition and subconscious wisdom. As the name suggests, this chakra is based in the center of our brow just above our eyes. It is tradition for many Jain and Hindu worshippers to place a bright red bindi (colored dot) on their forehead to show their admiration for this chakra.

The Ajna chakra is responsible for our ability to connect to the spiritual side of the world. It is said that someone with an opened third eye chakra can receive messages from the past and future. Whether we know it or not, this energy point plays a major role in guiding us through our lives. Even those with a closed third eye will still occasionally receive messages of great importance; these are the gut feelings and unexplainable pulls towards decisions that we sometimes feel.

This chakra is most associated with knowledge, intuition, perception of our world and others, wisdom, inspiration, and spiritual leadership. It is not only responsible for guiding us in our times of need, but those with an opened third eye are capable of spiritually guiding others toward enlightenment. Once one opens their third eye, they gain the ability to act as a spiritual lightning rod. They will behave like a magnet for wisdom and premonition, being able to guide themselves and others through times of spiritual uncertainty. The Ajna also directly affects our ability to detect lies. Thus, those with an opened third eye are far more aware of the truths of the world around them.

The third eye chakra is closely linked to what is known as the "supreme element". This is simply every element together in their purest form. It represents the chakra's place outside of the physical world. This chakra is completely spiritual; it is pure and unsullied by earthly faults. The color of the Ajna chakra is purple, though the quality of this energy point is not defined by its color, but rather by the luminance of that color. Purple represents the color of moonlight, the moon being a symbol of purity and spirituality.

The Ajna chakra is visualized as a transparent or lightly-colored lotus flower with two white petals that are placed horizontally on the left and right of the flower. These petals are believed to represent the two nadis (channels of psychic power), Ida and Pingala, which travel along the two sides of the body and meet the central channel, Sushumna nadi, at the third eye.

Once these three channels meet at the third eye, they then travel up to the crown chakra. The letter "ham" is found on the left petal and represents the deity Shiva, while on the right petal we will find the letter "ksham" which represents Shakti. In the center of the lotus is a depiction of Shakti sitting cross-legged with six faces and six arms, holding a skull, book, drum, and rosary. With their two free hands, Shakti is making gestures of giving gifts and dispelling fears.

As we have already seen, the Ajna is heavily linked to the deities Shakti and Shiva. These two are often seen as two sides of the same whole. In the context of this chakra, Shiva symbolizes consciousness and the masculine side of our minds, whilst Shakti symbolizes the activation of power and the feminine side of our minds. Shakti and Shiva work hand in hand to provide us with the power and knowledge to enlighten ourselves.

Crown Chakra

The final chakra on our journey to enlightenment is the crown chakra, or Sahasrara. Sahasrara translates to "thousand-petalled", this name stems from the thousands of different aspects of consciousness which this chakra is responsible for. As the name suggests, this chakra is found in the crown of our heads. It is said to be the most subtle and detached chakra in our bodies, only ever being utilized by those who have dedicated themselves fully to the pursuit of enlightenment. It is said that all the other chakras emanate from this one chakra.

When one is able to raise their Kundalini up through all of the chakras and into Sahasrara, they achieve Nirvikalpa Samadhi. This is a state of bliss and higher consciousness in which we are unwavered by whatever happens in the physical world. Those with the crown chakra opened can invoke a state of higher spirituality—one in which they are able to sever their ties to the earthly world and spiritually travel to other realms, see the past and future, and convene with spirits.

The Sahasrara is often associated with consciousness, connection to the spiritual world, liberation from earthly bonds, spiritual bliss, and higher wisdom or divine knowledge. This chakra is our primary link to the universe outside of our plane of existence. This is our source of divine energy and the consciousness that makes us human. This chakra is a cork in our bottle; it holds us in our physical body, often for our own good. But those who master themselves and the world around them are given the strength to remove that cork and venture outside of the world they knew before.

The crown chakra has no element per se but is rather represented by the universe and the divine light that fueled creation. This chakra is completely detached from our world, and therefore no earthly element could represent it. This chakra's link to the divine light is because the Sahasrara is the center of our consciousness, and our consciousness is what makes us. The colors of this chakra are pure white and gold. White represents the purity of mind and spirit needed to reach here, as well as the purity of the spiritual world. Gold symbolizes the divine light of creation and the power of the Kundalini that has awakened us.

The Sahasrara chakra is visualized as a thousand-petalled lotus. These petals are arranged in 20 rows each with 50 petals. The petals of this flower are multicolored and surround the center like a rainbow. The center of the flower is golden and within it is a shining triangle. This triangle can be both upward- and downward-facing. The Sahasrara chakra has no specific connections to any diety. This chakra is more representative of our journey to divinity. If a human is able to unlock it, they reach apotheosis, a level of divinity and spiritual strength that is celestial in its power.

SYMPTOMS OF CHAKRA IMBALANCE

Root Chakra

The root chakra is our source of emotional strength and is representative of the colon, bladder, legs, feet, and lower back. When we have a blockage or imbalance in our root chakra, we can see a variety of physical issues manifest such as incontinence, constipation, joint inflammation, gout, lower back pain, and stomach pain.

Because of the root chakra's importance in maintaining our emotional strength and mental wellbeing, it is crucial that we put time into making sure it is clear for our own mental health. Some mental symptoms of a blocked root chakra are anxiety related to basic needs, insecurity about money, feelings of being unsafe, abandonment anxiety, and codependency.

Sacral Chakra

The sacral chakra is our source of love and pleasure and is representative of our reproductive organs, kidneys, and bladder. An imbalance in our sacral chakra can bring about many physical issues such as urinary / kidney infections, menstrual problems, gynecological cysts, impotence, infertility, and premature ejaculation.

The sacral chakra plays one of the most important roles for us in regards to mental health. Our ability to interact with people in meaningful ways and show love are reliant on the balance of this chakra. Therefore, blockage of it can lead to conditions like depression, insecurity, and jealousy. It can also result in self-esteem issues and self-isolation.

Solar Plexus Chakra

The solar plexus chakra is our source of energy and dynamism and represents our stomach, metabolism, and digestive system. An imbalance in it can cause a whole plethora of physical and psychological issues. Some of the physical issues that can indicate a blocked solar plexus chakra are stomach pains, indigestion, constipation, stomach ulcers, hypoglycemia, pre-diabetes, and weight gain.

The solar plexus is often seen as the source of our drive and inner strength. Because of this, a blocked solar plexus can lead to mental conditions and issues such as feelings of powerlessness, depression, low self-esteem, and lack of motivation. On the other hand, an overactive solar plexus chakra can lead to things like egomania, manic behavior, and hyperactivity.

Heart Chakra

The heart chakra is responsible for our love and connection to our spiritual side, and it also represents our heart and vascular system. An imbalance in this chakra can bring about plenty of emotional and relationship issues, as well as some physical discomforts. Some of the physical issues that can indicate an imbalanced heart chakra are upper back and shoulder pain, chest pain, heartburn, and high cholesterol.

The heart chakra is our source of love and is crucial to our relationships, and due to this, a blockage can be devastating to our personal lives. A blocked heart chakra can lead to plenty of emotional issues such as anxiety, fear of abandonment, feelings of loneliness, detachment, and irritability.

Throat Chakra

The throat chakra is responsible for our ability to communicate with others and make our thoughts a reality. An imbalance in it can bring about various physical and emotional symptoms due to the importance of this chakra in motivating us to be active and creative. Some of the physical symptoms of an imbalanced throat chakra are a sore throat, persistent coughing, vocal cord issues, thyroid dysfunctions, neck stiffness, jaw pain, and mouth ulcers.

The throat chakra is crucial to our personal and professional lives. It not only represents our ability to communicate, but our motivation to do things in life. Some symptoms of throat chakra imbalance are feelings of introversion, emotional instability, insecurity, and lack of motivation.

Third Eye Chakra

The third eye chakra is the driving force behind wisdom and intuition. Because of the important role it plays in our head, many of the issues caused by its imbalance are based around the brain. Some of the physical problems that may be caused by a blocked third eye chakra are as follows: headaches (particularly around the frontal lobe), ear infections, eye infections, inflammation around the eyes, and dizziness.

The third eye chakra has a key role in our mental wellbeing. This chakra plays a large part in our ability to problem-solve, learn, and interpret the world around us. Some psychological symptoms of an imbalance in this chakra are mental fog, difficulty in decision-making, inability to focus, over-analyzation, confusion, and lack of willpower.

Crown Chakra

Lastly is the crown chakra. It is the source of our spirituality and divine energy. Although this chakra is completely detached from our body, it can still have an effect on some areas of our brain, particularly the pineal gland and parietal lobe. Some of the physical issues that may be brought upon by an imbalance of this chakra are insomnia, lethargy, migraines, and mental fog.

The crown chakra is linked to our pineal gland, which controls our sleep cycles and states of consciousness. This means that imbalance in this area can cause sleep deficiencies which can lead to psychological issues and changes in one's personality if not dealt with. Some of these psychological issues may be cynicism, agitation, feelings of vulnerability, fear, and misanthropy.

WHAT CAUSES CHAKRA IMBALANCE?

In this section we're going to cover what the main causes of imbalance are for the seven major chakras. Some of them are simple to fix and others are more difficult, but all can be overcome with enough determination, meditation, and meaningful introspection.

Root Chakra

An imbalance or blockage of the root chakra can be brought upon by many things related to fear, trauma, laziness, and unhealthy eating. Fear and trauma are the two most common causes of a blocked root chakra. These tend to be deep-seeded issues that may take many sessions of meditation and introspection to overcome. Especially in cases of trauma, you may need the assistance of a professional psychologist. In the case of laziness, this can cause a chakra imbalance because of our root chakra's relation to Kundalini and the search for self-improvement. Lastly, unhealthy eating can also be a cause of chakra imbalance because of the root chakra's close association to the stomach. A bad diet or eating disorders can cause a blocked Muladhara chakra by interfering with the health of one's stomach and gut.

* * *

Sacral Chakra

The sacral chakra is one of the most commonly blocked or imbalanced chakras in today's high-stress, low-empathy world. Its blockage is often brought about by overindulgence in sexual desires, repression of sexual desires, codependence on a person or substance for pleasure, and emotional conflict. Both the overindulgence and lack of indulgence in sexual desires can cause a blockage of this chakra, because as with most things, we need to find balance. One should feel comfortable in their sexual freedom while still maintaining control over their instinctual desires.

Codependency is another major cause of blockage for this chakra. The sacral chakra is not only about loving others but also plays a big role in self-love. We should not need to rely on others to feel loved; rather, love should come from within primarily.

Lastly, emotional conflict can cause imbalance of this chakra. The sacral chakra is key in influencing our relationships with others, so emotional conflicts, especially ones with people we love, may impact the balance of this chakra.

* * *

Solar Plexus Chakra

The Manipura is one of the most important chakras for us to cultivate and work on. Without a balanced solar plexus, it may feel like we put in a lot more than we get out of life. Blockage of this chakra can be brought about by many factors, but mainly bad habits are to blame for imbalance here. As we've already mentioned, this chakra is our source of inner power and motivation; if we don't put that power to use, we could see an imbalance occur.

Idleness and indecisiveness are two of the primary causes of solar plexus chakra imbalance. An overflow of the power in this chakra can lead to either a blockage, which causes us to spiral further into inactivity, or an overload, which can cause us to become manic or hyperactive. Past trauma can also have a hand in causing imbalance in this chakra, and being spoiled and doted over as a child can lead to a shortage of willpower later in life. Conversely, early life neglect and oppression can lead to a restless spirit unable to focus itself on tasks. Either way, expert help may be needed to find closure and balance this chakra.

Heart Chakra

The Anahata chakra is definitely one that we want to put plenty of time and effort into keeping balanced. For all of our personal relationships to stay strong and well, we need to focus on maintaining its health. A blockage or imbalance of this chakra can be brought upon by many things, but it's usually caused by emotional trauma of some sort. Heartbreak and betrayal are the two most common forms of emotional trauma that affect it. These are things we must learn to come to terms with and move on from in order to restore balance.

A blockage can also occur in this chakra if we fail to share our love with others. Share love with our friends and family, commit acts of kindness toward strangers, and contribute to charities. By sharing our love with others, we allow for a healthy flow of energy in and out of our heart chakra.

Throat Chakra

The throat chakra is deceptively difficult to keep balanced. It requires us to be honest and authentic with everything we say and do in life. In today's world, white lies often seem like the lesser evil in social and professional matters. If we continue with this philosophy, we may find ourselves with a horribly imbalanced throat chakra. An imbalance of this chakra if most frequently caused by not living authentically and hiding our true selves from the world. It is responsible for much of our expression and social skills. If we withhold our true selves from the world, we stop this chakra from being able to fulfill its purpose.

A blockage of the throat chakra is also frequently caused by creative frustration. Failed previous attempts at expression can lead to negative thoughts which make us insecure and afraid to express ourselves further. One of the key methods for keeping this chakra in a balanced state is simply through consistently expressing one's personality and creative side.

Third Eye Chakra

Our third eye chakra is the source of much of our mental power and knowledge. When it suffers a blockage, it's usually due to a failure to exercise or an overuse of our intelligence. Both of these stem from the same basic cause of confusion and lack of clarity on our goals and desires. The third eye chakra needs constant stimulation, so we should never stop learning and training our minds. Enlightenment comes from wisdom and knowledge. But as with all things, we need balance. If we overwork our brains by overanalyzing simple thoughts and overwhelming ourselves with too much information all at once, we can also bring about a blockage.

Another potential blockage of the third eye chakra can come from not listening to our inner wisdom or "sixth sense". If we ignore the subtle signals that this chakra sends us, it may start to lose balance and potentially become blocked.

* * *

Crown Chakra

Finally, we have the crown chakra. This is a tough one to diagnose as it has few clear physical or psychological aspects. The crown chakra is the source of all chakras and, therefore, is directly affected when one of them falls into imbalance. Fear of death is one of the few psychological aspects of this chakra; whilst other energy points deal with fear as an emotion, the crown chakra deals specifically with our instinctual fear of death and our anxiety as to what lies beyond death. This form of existential fear and spiritual uncertainty can cause imbalance in the crown chakra.

Along with that, past traumas can also play a big role in unbalancing this chakra. Sudden losses of consciousness such as those caused by near death experiences and serious accidents can cause premature spiritual experiences in those who are not ready. This can cause the mind to actively avoid such occurrences in the future.

Benefits of Chakra Healing

WHAT IS CHAKRA HEALING?

Chakra healing, or chakra balancing, is simply the process of making sure your chakras are functioning in ways that benefit you. There are many different stages of chakra health that one can reach. Some people put years of their lives into perfecting the health of chakras and opening them to their fullest. Most are content with having them in a balanced and healthy condition.

For those of us trying to balance our chakras in our day-to-day lives, we have a whole plethora of options available to us. From this point onward in the book, we will cover all the various conventional techniques for healing and balancing our chakras. Some require expert help, like reiki and massage, while others can be comfortably done every day regardless of work or studies.

But, before we get into the techniques needed to heal our chakras, let's go over the reasons you want your chakras to be healed. It's all fair and well saying it's good for you, but it's understandable if you want some more details. Thus, below you will find details about the physical and mental benefits of healing and balancing each of the chakras.

THE BENEFITS OF HEALING YOUR CHAKRAS

Root Chakra

Healing the root chakra is the first step we should take toward attempting to heal and balance all of our chakras. As we have already established previously, this chakra is responsible for much of the lower body, and it's psychologically linked to our basic needs as humans. Healing it can be a fantastic quality of life improvement for anyone considering its important role in our day to day lives. By healing and balancing this chakra, we bring about feelings of comfort, security, and a general feeling of being at ease with the world around us.

Healing this chakra can also help to prevent various physical ailments such as constipation, joint pain, arthritis, stomach issues, and back pain. These physical ailments are easily treated and reduced by many of the healing techniques we will cover later in this book like meditation, massage, and healthy eating.

* * *

Sacral Chakra

As has already been mentioned, the sacral chakra is our source of love and pleasure. It helps us enjoy life and interact with other people in meaningful ways. The sacral chakra is heavily linked to our reproductive organs, our emotions concerning love and relationships, and our extraversion. Keeping this chakra balanced and healthy is crucial to maintaining a happy love life and an active social life. By healing it, we can ensure feelings of self-confidence, self-love, extraversion, and satisfaction.

We can help prevent or improve a multitude of physical conditions by healing this chakra. Some of the conditions we can easily help treat are impotence, premature ejaculation, gynecological cysts, and pelvic discomfort. All of these phys-ical ailments can be treated by meditation, yoga, healthy eating, and massage.

Solar Plexus Chakra

When healing our chakras, we can never overlook the solar plexus. This chakra is so crucial to our general health and wellbeing that it should be a priority to keep it balanced at all times. Those of us who are hard-working professionals espe-cially rely on this chakra as our energy source and the driving force behind our metabolism. Have you ever had one of *those* weeks? You know, the ones when you wake up every morning and feel completely exhausted and barely have the energy to make it to lunchtime. That is probably the result of an unbalanced solar plexus.

Having a balanced solar plexus can make a massive difference to our daily lives by giving us plenty of energy and feelings of power, optimism, and motivation. We can also alleviate a load of different physical problems by balancing this chakra. Issues like stomach ulcers, indigestion, high and low blood sugar, and other digestion-based ailments can easily be treated with healthy eating, aromatherapy, and yoga, among other things.

Heart Chakra

Just like the solar plexus, the Anahata chakra is incredibly important and should be a definite focus for anyone looking to balance their chakras. Physically, it influences the health of our heart and circulatory system. Psychologically, this chakra is the source of our ability to feel and show love. Therefore, balancing it is crucial for our general health of both body and mind. I'm sure most of us have felt the heartbreak of a relationship ending. Well, that feeling can be reduced or even fully negated with a balanced heart chakra. By balancing it, we can improve our abilities to forgive, move on, and love again.

There are many physical ailments that a balanced heart chakra can help to treat and improve. Conditions like heartburn, high blood pressure, high cholesterol, poor circulation, heart palpitations, and shoulder/upper back pain.

Throat Chakra

Everyone has an artistic side. Some of us love to sing, others love to paint, and some play instruments. Whatever our chosen art is, we rely on this chakra to do it. The throat chakra is the source of our creativity and communication skills, so keeping it balanced is key for those of us who consider ourselves artists or just like to express ourselves freely. The positioning of this chakra is also important for our physical health and comfort. Our throat, lungs, and mouth all fall under it, and these regions are key areas to keep healthy. By balancing this chakra, we can improve our creativity, problem-solving skills, and our ability to communicate and persuade others.

There are a number of physical ailments that we may be able to help too. Conditions such as chest colds, mouth ulcers, thyroid issues, laryngitis, and jaw pain can all be helped by balancing this chakra.

* * *

Third Eye Chakra

If we've ever had one of those weeks where our luck just seems to be terrible, every gut decision we make backfires, or we feel like our judgment is wrong in everything, we probably have a blocked or unbalanced third eye chakra. As we've already covered, this chakra is our center of wisdom and knowledge. For all of us who are working and studying daily, it can be the difference between success and failure. This chakra doesn't have many effects on the physical body, but the negative ones that an imbalanced third eye can have are very painful and distracting.

Having a balanced third eye chakra can massively help with treating insomnia, nightmares, sleep-walking, and even mild depression. When it comes to physical issues, an imbalanced third eye chakra can be responsible for headaches, blocked sinuses, dizziness, exhaustion, and tired eyes. By balancing it, we can effectively lessen the impact of, or altogether treat, these illnesses.

Crown Chakra

Last of all comes the crown chakra. This is a difficult one to balance, but the benefits far outweigh the costs once you do. This chakra is inherently a purely psychological one. Its physical effects are few and are mainly felt through neurological disorders. By balancing it, not only are we helping to prevent all the symptoms of an unbalanced crown chakra, but we are helping to balance our whole being.

All the energy that every chakra needs to function comes from the crown chakra, thus a healthy crown chakra means a healthy flow of energy everywhere else. Balancing it results in having more clarity when choosing our direction in life, a better ability to stick to goals and targets, and a stronger connection to our spiritual side. On top of that, the neurological issues that we can avoid by working on this chakra include pineal gland disorders, migraines, depression, anxiety, and memory loss.

Meditation and Chakra Healing Techniques

YOGA AND EXERCISE

Undoubtedly one of the best ways to balance and heal our chakras is through exercise and yoga. For thousands of years, Hindu, Buddhist, and Jain teachers have been stressing the importance of activity in opening one's chakras. This is especially true for our primarily physical chakras like the root, sacral, solar plexus, and heart chakras. These and the areas of the body around them need to be exercised.

The three big Indian religions all extensively teach about the holiness and sanctity of hard work and self-improvement. Although each chakra represents a different region of our physical form, our spirit as a whole benefits from self-care and a healthy body.

Root Chakra

The Muladhara chakra is balanced and healed through exercises and yoga that concern the lower body. In particular, exercises that strengthen the calf, quads, hamstrings, and glutes are fantastic for strengthening our grounding and improving our health. In terms of yoga poses, the root chakra has a few very useful ones that not only help channel spiritual energy up our spine, but help improve the blood flow and strength of muscles in the lower body.

The Ashwini mudra is one of the best known techniques for channeling Kundalini up the spine into the sacral chakra. In this yogic exercise, we want to seat ourselves comfortably on the floor, ideally in a lotus pose or easy pose. Once in position, we should take a few deep breaths, centering ourselves and controlling our breathing. Once we feel at peace we take another deep breath, hold it, contract the pelvic floor muscles, then relax them, and exhale. We should do up to five contractions, then take a break for a few breaths.

The Mahamudra is a common beginner pose that focuses on the root chakra. To do it, we want to start by sitting on the floor. One leg should be straight in front of us, the other is bent so that our foot is tucked under our buttocks. Take in a deep breath, and bend forward, exhaling. Grab hold of the foot of your straight leg with both hands. Lift your head and look forward. Hold this position for a few minutes, breathing normally, then switch legs.

Lastly comes the Manduki mudra (Bhadrasana). This is a slightly more difficult pose meant for intermediate and experienced yoga practitioners. Our starting position is Vajrasana, a kneeling pose in which our heels are tucked under our buttocks. Next we spread our legs slightly and, exhaling, we bend forward and place our hands on the floor in front of us. Make sure the fingers point outward. Remain in the position and breath normally for a few minutes.

Sacral Chakra

The Svadhisthana chakra can be balanced and healed through exercises and yoga that focus on the pelvic, lower back, and lower abdominal areas. In particular, this includes exercises like kegels, bridges, crunches, and leg raises. In regards to yoga poses, the sacral chakra has a multitude of useful positions that both raise the spiritual strength of the chakra and help to increase blood flow and muscle health in the area.

The cobra pose, or Bhujangasana, is one yoga position that is very popular among yogis trying to balance their sacral chakra. One must start by laying on the ground on their abdomen. We then inhale and lift our upper half to a near-vertical position, pivoting on the Svadhisthana chakra. Once we are in the cobra pose, we exhale and hold the position for as long as comfortable. We then end the pose by exhaling as we slowly lower ourselves to the starting position. Repeat this pose up to three times before taking a break.

The bridge pose, or Setuasana, is another very popular pose for this chakra. This pose is fantastic for relieving lower back pain and building strength in that muscle area. We start by sitting upright with legs straight in front of us. We concentrate on the sacral chakra and place our hands on the floor behind our body with fingers pointing backward. Then, while inhaling, we lift our upper body and pelvic area. Our hands should support our weight. Relax the neck and let the head hang back. Breathe normally and remain in this position as long as possible before exhaling and slowly returning to the starting position.

The Yoga Mudra is a mudra focused on helping increase the flow of energy into the sacral chakra and promoting the movement of Kundalini. This mudra starts in the Vajrasana position, kneeling with your feet tucked under your buttocks and your hands on your lap. Relax the whole body and close the eyes. Then, take in a deep breath and raise your arms above your head. Now exhale and keep the back straight as you slowly bend forward until your forehead touches the floor. Rest your arms beside your body with the palms facing upward. Relax in this position and breath normally for as long as you wish. Then inhale and bring the body back upright with arms raised. Lastly, exhale and return to the starting position.

Solar Plexus Chakra

The solar plexus, or Manipura, can be healed and empowered through various yoga poses and exercises that focus on the abdominal muscles and the back. In regards to exercises, there are quite a few easy-to-do and very effective exercises for this chakra. Some of those exercises include sit-ups, planking, back extensions, leg raises, and cat curls. When it comes to yoga poses, the solar plexus has a bunch of incredibly effective poses that help to stimulate your central organs, strengthen your core, and assist the channeling of vital life force energy around your body.

The full boat pose, or Paripurna Navasana, is a favorite among yogis looking to empower their core muscles and strengthen their focus. To achieve this pose, you must start in an upright, seated position with your legs straight and arms at your side. This position is known as the staff pose. You engage the muscles along your core and spine to keep your posture completely erect. You then move your shoulder blades up and back and push out your chest. Your upper body and lower body should now form a 90-degree angle at your hips.

Now you tilt your back slightly and take your weight onto your sitting bones, keeping your back engaged so you don't hunch. Next, raise your legs, regaining the 90-degree angle you had. Lastly, raise your arms and keep them parallel with the floor, forming a bridge between your torso and legs. Hold this position for as long as possible, and then repeat the instructions in reverse, coming back to your seated position.

The firefly pose, or Tittibhasana, is an intermediate-to-advanced yoga pose which focuses on improving balance, core strength, and arm strength. In order to perform this pose, you must start in a low squat with your feet shoulder-distance apart and your pelvis at knee-height. Next take your left hand and place it on the floor next to your left foot, fingers pointing forward. Do the same for your right-hand side. Very slowly, rock back and feel your center of gravity tilt. Your hands should now be taking most of the weight of our body. Inhale as you lift your legs off the floor and take all of your weight onto your hands. Your pelvis should be high so that your legs are parallel to the floor at this point. Without tensing your neck, look forward and breathe slowly for 15 seconds or longer if possible. Finally, with an exhale, you can lower your legs to the floor and rest.

Lastly, we have the Bharadvaja's twist, or Bharadvajasana. This is a relatively simple, seated yoga pose that helps to activate energy flow up the spine, strengthen the back, and encourage better posture. The first step of this pose starts with the same seated position as the Paripurna Navasana, with the legs straight and torso upright. Imagine a central axis running along your spine, from your pelvic floor to your crown. Your back should at all times be as straight as possible; this axis should never bend or curve.

Keeping this in mind, shift your weight onto your right hip, and swing your legs to the left. Your left leg should rest under your left buttock. Your right leg should be resting on your left thigh. Recenter your balance back onto both hips. Now, you must twist your body, using the abdominal muscles, to the right. Lastly, place your right hand onto your left knee, and wrap your left arm around your back. Hold this position for up to 10 breaths, and then release back into the original seated position. Repeat this, mirroring your actions on the other side.

Heart Chakra

The heart chakra is actually one of the easier chakras to balance and strengthen through exercise and yoga. It focuses on the chest, heart, circulatory system, and blood. Exercises for this chakra are pretty straightforward. The cardiovascular system is greatly benefited by cardio like running, cycling, rowing, and swimming. Along with that, you can strengthen the muscles of the chest through push-ups, bench presses, and butterfly chest presses. When it comes to yoga, there are plenty of poses that focus on building stamina, aiding blood flow, lowering blood pressure, and helping the flow of energy out of the heart chakra.

The first heart chakra pose we will explore is the cow face pose, or Gomukhasana. In order to achieve this, you must start in the staff position with your legs straight ahead of you and torso upright. Continuing, you need to bend your knees and place your feet onto the ground. Then slide your left foot under your right knee, and cross over your right knee to the left. You want your two knees to be stacked on top of each other with your feet next to your hips. Once your legs are in position, rest evenly on your sitting bones. Next, take your right arm and reach it straight out to your right, parallel to the floor. Turn the arm inwardly, first with your thumb pointing to the floor, then again with your thumb pointing behind you with the palm toward the ceiling. While exhaling, swing the arm behind and into the hollow of your back.

With your arm parallel to your waist, roll your shoulder back and work your forearm up until it is in line with your spine. The back of your hand should now be resting between our shoulder blades. Next, take your left arm and stretch it out toward the wall in front of you, palm-side up. Continue this movement by lifting this arm up to the ceiling, and in one fluid movement, bend at the elbow and reach down behind you to meet the other hand. Attempt to interlock the fingers of both hands and hold that position for a minute, maintaining normal breathing. Repeat the process on the opposite side.

The second yoga pose that we will look at is the eagle pose, or Garudasana. To start, stand upright with arms at your side; this is called Tadasana, or mountain pose. Continue by bending your knees slightly and lifting your left foot up. Cross your left leg over your right and hook your left foot behind your lower right calf. Your next move is to raise your arms up parallel to the floor. Turn them palm-side up and cross them over at the elbow.

Continuing this movement, bend your arms at the elbow and rest your left arm in the crook of your right elbow. The backs of your hands should be facing each other now, and your fingers should be pointing at the ceiling. Lastly, you want to twist your right hand to the right and left hand to the left; this should cause your palms to both face each other. Hold this position for up to 30 seconds, unwind, and repeat for the opposite side.

Our last heart chakra pose is the camel pose, or Ustrasana. You begin this pose by kneeling on the floor. Your thighs and torso should be vertical. Keeping your knees hip-distance apart, you want to press the top of your feet down onto the floor and straighten your ankles. Next bring your palms together in front of your chest and drop your chin down into the chest. Take a deep breath, and push your palms out so that they face in front of you. With the following exhalation, move your hands around your body and down to your heels. Then press upward with the spine, and puff out your chest as far as you can before relaxing your neck and letting your head hang back. Hold this position for 10 breaths, and then return to the kneeling pose.

Throat Chakra

The throat chakra is the first of the three spiritual chakras. This is the point where physical exercise becomes less important; spiritual exercise is more instrumental in developing this chakra. There are plenty of yoga poses that are still very effective at helping to develop, heal, and open up this chakra despite its ethereal nature. In regards to physical exercise, you can still rely on neck, shoulder and upper back exercises to help activate and balance it. Exercises like neck rotations, shoulder rolls, chair rotations, thoracic extensions, and dumbbell rows are all fantastic for building strength and flexibility in the region of the throat chakra. For yoga, there are plenty of poses that focus around stretching and loosening up the throat and neck, as well as help with the expression of energy from the throat chakra.

The first pose we are looking at is the fish pose, or Matsyasana. This is a very simple, yet effective pose for opening up the throat chakra. You start with your back to the floor, knees bent and feet planted flat on the ground. Pressing down with your feet, lift your hips off the ground. You can then proceed to place your hands on the floor with your palms down, and then slide your hands under your hips.

At this point, your buttocks should be resting on your hands. Then, with one foot at a time, you lower and straighten your legs. You should try to stretch your big toes and flatten your feet as far as possible. Going back to your torso, you should now puff out your chest and engage your spine. Be sure to engage only the spine and not the neck.

Your neck and head should be relaxed and hanging. Hold this pose for 10 breaths, and then return to your starting position.

Our next throat chakra pose is the supported shoulderstand, or Salamba Sarvangasana. This is an intermediate pose that is especially good at unblocking and activating the throat chakra. To start, you need two or more yoga mats or thick blankets folded into one by two foot rectangles. Stack these rectangles on top of each other, and then lie on them. Be sure that when you lie on these mats, your shoulders are on the mat but your head is on the floor.

Once comfortable, you can lay your arms beside your torso, bend your knees up, and lay your feet flat onto the floor. Exhaling, try to press your feet and arms into the floor, lifting your body up. Continue to slowly lift yourself up, pushing the pelvis away from the floor and using your arms to support you by bringing them out to your sides and in line with your shoulders. Moving your arms further, you should bend your elbows, rest your upper arms on the mat, and bring your hands up to your back.

Now, raise your pelvis over your shoulders so that your torso is nearly perpendicular to the floor. Next, you can inhale and lift your legs up toward the ceiling, starting with your bent knees, then extending further to include your whole legs. Finally, relax the neck and throat, tense the shoulders, and push the chin outward. Your forehead should be parallel to the floor, and your shoulders should be holding a majority of your weight. Start by holding this pose for only 30 seconds, and gradually add more time as it becomes easier and more comfortable.

Lastly is the child's pose, or Balasana. The first step is to kneel on the floor and spread your knees hip-width apart. You will then exhale and lay your torso down onto your thighs, arch your back slightly so that there is no pressure on your spine, and extend your neck out, bringing your forehead parallel to the floor. Continue by laying your hands on the floor, palmside down, out in front of your body. Your shoulders should be relaxed and your arms should hang to the floor. Hold this pose for a few minutes while maintaining normal breathing.

Third Eye Chakra

The third eye chakra is a primarily mental chakra. As such, normal physical exercises won't do too much to help heal or strengthen this chakra. However, mental exercises are incredibly effective in keeping the mind healthy and helping this chakra to open up. Doing a few daily exercises such as a jigsaw puzzle, crossword, sudoku, practicing an instrument, learning a language, or doing a memory training exercise can all provide massive benefits toward healing and strengthening this chakra. In regards to yoga poses, we are mainly going to be focusing on resting poses, which encourage relaxation and better blood flow to the brain.

First off is the downward-facing dog pose, or Adho Mukha Svanasana. This is one of the most well-known poses in the practice of yoga. The position we will take up here is perfect for increasing blood and energy flow to the brain. Starting off, you position yourself on your hands and knees. You need your wrists to be in line with your shoulders and your knees to be in line with your hips. In one swift movement, tense your legs, curl your toes under your feet, and lift your legs and hips up into a straightened position. You should try to engage your quads and avoid locking your knees.

Next, you can extend your arms and lift your torso up with your quads carrying most of your weight. Again, make sure not to lock your elbows. Hold this position for 10 breaths or as long as you are comfortable. Once done, you can exhale and bend your knees to release the pose and come back down into your starting position.

The next pose is the hero pose, or Virasana. This one is a simple seated resting pose that is often used as an alternative to the lotus pose. Although this is one of the least physically intensive poses in yoga, it is an incredibly powerful position for meditation. You will start by positioning yourself on your knees. Your thighs should be perpendicular to the floor, and your knees should be touching. Following that, you will slide your feet apart slightly past your hips, and angle your big toes slightly inward.

Next, exhale and sit down between your feet. If your buttocks is not resting on the floor, feel free to use a book or folded mat to support it. Next you will proceed to lay your hands palm-side down on your kneecaps, firm your shoulders, and puff out your chest. Be sure to keep good back posture. Maintain this pose with normal breathing for as long as comfortable. Also, feel free to try meditating in this pose once comfortable.

Our last third eye chakra pose is the big toe pose, or Padangusthasana. This position is incredibly effective at directing energy down the spine and into the third eye. In order to achieve this pose, you must start in a standing position. Your feet must be roughly six inches apart, and your legs should be completely straight without locked knees. Proceed to bend over, bending the knees slightly if needed, and hook your index and middle fingers into the space between your big and second toes. Next, with a deep breath in, you will lift our upper body as if you were going to stand again, straightening your arms. As you exhale, you will flex and release your glutes while relaxing your lower back.

Following that, you should push out your chest and straighten your neck, taking care to not compress your neck and put pressure on it. Take another few deep breaths, and with each inhale, you should try to lift your torso, flex your quads, and flex your glutes. Finally, stretch forward into a comfortable bend, and hold the position for one minute, breathing normally. Afterwards, you can release your toes, bring your hands to your hips, and in one motion, swing your torso and head back up in a controlled manner.

Crown Chakra

The crown chakra is a completely spiritual chakra, and for this reason, no exercises of a mental or physical nature are going to affect it directly. The only way for us to heal and strengthen this chakra is through spiritual exercises, such as meditation, fasting, abstinence, crystal healing, and aligning all of the other chakras.

Our first crown chakra position is the plow pose, or Halasana. This is a relatively difficult position but works wonders for healing and empowering the crown chakra. The plow pose is an extension of the supported shoulderstand, which is the starting point. Once in the supported shoulderstand position, you exhale and bend forward from the hips, bringing your legs above and over your head. You should try to keep your torso as vertical as possible and ensure that your legs are straight at all times.

With your toes touching the floor, you should tense your thighs and tailbone while flexing your pelvic floor. Your arms can either stay in the supported shoulderstand position of supporting your back, or if more comfortable, you can lower your arms and stretch them out behind you. Continue to flex the pelvic floor and take your weight on your thighs. Hold this pose for up to five minutes. To exit this position, simply lift your legs back into the supported shoulderstand and roll down onto your back.

Secondly, we have the seated forward bend, or Paschimottanasana. This pose is a relaxed resting pose and serves to help relax our mind, body, and spirit. To start out, you want to sit on the floor with your buttocks on a folded mat and your legs directly out in front of you. Following that, you can shift your weight onto your left buttock and stretch your right leg completely. Then you will switch sides and do the same for your left leg. Next, place your palms onto the floor next to your hips, and push your chest out toward the ceiling. You need to then inhale and lean forward from your hips. If possible, reach for the sides of your feet and hold them with your hands as you bend forward.

Once comfortable, you continue the forward bend by bringing your belly down onto your thighs, then your ribs, and finally your head near your feet. Always try to keep good posture and avoid bending your elbows. With each breath, flex the muscles of your torso and increase the forward bend. By doing this, you gradually increase your flexibility and lengthen your reach further. Stay in this pose for up to three minutes. To return to normal, you can gradually lift your torso away from your thighs and relax your arms.

The final pose for the crown chakra is the reclining bound angle pose, or Supta Baddha Konasana. This position is an extension of Baddha Konasana, a simple seated pose in which you sit upright with the bottoms of the feet touching. To perform this pose, you start in Baddha Konasana. Your first move is to exhale and recline your lower back toward the floor, leaning on your hands. Then lower yourself further so that now your forearms are bearing your weight. Using your hands, you support your lower back as you bring your torso all the way down onto the floor.

Next, you will position your arms at a 45-degree angle from your upper body, palms up and relaxed. To stretch your pelvis, you need to engage the muscles in your groin and flex them; this will relax your glutes and improve the stretch you receive from this pose. You must be careful to not press your knees down into the floor, as it can actually lessen the effect desired from this position. Rather than letting your knees drift toward the ceiling, let them hang in the air weightlessly.

Stay in this pose for one minute at the beginning, but feel free to increase the duration once you are more comfortable. To come out of this pose, you will use your hands to push your legs together. Then, you can roll to one side and push your-self up onto your hands and knees.

MEDITATION

Meditation is arguably the most ancient and sacred form of spiritual empowerment. Nearly every religion from Buddhism and early Abrahamic religions, to Native American religions and everything in between has used meditation as a way of aligning oneself and reaching higher planes of consciousness. Meditation is one of the longest studied and practiced skills in human history. Intellectuals throughout time have explored the intricacies of this practice. But those of you who are inexperienced in the matter may wonder what meditation actually is.

Well, meditation is simply a deeper form of concentration. That is what we hope to achieve whenever we meditate. Every time we close our eyes, control our breathing, and chant a mantra, we are trying to reach that deeper level of focus, awareness, and concentration. It sounds a lot more simple than it is because, in truth, meditation is a skill that has many levels to it. Almost anyone can sit in a quiet room and meditate to calm themselves, but not everyone can heighten their senses, achieve emotional clarity, or heal their chakras.

These are only some of the things which will come with practicing meditation. One of the key goals of any meditator is to reach a stage of total self-awareness. After achieving complete calm and concentration, we can perceive ourselves within ourselves. In other words, we are able to look at ourselves from an outside perspective—one free of bias or ego. From this position, it is possible to make the best decisions for ourselves, notice our errors, and appreciate our successes.

Meditation has been scientifically observed to have multiple benefits for our physical and mental wellbeing. Regular meditation may significantly lower feelings of stress, depression, anxiety, and chronic pain. Meditation has also been shown to lower blood pressure, increase attention span, and improve quality of sleep. It results in all of these benefits with no known downsides aside from the 30 minutes you need to take out of your day to perform it.

As with yoga, meditation is something that is best taught by a master rather than learned on one's own. Luckily, guided meditations are incredibly easy to come across, and it's almost guaranteed that whatever we may need from a guided meditation is already available somewhere online. In the sections below, we will go over the meditations for each chakra, what we hope to focus on, the best places to meditate, and the goals of each meditation.

Preparations

Before we cover the intricacies of meditating on each chakra, let's go over the key areas of any meditation. These are the initial steps and tips to follow while starting a form of meditative practice. Although there are hundreds of different types of meditation, they all have the same core concepts of breathing control and relaxation.

- **Position yourself comfortably.** Seat yourself on the floor, a mat, or a chair in an upright position. Make sure your spine is straight and that you are at a comfortable temperature.
- **Slow your breathing.** Typically we want to keep a pattern of breathing in for three to five seconds, holding the breath in our lungs for three to five seconds, and then exhaling fully for three to five seconds. Find the rhythm you're most comfortable with and stick with it.
- **Relax your muscles.** Once you fall into a comfortable breathing rhythm, you will start to feel your muscles relax. Ignore the temptation to move fingers, flex muscles, or scratch your nose. If you do need to move, make sure that it is in slow and fluid movements.
- **Close your eyes.** Your eyes should be naturally closing themselves at this point. It is possible that your eyelids will be feeling very heavy, and your eyes may even lose focus as you drift into an ultra-relaxed state.
- **Clear your mind.** Some of us have an easier time clearing our mind than others. Personally, I have an overly active imagination, so I find it hard to completely empty all my thoughts from my head at times. I find it often just takes time to learn how to do this. You may need a few more minutes than you expected, but just try your best to persevere and stick

with it. As long as you keep focusing on your breathing, your mind will declutter itself naturally.

- **Don't force it.** This is arguably the most important point to take note of for anyone new to meditation. Do not force any stage of the process. Focus on your breathing, and with time, everything will come naturally to you.

Root Chakra

The root chakra is the first chakra that we will look to heal and strengthen. Meditation on this chakra usually involves focusing on your basic needs and insecurities. Your primary goal when meditating on this energy point is grounding. You are stripping away your material worries and reminding yourself of your connection to the earth. If you often feel worried about your needs and wants in life, then meditating frequently on this chakra may bring you peace.

Below, we will cover some of the common themes and ideas behind root chakra meditations.

- **Meditate outside**: The root chakra is your grounding point to the world that surrounds you. By meditating outside, on the ground, and in nature, you can absorb the energy around your body which is related to this chakra. Meditating on dirt, rock, or at least with a pot of soil next to you will massively strengthen the connection you make with the earth around you.

- **Focus on the position of this chakra**: The root chakra is located at the base of your spine. Try to think of it as a well that you need to dip a bucket into in order to get spiritual energy from it. Focus on channeling energy from the root chakra up your spine. Imagine a trickle at first that with every breath grows until it eventually becomes a torrent.

- **Visualize the color**: The color of this chakra is a deep, earthy red, the color of hot lava, a beautiful lotus flower, and of soft pottery clay. Imagine that color radiating from the base of your spine, up into your torso, and down into your legs. The color of this energy point is warm and comforting. If you feel anxious outside of meditation, try to imagine that same red glow spreading through your body.

- **Use the mantra**: The mantra that corresponds to this chakra is "Lam" (pronounced L-ahm). Once deep into your meditation, using a clear mind, formulate the Lam mantra. You will want to picture the letters of the mantra entering your mind as you say them. Focus completely on the word as you slowly chant it out loud in time with your breathing.

Sacral Chakra

The second chakra that we will look to meditate on, the sacral chakra, is one we will very commonly feel is locked. To heal and unblock this chakra, you will find yourself focusing on your creativity, sexuality, and self-image. Your primary goal when meditating on the sacral chakra is to build a better sense of self-worth, creative freedom, and self-confidence. If you often feel insecure, struggle with creativity, or feel guilty about sexual emotions, then meditating frequently on this chakra is something you need to do.

Below, you will find some of the common themes behind meditating on the sacral chakra.

- **Meditate near water**: Water is the element of this chakra as it reflects the fluid and flowing nature of this chakra's energy. Try to meditate near water, whether that be the ocean, a lake, a pool, or even a bowl filled with water. Great rivers are massive sources of sacral chakra energy and thus make the best meditation locations for this chakra.
- **Focus on the position of this chakra**: The sacral chakra is located between the navel and sexual organs. The power from this chakra flows down into the sexual organs and up into the solar plexus. Try to imagine that flow of energy in both directions when meditating on this energy point.
- **Visualize the color**: The color of this chakra is a bright, radiant orange. It is the shade of a juicy orange or a perfectly ripened pumpkin. Picture this

refreshing and exciting color in your mind whenever you need to focus on this energy point.

- **Use the mantra**: The mantra of this chakra is "Vam" (pronounced V-ahm). Once you're into a meditative state and are successfully visualizing the movement of this chakra's energy, try repeating the mantra. Focus on it completely, and imagine it aiding the flow of energy from this energy point.

Solar Plexus Chakra

Our third chakra on the journey up the spine, the solar plexus, is another energy point that is very commonly in some stage of imbalance. Often people who work in high stress environments and don't take care to eat properly will suffer blockages here the most.

In order to heal and unblock this chakra, we will be focusing on willpower, drive to work, and feelings of pride and achievement. Your goals when working on this chakra are to achieve a more rigid sense of self-discipline, a greater drive to work toward things, and a feeling of pride in who you are and what you have accomplished. If you often suffer from feelings of helplessness, lack of motivation, or a lack of self-respect, then it may be good for you to spend some time working on this energy point.

- **Meditate near fire**: The solar plexus is the source of

our inner fire, and therefore, meditating near fires is a fantastic way of recharging and rebalancing this chakra. That fire can be anything from a burning candle to a simple campfire or raging bonfire. As long as you have your fire in a safe place, it will work for this meditation.

- **Focus on the position of this chakra:** This chakra is found in the middle of the torso, above the navel and below the lungs. This chakra radiates energy all around the body from this central position. Imagine a network of bright yellow veins networking out from the center of your body into the extremities.

- **Visualize the color:** The color of this chakra is yellow which represents the brilliant vibrancy of the energy that it produces. Think of a ripe lemon or a brilliant ray of sunlight; that is the color you should visualize if you ever need to connect yourself to this chakra.

- **Use the mantra:** The mantra of the solar plexus chakra is "Ram" (pronounced R-ahm). Whenever you meditate on this energy point, repeat this mantra in long, elongated syllables with every exhale. By doing this, you will be mimicking the flow of energy out of your solar plexus.

Heart Chakra

The heart chakra is the halfway point toward enlightenment. The chakra is the middle ground between the physical and spiritual, which means it can be pretty temperamental and complicated at times. This chakra is most commonly upset by failure in things that mean a lot to us, whether that be relationships, work, or personal goals. In order to heal and balance this energy point, you will be focusing your meditations on your ability to show love, receive love, and forgive others and yourself. Your goals with heart chakra meditation are to strengthen your emotional strength, improve your ability to love, and heal any feelings of hurt or betrayal.

If you often experience feelings of being unloved, feelings of being distant from others, and feelings of abandonment, then meditation on the heart chakra is definitely needed.

- **Meditate in nature**: The heart chakra is intrinsically linked to nature. In order for us to thrive as humans, we need to show love to the world around us, and that world is the nature that we see everyday. Our heart is also the part of our body that we have to keep healthy above all others. Nature represents health; where plants and animals are healthy, everything else is healthy too. Try to meditate surrounded by plants, in grass, or even with your pets (if they aren't too distracting).
- **Focus on your heartbeat**: This chakra is located in the center of your chest but it directly channels energy through the heart. Focusing on your heartbeat during meditation can bring you to a deeper state of relaxation and closeness to this chakra. Just imagine,

with every beat, your love for the world around you grows, and with it your health.

- **Visualize the color**: The color of this chakra is the shade of healthy nature: green. Think of a lush green pasture or a strong vine growing up a temple wall. Visualizing this color pumping through your veins and enveloping you while you meditate is a powerful way of boosting the energy of this chakra.
- **Use the mantra**: Lastly, make use of this chakra's mantra, "Yam" (pronounced Y-ahm). Repeat this mantra in times of emotional uncertainty. Use long elongated syllables and sync it to your breathing for the best results.

Throat Chakra

The throat chakra is the first of our spiritual chakras, and therefore, meditation is particularly effective in helping to heal and balance this energy point. Being your center for expression, this chakra is one that can be upset on a daily basis by any number of factors. Typically, you may see imbalances being caused if you don't voice your concerns or opinions, don't express yourself, or even try to suppress others from expressing themselves.

Your goals when meditating on this chakra are to build confidence in speaking and expression, help clear your mind to make room for creative thoughts, and create a more open-minded view of others' expressions. If you have feelings of shame about your art, a mind cluttered by ideas, or an anxiety when it comes to speaking to others, then you need to work on the throat chakra.

- **Meditate with ambient noise**: This chakra is represented by sound in our world, specifically sounds of expression like chants, prayers, music, speeches, poetry, or even an audiobook. These are all sounds of expression that will nourish this chakra and perhaps provide you with the inspiration you need. So next time you plan to meditate on this chakra, play some calm ambient music, rhythmic drums, quiet poetry, or even a soft spoken audiobook in the background.
- **Focus on sounds**: Continuing from the last point, now that you have something playing in the background, try to focus on it. This may seem difficult at first, but focusing on a specific beat, sound, or frequency can help you easily fall into a deep trance. Meditating in this manner also allows you to directly connect with the primary source of energy for this chakra, making it a very efficient way of empowering it.
- **Visualize the color**: Violet and deep blue are the key colors that represent this chakra. These are the colors of the night sky and heavily-burdened storm clouds. Picture a calming rain or a violet sunset while meditating on this chakra. These scenes are both cool

and relaxing yet warming and active at the same time.

- **Use the mantra**: Finally, we want to make use of this chakra's mantra, "Ham" (pronounced H-ahm). This mantra in particular resonates and vibrates strongly in the throat when chanted, which can be therapeutic for those of you who suffer from a sore throat.

Third Eye Chakra

The third eye chakra is the penultimate chakra in this journey to enlightenment. Meditation on this energy point is a key part in balancing it, because doing so helps to clear and calm the areas of the mind that this chakra influences most. You will typically see imbalances in the third eye chakra caused by a lack of clarity in your goals, ignoring your intuition, and refusing divine guidance.

Your goals when meditating on this chakra are to bring clarity to your mind, open yourself up to wisdom, and allow for divine guidance to positively influence you. If you have feelings of confusion in life, a feeling of being without purpose, and feelings of disconnection from your inner wisdom, then you need to spend time working on the third eye chakra.

- **Meditate in a place with multiple elements**: This chakra is represented by the supreme element, a combination of all elements in one. Now, it may be hard to find all elements in one place, but you can at least meditate near a few that will definitely have a beneficial impact. Another option is to set up an altar with a bowl of water, a bowl of soil, a healthy plant, and some ambient noises.

- **Focus on space**: This chakra is associated with space —with the emptiness and calm of the void. If you clear your mind and free your consciousness, you can gain access to so much room for thought, inspiration, and deliberation. Meditating in this manner allows you to make direct contact to the realm from which divine wisdom flows.

- **Visualize the color**: The color of this chakra is purple, between the vibrancy of lavender and the darkness of distant space. When meditating on this energy point, try to picture a warm, purple void through which you are drifting. Allow it to encircle and envelope you.

- **Use the mantra**: This mantra has two parts. The first is "Ksham" (pronounced Sh-ahm), and the second and most well-known is "Om". Yes, this is the same Om that people say to imitate Buddhist monks. It is the basic sound of the universe and is believed to contain all other sounds.

Crown Chakra

Last of all, the crown chakra is the source of all our other chakras. This hub needs regular maintenance and attention, otherwise everything could fall into imbalance. This energy point can be sent into imbalance by a number of things, including other chakras being severely thrown off track, spiritual ignorance, and a lack of divine energy finding its way into your body. Your goals when meditating on this chakra are finding inner peace, opening yourself up to divine energy, and searching for spiritual enlightenment.

Feelings of spiritual doubt, a disconnect from the world, and apathy may be caused by issues relating to this chakra and should be dealt with right away with meditation and other healing techniques.

- **Meditate in the midday sun**: The crown chakra is not associated with any earthly element but rather with the divine light and the greater universe. In order to tap into this source of energy and connect to this chakra in a deeper way, you can meditate in the midday sun. The sun you feel in the middle of the day is not only the hottest and purest, but it shines directly down onto the crown of your head.
- **Focus on the divine**: When meditating on this chakra, try to focus on the divine. Picture your gods or spirits —picture the creation of the universe and the brilliance of the sun shining light down onto the earth. Meditating on these images helps your crown chakra to open and, in turn, it opens you up to divine wisdom.

- **Visualize the color**: The colors of this chakra are gold and white. When you meditate on this chakra, make sure to incorporate these divine colors into your clothing, surroundings, and thoughts.
- **Use the mantra**: Finally, the mantra of this chakra is the universal sound of "Om". However, complete silence is also a powerful catalyst for this chakra. After all, the universe is silent and so should be our minds when meditating on this chakra.

VISUALIZATION

Visualization is a very simple yet effective technique for improving your mental and physical well-being. The name is rather self-explanatory; we visualize what we want, and through the focused power of our chakras, we can make it so. Now, visualization isn't going to make a sports car appear in front of you, and it definitely won't turn your home into a mansion, but it can heal your chakras and help you make changes to yourself that you truly desire.

Visualization is most powerful during moments of calm and meditation. The process is rather simple. You get comfortable, bring yourself into a state of meditation, and then visualize the changes you want to make while maintaining a state of total calm. The types of changes you can bring about are nearly endless, but most revolve around the way you perceive yourself and the world around you.

If you feel symptoms of a blockage in your solar plexus, visualization may be an efficient way of clearing it away by focusing on the color, mantra, and element of the chakra. Along with focusing directly on chakras, you can also direct your attention to the causes of chakra imbalance themselves. Let's say, for example, that you are insecure about your weight, and it is impacting your ability to love yourself. This is causing a blockage in your heart chakra. By visualizing yourself loving yourself and others loving you as you are, you can overcome those insecurities.

Visualizing goals is another way to utilize this mindfulness technique. Our brains certainly are not perfect machines. In fact, they can be fooled pretty easily. We can use that to our advantage, however, by visualizing our goals. While doing so, you can trick your brain into thinking that those goals have already been achieved. Although you know they haven't been, a part of your brain will feel more confident and capable of achieving those goals.

This is all due to a phenomenon called neuroplasticity. The images that we put in our brain evoke certain feelings, whether those images are actually real or not. These feelings can come back into use whenever we are reminded of those images. Thus, we can program ourselves to feel more confident when we are approached with certain situations.

AFFIRMATIONS

Affirmations are a key part of healing our chakras. These are truths that we tell ourselves to counteract the lies that we believe about ourselves. When our chakras are unbalanced, we may feel insecure, uncomfortable, and unhappy about aspects of our lives and ourselves. In order to balance and heal those chakras we need to acknowledge and accept that those insecurities are false and do nothing but poison our self-image. Through affirmations, we condition ourselves to think positively and to reject insecure thoughts. Each chakra has different affirmations that target certain aspects associated with those areas of our body and mind.

Affirmations can be used in multiple ways but the two most common are through meditation and daily repetition. When using affirmations in meditation, we wait until we are in a deep meditative state, and then we visualize the affirmations we need to hear entering into our mind one by one. We focus on every word and imprint each onto our consciousness. By repeating these affirmations to ourselves in this heightened state of awareness, we nullify our own mind's ability to contradict us. In our state of deep meditation, our mind is only open to truths, so every affirmation will be taken into our mind as the whole truths that they are.

When using affirmations in daily repetition, the name is pretty self-explanatory. The idea is that we set up multiple times throughout the day where we repeat a few affirmations to ourselves. These affirmations can be targeting a specific chakra, or they can be targeted toward our whole being in general. Most of the time, we tend to do these repetitions around three times a day—after waking, at the middle of our waking hours, and before we sleep. However, we can actually repeat these affirmations whenever we feel we need them. If you happen to be in a situation that makes you feel insecure, repeat the necessary affirmations to yourself and take in some deep, meditative breaths.

Root Chakra

For the root chakra, our affirmations primarily revolve around safety, security, and stability. This energy point is most commonly associated with being the spiritual base and the source of our connection to the world around us. Therefore, any affirmations you read, say, and create will have some link toward reassuring the support you need and get from the world around you.

Some affirmations for the root chakra are as follows:

- "I will be safe and secure wherever I am."
- "I am safe and content in my home."
- "My safety needs will always be fulfilled by the earth."
- "At this moment, I am grounded, stable, and at peace."
- "I am grounded to the earth, and I am supported by the universe."

- "I am deserving of support whenever I need it."
- "I will receive support whenever I need it."
- "I have a strong body, a healthy mind, and a balanced spirit."
- "The world will always support me and provide for me."
- "My root chakra is opening, and I feel myself becoming balanced."
- "I feel the energy of the earth spread through my body."

Sacral Chakra

For the sacral chakra, our affirmations are primarily based on expression, creativity, and self-love. This chakra is our source of sensual energy, self-confidence, and creativity. This means that any affirmations you use for this chakra will be very personal and intimate in nature. These affirmations may be hard to say at first because of this very personal nature, but they are important for us to hear.

- "I am a strong, imaginative person, and I love the things that I create."
- "I am sure that what I offer to the world is enough."
- "I deserve to feel pleasure and have my needs fully met."
- "I feel safe expressing my sexual self in enjoyable, healthy, and creative ways."

- "I am a magnet for good, loving people who will assist me when I need them."
- "My body is perfect, and I am comfortable with who I am."
- "I am happy embracing change."
- "I will make the most of my future."
- "Each day, my joy and satisfaction with myself increases."
- "I am ready for great personal growth and deep positive change."

Solar Plexus Chakra

For the solar plexus chakra, our affirmations are concerning our self-esteem, self-control, and inner peace. This energy point is our source of willpower and inner strength, and it is our driving force. The affirmations that we will be repeating for this chakra are fantastic for boosting your confidence and hyping you up for occasions.

If you have a big presentation at work or an important college exam coming up, try using these affirmations to get yourself into the right frame of mind:

- "I'm capable, ambitious, and determined to fulfill my purpose in life."
- "I am powerful, and I am confident in my power."
- "Inner peace and confidence flow through me."

- "I believe in myself, and I feel more confident in myself every single day."
- "I don't always need to be in control, and that's okay."
- "I feel capable and driven to pursue my goals."
- "I feel no guilt for past experiences."
- "I free myself from the pain of negative past experiences."
- "I know that I am strong, good, and worthy of success."
- "I forgive myself for any previous mistakes. I will learn from them."
- "The only thing I can control is how I approach situations."

Heart Chakra

For the heart chakra, our affirmations are about loving others, feeling love ourselves, and healing past wounds. This chakra is our source of love, our ability to make important decisions, and inner peace. The affirmations that we will recite for this energy point are designed to help you overcome emotional wounds, listen to your heart when making decisions, and find inner peace in your ability to make choices for your own happiness.

- "I love who I am unconditionally, and I offer the same love to others."

- "I choose to love myself, take joy in who I am, and show compassion to myself and others."
- "I am happy and well because my heart chakra is open."
- "I am free of the wounds of my past."
- "I accept whatever form my emotions take, and I will keep control."
- "I forgive myself, and I forgive others."
- "I freely give love to others, and it makes me feel happy and whole."
- "I aim to fulfill my heart's desire every day, and I do."
- "I open myself to love, and every day I receive and give more."
- "I create healthy and loving relationships that are beneficial for all involved."

Throat Chakra

For the throat chakra, our affirmations are centered around our creativity, communication skills, and ability to turn ideas into reality. This chakra is our source of change bringing willpower, problem-solving, and people skills. Thus, all the affirmations listed below will be very useful for those of you needing a boost in social situations.

These affirmations are said to help us feel more confident in expressing ourselves and our artistry:

- "I speak the truth with ease, and others know this."
- "I trust my true voice, and I let it speak for me."
- "My thoughts and words have an impact on the world."
- "I am a caring listener and a great communicator."
- "Others listen when I speak."
- "When I speak to others, they take my opinions and contributions into account."
- "I don't second guess the words I speak. I'm confident in my thoughts."
- "Others always understand and respect me."
- "I can find the right words for any occasion."
- "My creativity has no limits and neither does my ambition."
- "I am an artist, regardless of my chosen art."

* * *

Third Eye Chakra

For the third eye chakra, our affirmations target our spiritual doubts, gut instincts, and sense of purpose in life. This chakra is the source of our spirituality and inner wisdom, and therefore, any doubts you have about your spirituality or ability to make the right decisions for yourself come from here.

The affirmations below are meant to help you feel more secure in your spirituality and intuition:

- "I follow the lead of my inner wisdom and knowledge."
- "I am following my true path in life."
- "Every day, I take a step toward fulfilling my purpose in life."
- "I listen to my intuition, and I know it will lead me down the correct path in life."
- "I know how to make the best decisions for myself, and I do it with ease."
- "I trust my third eye to guide me safely through life."
- "The world is open to me, and everything is possible."
- "It is wise and safe to follow the guidance that my third eye gives me."
- "My third eye is opening, and my full purpose will soon be revealed to me."
- "I am wise, I am intuitive, and I know what is best for me."

* * *

Crown Chakra

Lastly, for the crown chakra, our affirmations are concerning our connection to our spiritual side, our divine knowledge, and our oneness with the world around us. This chakra is most commonly associated with being the source of all the other chakras, our primary link to the spiritual world, and our source of divine knowledge and wisdom. Because of these associations, the affirmations we need to say are based around reassuring ourselves of our spirituality.

- "At this moment, I am happy, sure of myself, and aware of my worth."
- "I radiate love, I radiate joy, and I radiate light."
- "Every day, I open myself to divine guidance."
- "I am in a constant connection to my divine self."
- "We all exist in this world to make a difference."
- "I glow with love and light that attracts others who glow with love and light."
- "I feel at one with the world in which I reside."
- "I feel connected and tuned into the divine energy of the universe."
- "The world is beautiful, and I embrace this beauty in whatever form it takes."
- "I know my spiritual path, and I live my life to fulfill it."

* * *

MASSAGE

Massage is an ancient healing therapy that has been used by Indian religions since at least 3000 BCE. For thousands of years, Ayurveda practitioners have used massage to alleviate pain, heal injuries, and prevent illness. A key part of the success behind Ayurvedic massage healing comes from its effect on the chakras. Although massages are fantastic for bodily health by stimulating blood flow and relieving muscle tension, chakra massages also target the specific locations of chakras and help to relieve blockages.

By massaging specific chakras, we can reduce tension in the region, lower stress and anxiety levels, improve blood pressure, and release toxins that may be polluting the organs, muscles, and glands associated with certain chakras. Most chakra massages combine the usage of essential oils, incense, and crystal therapy for a complete chakra-healing experience.

Root Chakra

The root chakra is a very simple one to heal with massage. Because of the location of this energy point, we have the feet, legs, and glutes that can all be focused and massaged in order for this chakra to benefit. Glutes may be an awkward area to have massaged, but this region is closest to our root chakra and provides the most benefits for us. Most full body massage packages will cover the glutes. Any chakra massage package will definitely focus in this area.

* * *

Sacral Chakra

For the sacral chakra, we ideally want any massage to focus on the lower abdomen and lower back. Most commonly, sacral chakra massages pinpoint the lumbar section of the lower back, the area just below the belly button, and the hips. Oil massages around the lumbar region are particularly effective at opening up this chakra and double up as incredibly good for general back and posture health.

Solar Plexus Chakra

Massages for the solar plexus chakra usually focus on the area around the middle to upper abdomen and the middle back area. For the most part, you will see solar plexus massages happening over the area of your solar plexus in your central abdomen. Chakra massages in this area usually consist of pressured clockwise movements that are designed to activate the flow of energy in the chakra.

Heart Chakra

There are two distinct types of massage that are effective for the heart chakra. One is traditional chakra massages, and the other is trigger point therapy. Trigger point therapy is a complex and potentially painful type of massage therapy that targets specific areas of tension. This is something that is done by a trained professional, and although it is incredibly effective for balancing this chakra, it can be painful and intense at times. Otherwise, for traditional chakra massages, you will often see these being conducted on the upper back, shoulders, and over the heart.

Throat Chakra

The throat chakra benefits mainly from massages to the back and front of the neck, jaw, and sternum. Massages involving aromatherapy are very common for this energy point. Most commonly, you will start with a deep tissue massage to the back of the neck to loosen up the area around the chakra. Following that, lighter oil massages are done from the sternum, up through the throat, and onto the jaw area. This process is the optimal way to relieve blockages and imbalances in the area of the throat chakra.

Third Eye Chakra

For the third eye chakra, there is a specific technique that is used called brow stripping. In brow stripping, long and pressured strokes are done along the length of the muscles in the brow. Often, we will also see massages for this chakra done near the ears and temples as well. Essential oils are very commonly used in this area for their beneficial effects in relieving stress and anxiety.

Crown Chakra

Finally, we have the crown chakra. Typically, scalp massages are the go-to for this energy point. Scalp massages are amazing at increasing the blood flow to the brain, relieving tension in skull tissue, and relaxing muscles in the head and neck. Massages in this area typically follow the lines of the skull. By activating the blood vessels in these areas, we can greatly increase blood and energy flow to and from this chakra.

COLOR THERAPY

Color therapy, also known as chromotherapy, is one of the best passive ways of healing our chakras. But, what is it, and how does it work? To put it simply, color therapy is the practice of using the frequency of colors in the world around us to promote healing in our chakras. Earlier on, in the first chapter, I had mentioned that each chakra has a color which it is visualized as. The colors associated with these chakras represent different aspects of our world. If we take one of these colors and surround ourselves with it, we allow its energy to resonate with the chakra that it represents. This flow of energy helps to heal and rebalance the chakra, and it gives us a source of energy outside of our own bodies.

There are multiple ways to carry out color therapy. The simplest and most organic way is through nature. Below I have listed some examples of using nature to heal each chakra:

- **Root Chakra**: If we want to heal our root chakra, we may want to meditate on a patch of bare soil or on a large stone. This direct connection to the reddish-brown ground below us will help the chakra absorb energy from the parts of our world that it is most deeply connected to.
- **Sacral Chakra**: For our sacral chakra, we can look to spend time around orange areas of nature or things. Places like orange sandy beaches and citrus orchids are fantastic. Neither of those are very common

depending on where you live, though. Some simpler-to-find options are fire, the orange glow of a sunset, or even a patch of autumn leaves.

- **Solar Plexus Chakra**: The solar plexus is primarily linked to the color yellow, so we want to try and surround ourselves with yellow aspects of nature. Some of these include yellow sand and yellow flowers.
- **Heart Chakra**: The heart chakra is an easy one to heal in nature with color therapy. With the primary color being green, we need to simply take a walk in a forest or meditate on some green grass.
- **Throat Chakra**: The throat chakra is another rather easy one to heal through nature. This energy point is linked to the colors blue and violet. Violet may be a bit difficult to come across in nature but blue is pretty common. In order to heal the throat chakra through interaction with nature, we can take a trip to the sea or a lake. Large bodies of water are a wealth of energy. Blue flowers are also rather common in nature and can be planted in your garden to provide a nearby source of energy.
- **Third Eye Chakra**: The third eye chakra needs purple. This may seem a bit tough to come by, but there are some pretty simple options. One of these options is lavender. This flower is very easy to come by and can be planted in any garden. Along with that, the third eye chakra has a deep connection to the moon. Moonlight is often considered to have a purple

hue and meditation or walks in the glow of the moon can heal this chakra very effectively.

- **Crown Chakra**: Lastly, we will discuss the crown chakra. This energy point is represented by the colors gold and white. We may think we're out of luck unless we are rich or live in a snowy region, but don't worry—there are options open to everyone wanting to heal this chakra. The best way to heal this chakra is through the golden rays of a midday sun. Rays of light shining directly down onto our crown is the most effective way to absorb the energy of the world around us into this chakra. White flowers, snow, and chalk are examples of aspects of nature we can also use.

Aside from nature, color therapy can also very effectively be performed by wearing clothes, jewelry, and makeup in the color of the chakra we wish to empower. If we're artists, we may wish to decorate our art studio with the color blue to empower our throat chakra. In fact, decorating rooms to empower certain chakras is a very effective way of energizing our energy points during our day-to-day lives. Curtains, rugs, blankets, cushions, wall paint, and even colored lights can be used in this way to boost the energy of a room.

* * *

MUSICAL HEALING

Music has been an integral part of traditional Indian religious ceremonies for thousands of years. Music, as with color, gives off powerful spiritual energy. Just as with every chakra, there is a corresponding color, each chakra has a corresponding type of sound too.

- **Root Chakra**: For the Muladhara chakra, the sound of large drums are most closely linked. These bass-filled sounds imitate the noise made by earth and rock moving.
- **Sacral Chakra**: The sacral chakra is represented by the sounds of small drums. Small drums mimic the sounds of movement and activity, the stomping of feet, and the rhythm of love-making.
- **Solar Plexus Chakra**: Trumpets and large wind instruments affect the solar plexus chakra. These instruments imitate the sounds of our stomach, and it is believed that the breath used to play them originates in that area.
- **Heart Chakra**: Strings have their influence on the heart chakra. There is a reason "pulling on my heart strings" is a commonly used phrase. Anyone who has heard a brilliant violinist play can confirm the effect those instruments have on their heart.
- **Throat Chakra**: Small wind instruments such as flutes and pipes are representative of the throat.

These instruments mimic the action of talking and require great control over one's breathing to fully utilize.

- **Third Eye Chakra**: The third eye chakra is a fan of bells and the sounds of nature, like bird song and dripping water. These calming sounds help us focus which, in turn, empowers this chakra.
- **Crown Chakra**: The crown chakra values all of the instruments put together as one. Just as we need all the other energy points to be balanced for our crown chakra to feel balanced, we need all instruments played as one for our crown chakra to gain from them.

If we watch any Indian rituals, we will see this in action. In temples, during ceremony, the large drums are furthest to the back and sides. Then come the smaller drums, and just in front of them are the large wind instruments. Next come the strings and small wind instruments. And lastly, in the very center, are the bells, which are often held by the ceremony leader.

For those of us who don't have access to temples and ceremonies, there are plenty of resources available online and in CD form. Many people like to use classical music during meditation to empower certain chakras. One of Mozart's piano concertos, for example, may be exactly what you need to open up your heart chakra. Similarly, a full orchestral piece may help to center your crown chakra. There is plenty of modern music also made for the specific goal of empowering and healing the chakras. Feel free to explore and experiment. Musical healing works wonders for me, and it may work wonders for you too.

REIKI

Reiki is an ancient Japanese healing technique that has been practiced throughout East Asia for centuries under various names. The core belief around reiki is that we have the ability to manipulate, move, and transfer vital life energy (ki, chi, prana) in ourselves and others to heal physical and spiritual aspects of our bodies.

A trained reiki master can help us heal and balance our chakras by radiating their energy into our chakra centers through the palms of their hands. In a physical sense, reiki is different from massage in that the touches are very light and non-invasive. The primary goal of reiki isn't to encourage physical changes like blood flow or muscle relaxation, but rather to directly energize the chakras.

A skilled reiki practitioner can energize chakras that are starved of energy, divert the energy from overactive chakras into other parts of the body, and free up blockages that are stopping the movement of energy up the spine.

Foods and Chakras

Food is one of our most primal needs as human beings. This deep, intrinsic link that we have to food has both physical and spiritual aspects, especially in regards to our chakras. The colors of many foods help to describe their mineral and vitamin contents. For example, red foods are very high in certain antioxidants which cause the red coloration. These antioxidants also happen to be very good for gut and bowel health, and as such they directly influence the area around our root chakra.

Similarly, the specific type of antioxidants found in berries and other deep blue or purple foods are particularly good for improving memory, cognitive function, and defending the brain against deterioration. These foods are the ones most closely linked with our third eye chakra for these exact reasons.

THE RELATIONSHIP BETWEEN CHAKRAS AND FOOD

Root Chakra

Of all the chakras, the root chakra is the one most easily healed and balanced through food. All foods naturally come from the earth, and so all have at least some energy from the earth in them. This earth energy is what powers the root chakra and helps it to maintain balance. Because of how easy this chakra is to nourish, if you simply make sure to eat healthy, well-balanced meals on a regular basis, this is often enough to keep it open and relatively unblocked.

However, if we do need to focus on specific root chakra foods to help heal the chakra or unblock it, we should look toward red foods and root vegetables. Because earth is an element responsible for building structure, these foods may cause a large increase in body mass if eaten in too high of quantities. As in all things in life, moderation is key.

Take a look below at some examples of foods that can help keep your root chakra balanced:

- Meat
- Red peppers
- Tomato
- Pomegranate
- Chillies
- Red berries
- Beetroot

- Garlic
- Red apple

Sacral Chakra

As we have already covered, the sacral chakra is our source of sensual energy and passion. This specific chakra is responsible for our energy in romance and in passion projects. So whether you are making love, playing your favorite sport, or playing your chosen instrument, the foods associated with this energy point will give you the boost you need. This boost comes from the high electrolyte and vitamin content of these foods, when we sweat or spend long periods of time in deep focus, we quickly burn through our body's supply of vitamins and minerals.

All the foods associated with this chakra are dense in the vitamins and minerals needed to replenish our reserves; in many cases, they contain plenty of refreshing liquid for your body, too. Here are some of these foods:

- Carrot
- Peach
- Apricot
- Orange
- Mango
- Pumpkin
- Mandarin

- Peanuts
- Tofu

* * *

Solar Plexus Chakra

The solar plexus chakra is our body's primary source of vital energy. The foods associated with this energy point are, as such, packed full of the energy that is needed to power us as we go about our daily routine. Foods high in carbohydrates, the human body's primary energy source, like grains, potatoes, and meaty fruits are excellent sources of raw energy for our body. This raw energy is then distributed where it is needed by the solar plexus.

As well as carb-heavy foods, the solar plexus chakra is also linked to pungent and strong-flavored foods. These foods are believed to contain the fire of vital energy. Some of these vital energy-flavored foods include ginger, lemon, and peppers. Other foods that are ideal for strengthening the solar plexus chakra are as follows:

- Grains
- Ginger
- Pineapple
- Banana
- Yellow pear
- Lemon
- Yellow peppers

• Potato

* * *

Heart Chakra

The heart chakra is a big fan of green foods. Green foods, in general, tend to be very high in fiber, as well as essential minerals. These are absolutely crucial to the health of our heart and vascular system. Fiber helps us to regulate our blood sugar levels, which play a huge part in our heart health and in balancing the flow of energy in and out of the heart chakra.

The minerals from these plants, on the other hand, are crucial for maintaining the health of our organs and blood vessels. Perhaps you are wondering why this is. Well, without the right cocktail of minerals, our blood vessels would be unable to transport oxygen, glucose, and vital energy around our body to the other organs and chakras.

Here are some of the foods that are wonderful for supporting the heart chakra:

• Watermelon
• Cucumber
• Zucchini
• Kiwi
• Avocado
• Green apple
• Mint

- Green grapes
- Leafy green vegetables

Throat Chakra

At this point, the chakras become less based on the physical body and more ethereal. This means that foods have less of a direct impact on the body and more of an impact on the soul. In a way, their effect is less tangible and more symbolic.

For our throat chakra, we want to mainly consume liquids. This energy point is heavily associated with water and the fluidity of communication and expression. Because of that, liquids and sea plants make fantastic foods to satisfy the spiritual needs of this chakra. Figs are also linked to this chakra because of their association with the Hindu god Vishnu, who was born under a fig tree. Vishnu is a creator, and the throat chakra represents our creativity.

Here are some of the foods and liquids you can incorporate into your diet if you wish to maintain a healthy throat chakra:

- Fruit juices
- Figs
- Seaweed
- Herbal tea
- Coconut water
- Soups
- Fish

* * *

Third Eye Chakra

The third eye chakra is located in the forehead—more specifically around the frontal lobe. This is the area of our brain that is responsible for emotions, problem-solving, language, memory, and judgment. All of the foods associated with this energy point are incredibly beneficial to this area of the brain, as they all contain a potent cocktail of useful antioxidants that protect against mental decay.

Blackberries and elderberries specifically are famed for their amazing benefits when it comes to mental cognizance and improving memory. Purple is one of the most powerful colors for color therapy. This is because the richness and depth of it helps to nourish the third eye chakra very efficiently. Thus, surrounding ourselves with foods of this color has a second effect of being a form of color therapy.

Take a look below at some ideas for foods you can eat to benefit your third eye chakra:

- Sweet potatoes
- Plums
- Red grapes
- Aubergine
- Prunes
- Passionfruit
- Blackberries
- Purple cabbage
- Elderberries

* * *

Crown Chakra

Finally, our crown chakra is a completely ethereal and spiritual chakra. Thus, no foods affect it as it is free from any earthly bonds. Fasting is viewed as the easiest and most effective way of purifying and unblocking this energy point. Fasting has long been viewed as a holy practice among many ancient religions, and now science is starting to recognize the benefits of it as well.

Intermittent fasting has become a regular fixture in many modern eating regimes. By taking short fasting periods of 24-36 hours, one allows the body to naturally detoxify itself, flush out toxins, and burn its natural reserves of energy. By fasting, you can also clear the mind by making your body slow down its energy production. Too much energy can cause an overactive mind and make it very hard for an individual to focus.

Sunlight, fresh air, and the ambience of nature also help to nourish this spiritual chakra. These are all outside sources of energy which our crown chakra can tap into:

- Purified water
- Sunlight
- Fresh air
- Nature
- Fasting
- Detoxing

DETOXING AND FASTING

Fasting has been a core concept of spiritualism in many cultures over thousands of years. Everyone from Tibetan Buddhists to Native American shamans and new age Pagans have noticed the incredible benefits of fasting and its effects on detoxing the body. Not only have spiritualists seen improvements, doctors, scientists, and dietitians across the world have taken notice of the potential benefits of frequent short-term fasting.

By practicing intermittent fasting, you can open yourself up to all of these amazing benefits:

- **Stabilize blood sugar levels**: By fasting regularly, you allow your body to naturally regulate its blood sugar levels by giving it periods to drain any excess blood sugar.
- **Lower insulin resistance**: During periods of fasting, the body drains itself of blood sugar. This means the cells that would usually use insulin to process that blood sugar are given a break. When you introduce sugar and insulin to these cells again later on, their resistance is lower and, in turn, they work more efficiently.
- **Reduce inflammation**: Chronic inflammation is a serious issue that many people face due to unhealthy diets. This form of persistent inflammation is one of the leading causes of heart disease, cancer, and various forms of arthritis. By fasting, you allow your

body time to drain itself of the toxins which can cause chronic inflammation to flare up.

- **Balancing of blood pressure and cholesterol levels**: Cholesterol is one of the leading causes of high blood pressure among adults. By fasting, you allow your body time to remove blockages and toxins from your blood which may otherwise cause high blood pressure. Consistent high blood pressure leads to serious cardiovascular diseases.
- **Larger amounts of growth hormone production**: Human growth hormone, which is also known as HGH, is the key hormone responsible for growth, metabolism, muscle strength, and weight loss. A number of studies have shown that fasting naturally increases the amount of HGH that is produced by the body.
- **Helps with weight loss and increased metabolism**: By fasting, you can obviously lower your overall calorie intake. This will lead to weight loss over the long-term. In the short-term, on the other hand, fasting can help boost your metabolism by increasing production of the neurotransmitter norepinephrine.
- **Increases brain function and mental clarity**: Fasting has been shown to encourage the production of nerve cells in the brain. Scientists are not exactly sure why this happens, but they know it directly improves the function of your brain and enhances mental clarity over a long period of time.

All of these benefits have been proven by science, and true to the theme of the crown chakra, they all affect our other six energy points in amazing ways.

Similar to fasting, detoxing is another way of helping the chakras heal and rebalance. Detoxing is simply the process of cutting any potentially toxin-causing foods out of your diet for a certain period of time. The longer you keep them out of your diet, the better the effectiveness of the detox.

Food-based toxins can be one of the leading causes in chakra blockages, and they are getting even more common in today's world of fast food and constant snacking. In order to detox effectively, there are some simple steps to follow and adhere to. Take a look at them below:

- Reduce or eliminate your alcohol consumption.
- Get eight hours of uninterrupted sleep every night.
- Drink more water; around half a gallon a day is recommended.
- Try to reduce or eliminate sugar and processed foods from your diet.
- Consume a lot of antioxidant-rich foods.
- Consume more fiber-rich foods.
- Reduce your amount of salt consumption.
- Exercise for at least 30 minutes every day.

Essential Oils and Chakras

I'm sure many of you who are reading this are familiar with essential oils and their overall health benefits. However, for those of you who are not so familiar or would like to learn more, let me give you a quick run-down.

Essential oils are extracts of various flowers, trees, roots, and herbs that have some absolutely amazing health benefits. Inside of these plants are particular compounds that have unique aromatic essences. These essences are distilled into an oil via distillation or cold pressing. This oil is then infused with a carrier oil in order to dilute it to manageable amounts. After this, it is ready for use. Essential oils are completely natural; anything that is made through chemical processes is *not* an authentic essential oil, so stay clear of these.

AROMATHERAPY

Aromatherapy is the most common way through which people make use of essential oils. The concept of aromatherapy is simple: we use aromatic essential oils to medicinally improve the health of the mind, body, and spirit.

For thousands of years, humans have made use of this practice. In fact, it is one of the oldest and most widespread medical techniques in existence. Ancient peoples in China, Egypt, and India all extensively made use of incense, balms, and oils that contain the essential oils of various medicinal plants. The precursor to modern essential oil distillation is attributed to the 10th century Persians, although it is almost certain that similar practices had been around before then.

Since at least the 12th century, it was common practice in many German abbeys to distill essential oils from sage, lavender, and rosemary for medicinal purposes. In the early half of the 15th century, the Swiss physician and father of toxicology, Paracelsus, extensively documented the utilization of essential oils in his experiments based around alchemy. In the 16th century, the first mentions of essential oils started popping up in German literature. Even up to the modern day, essential oils are a recognized form of therapy for multiple ailments and discomforts, and combining them with our knowledge of chakras can be incredibly life changing.

So, how does aromatherapy work? Well, there are two primary ways in which aromatherapy works: through smell and through skin absorption. There are a variety of products that help us with this and add to the usefulness of the oils that we are using. Some of the product types we will often run into are diffusers, bathing salts, hot and cold compresses, clay masks, and body creams, lotions, and oils. Be careful to only buy oils from reputable sources since they are not regulated by the FDA.

ESSENTIAL OILS FOR CHAKRA HEALING

Root Chakra

- Patchouli
- Ginger
- Frankincense
- Vetiver root
- Atlas cedarwood
- Australian sandalwood

Sacral Chakra

- Ylang ylang
- Geranium
- Bergamot
- Rose absolute
- Clary sage
- Sweet orange

Solar Plexus Chakra

- Juniper berry
- Cypress
- Rosemary
- Lime
- Lemon
- Fennel

Heart Chakra

- Fragonia
- Rose otto
- Tea tree
- May chang
- Melissa
- Jasmine

Throat Chakra

- Melaleuca
- Chamomile
- Basil
- Peppermint
- Spearmint
- Blue cypress

Third Eye Chakra

- Sage
- Rosemary
- Helichrysum
- Marjoram
- Sandalwood
- Eucalyptus

Crown Chakra

- Myrrh
- Lavender
- Patchouli
- Bergamot
- Fragonia
- Frankincense

WHERE TO USE OUR CHAKRA OILS

Now that we know what essential oils are suited to each chakra, we need to figure out where to actually utilize them. Each chakra has multiple points where we can place our essential oils depending on the ailments that our imbalances cause or the areas we want to give a boost to.

- **Root Chakra:** As we have already covered, the root chakra is tightly linked to our feet, legs, and bowels. The ginger essential oil is a powerful anti-inflammatory and can be used to help reduce joint pain in the feet and legs. Patchouli and vetiver have calming effects and can be used on the bowl region to calm an overactive root chakra. Cedarwood, sandalwood, and frankincense are all balancing essential oils that we can use at the base of the feet, behind the knees, and at the base of the spine to maintain normal function and level balance.
- **Sacral Chakra:** Being very closely connected to our

sexual organs and emotional links to people, this chakra can easily fall into imbalance without regular attendance. We can help open up a blocked sacral chakra by placing some bergamot or rose absolute just below our navel. An overactive sacral chakra can be slowed by placing some ylang-ylang or clary sage on the lower back or hips. And lastly, we can help to maintain balance of this chakra by using some sweet orange or geranium in a vertical line below the navel.

- **Solar Plexus Chakra:** As we mentioned earlier, the solar plexus chakra is located just above the navel in the center of the torso. For a blocked solar plexus chakra, we will need to place juniper berry or fennel in a vertical line just above the navel. If we have an overactive chakra, we can place some cypress or rosemary in the middle of the spine or above the navel. Lastly, we can maintain a balanced chakra by placing some lime or lemon above our navel in a circle or over our ribs.

- **Heart Chakra:** Being our emotional center, this chakra can be turbulent and quick to fall into imbalance. To help unblock this energy point, we want to use rose otto or fragonia over the central chest area. These are powerful anti-inflammatories that can help combat back and chest pain, and they also work toward rebalancing the heart chakra. Tea tree and melissa are both fantastic for calming an overactive heart chakra and should be placed between the shoulder blades. Finally, jasmine and may chang can be used very effectively to maintain balance of the chakra and help ward off negative emotions.

- **Throat Chakra:** As our communications center, this energy point is primarily based in our throat, lungs, and mouth area. Melaleuca, basil, and blue cypress oil are particularly good for cleansing the skin around the face and chest of acne and other skin conditions that may be brought on by an unbalanced throat chakra. Chamomile oil is used to calm an overactive throat chakra by placing some just below the chin. Lastly, peppermint and spearmint oil are fantastic for clearing blocked sinuses and soothing sore throats. Simply rub some around your nose or under your chin.

- **Third Eye Chakra:** For the third eye chakra, we are primarily looking to help with headaches, boosting our mood, and decreasing stress. For reducing the frequency and pain from headaches, we can use helichrysum, marjoram, and eucalyptus oil. We can apply these oils over the sinuses, behind the ears, and at the base of the neck. For boosting mood and reducing stress, we want to apply sage, rosemary, or sandalwood to our forehead or below the chin, or we can inhale it in vapor form.

- **Crown Chakra:** Finally, the crown chakra has very few links to the physical body. Thus, nearly all of the benefits we will get from using oils for this energy point are mental in nature. For insomnia and anxiety, myrrh, lavender, and patchouli oil are fantastic at helping us relax and sleep soundly when inhaled or placed on the forehead. To help boost moods and aid the flow of spiritual energy, frankincense, bergamot, and fragonia oil are all incredibly effective when inhaled or placed on the temples.

Crystals and Chakras

CRYSTALS FOR CHAKRA HEALING

Crystal healing is one of the most popular and straightforward forms of healing chakras. Along with being quite simple, crystal healing has been shown to be incredibly effective in rebalancing and encouraging healing in the chakras. Although there is little scientific research regarding the effects of crystals, it is clear that something is at work behind the scenes.

The traditional belief is that crystals work as conduits for energy. They are superconductors that allow positive and negative energy to flow through them incredibly effectively. Combine that conductivity with the correct colors for each chakra, and you essentially have a battery pack for every one of the energy points.

As well as being incredible sources of energy for our chakras, crystals can act as amazing cleansing tools. They behave like sponges for bad energy. If we feel that a chakra is blocked, we can place one of the corresponding gemstones on it and attempt to drain any negative energy from it, then replacing it with positive energy from the crystal.

A common theme is to describe the energy coming from crystals as vibrations. When something bad happens to us, it is an imbalance of too many low frequency vibrations. Low frequency vibrations cause our chakras to slow their spin or even become blocked. High frequency vibrations, on the other hand, speed up our chakras and re-energize them. These specific frequencies are found in all crystals.

Keep in mind that different crystals do have varying effects and work effectively in different areas of the body. The color of the various crystals corresponds to the colors of our chakras, and as such, those crystals help those specific areas of the body and the mental aspects of those particular chakras.

There are two basic techniques for healing the different regions of our body: targeted healing and general healing.

- **Targeted Healing**: For targeted healing, we try to pinpoint the specific location of the issue. If your stresses are manifesting as knee pain, you would place crystals alongside the knee on either side. Similarly, if negative energy manifests as bowel

issues, you would place crystals on your lower
stomach.

- **General Healing**: For general healing, we take a
direct approach to covering the chakra center itself. In
this technique, we focus on balancing the chakra first
and foremost, and hopefully by balancing the source,
any other issues will also clear up.

Most of the time, I would recommend doing a combination of
both techniques when trying to treat specific issues or
chakras. If you are only doing some routine maintenance,
however, general healing is usually the best option.

Root Chakra

When working with root chakra crystals, we are mainly
aiming to improve the health of the lower body and our sense
of security. The root chakra has the potential to be a hiding
place for a lot of negative energy. Any feelings of lack of security regarding basic needs goes here. If you're worried about
rent or grocery money, or if you are experiencing fear
regarding your general health, all of that stress will soak into
this chakra and manifest into issues surrounding this area.

Targeted healing areas for this chakra are typically found on
the tops of the feet, the ankles, either side of the knees, the
inside of the thighs, and the lower abdomen over the bowl.

Here are some of the best crystals to utilize if you want to balance your root chakra:

- Bloodstone
- Zircon
- Hematite
- Fire agate
- Black tourmaline
- Garnet

Sacral Chakra

Sacral chakra crystals are an incredibly potent form of crystal due to their brilliant colors and pure sensual energy. This chakra can be a source of a lot of personal negative energy. Due to the very personal nature of this energy point, any personal insecurities, embarrassing feelings, and sexual shames may end up poisoning the sacral chakra. Any kind of personal insecurities about body size, appearance, or sexuality can manifest in blockages of this energy point, and these blockages can lead to further issues in the areas surrounding this chakra.

Targeted healing areas for this chakra are the sides of the hips, on the lumbar of the spine, and above the sexual organs on the pubis.

The best crystals for the sacral chakra are as follows:

- Carnelian
- Copper
- Turquoise
- Orange fluorite
- Imperial topaz
- Moonstone

Solar Plexus Chakra

Solar plexus crystals are a particularly strong source of life energy. Some ancient cultures believed these yellow crystals to be sunrays in physical form. Maybe they had a point, because these crystals are incredibly effective at kickstarting our solar plexus chakra, the source of life energy in the body. Due to the nature of this chakra, any feelings of depression, lethargy, amotivation, and lack of willpower will linger in the energy point and affect its ability to produce energy for us.

The careful placement of some of these stones can massively help to rid the chakra of those damaging energies. Some of the targeted healing points for this chakra are along the sides of the ribs, on the solar plexus, on the center of the spine, and on the inside of the elbows.

Here are the ideal crystals to use for this chakra:

- Amber
- Yellow jasper
- Tiger's eye

- Yellow apatite
- Citrine
- Honey calcite

* * *

Heart Chakra

Heart chakra crystals are some of the most popular crystals out there for their effects not only in helping our love lives but also our cardiovascular health. This is the only chakra that has two different color crystals which represent its physical and mental aspects. Pink crystals represent its mental aspects while green crystals represent physical aspects of this energy point. Pink is a warm, nurturing color. It is the color of newborns, newly budded roses, and sweet berries. This color and its crystals help to combat negative energies surrounding love and relationships.

Past trauma from relationships, commitment issues, and fears of abandonment all manifest in this chakra and can be removed with pink crystals. Green, on the other hand, is the color of health in nature; green plants are healthy plants. It is the color of life and prosperity. Negative energy in this chakra can manifest as cardiovascular issues.

The accurate placement of crystals on this chakra and its targeted healing spots can help imbue some of that healthy life energy into it. The targeted healing areas for this chakra are the sternum (over the heart if using pink gems), between the shoulders and collar bones, in the crook of the armpit, and on the upper spine.

The following crystals can greatly benefit this chakra:

- Rose quartz
- Green aventurine
- Malachite
- Jade
- Pink tourmaline
- Rosasite

Throat Chakra

Crystals associated with this energy point have powerful creative energies to them. Lapis lazuli, in particular, has been used for thousands of years as a paint and dye by artists and crafters across the globe. Negative energies in this chakra focus on suppressing our creative elements and our ability to express ourselves. Because of this chakra being our source of creativity, any feelings of creative insecurity, stagefright, or artist's block can stem from imbalances here.

In regards to physical ailments, negative energy here can manifest as throat infections, neck pain, and thyroid dysfunctions, among other things. Our targeted healing points for this chakra are on either side of the neck, in our jugular notch, below the chin, and at the back of the neck.

The best crystals for balancing the throat chakra include the following:

- Angelite
- Amazonite
- Aquamarine
- Celestite
- Lapis lazuli
- Blue calcite

Third Eye Chakra

The crystals associated with this chakra are filled with frequencies that resonate very efficiently with those of our brain waves. Because of this resonance, these crystals can have an amazing brain-boosting effect for us.

The negative energies that affect our third eye chakra can not only cause anxiety, depression, and confusion, but they may also bring on migraines, mental fog, and even dizziness. The utilization of crystals to cleanse this chakra can help treat all these issues and also improve the health of our brain to an even higher level than before.

Targeted healing areas of this chakra are between the eyebrows, on the temples, behind the ears, and at the top of the brain stem.

Some of the crystals associated with the third eye chakra are listed below:

- Azurite
- Tanzanite
- Amethyst
- Obsidian
- Purple fluorite
- Lolite

* * *

Crown Chakra

Finally, we will discuss the crown chakra and its crystals. The crystals associated with this chakra are especially pure, containing energy that is untainted by any negative frequencies. They act as especially powerful conduits and can actually substitute for the crystals of other chakras too. This is due to the crown chakra's role as the source of all energy points. This chakra is the home of our spiritual energy and is the primary entry point of divine light and knowledge.

Because of the spiritual importance of this chakra, it's somewhere which can easily be affected by negative energies, meaning it is crucial that we cleanse this area frequently. Regular crystal cleanses in this region can help to prevent the spiritual doubt, tainted wisdom, and misdirection that is brought on by blockages here.

The most effective way of performing targeted healing for this chakra is by laying down and creating a halo of crystals around your head. This energy point is not a physical chakra, so it doesn't help to have its crystals in contact with the body.

Here are the crystals you can utilize to help balance your crown chakra:

- Quartz crystal
- White topaz
- Selenite
- White danburite
- Diamond
- White howlite

SETTING UP FOR CRYSTAL HEALING

Regardless of whether you are performing the healing on yourself or on someone else, it is incredibly important that everyone involved gets into a state of deep relaxation. We can achieve this by playing calming, melodious ambient music, diffusing essential oils into the air, burning incense, making sure the room is warm, and dimming the lights to a comfortably low level.

Once we have an ideal environment, everyone involved should take some meditative breaths in order to fall into a state of deeper relaxation. Continue to breathe in this manner throughout the process. If you are placing crystals on yourself, it's especially important that you make sure you're calm. Chakras are their most open and malleable when you're calm and relaxed, so it's key that you make sure you are in this state in order to get the best results out of your crystal healing.

How Long to Use

Crystal healing sessions can last as long as you feel you can maintain focus. If you can continue your calm breathing and stay focused on healing your chakras, you will be making an impact. Whether you only have five minutes or a whole hour to work with, you will be making a positive impact on your health.

Keep in mind that you should not force anything. If you feel yourself getting anxious or like you *have* to continue going, then stop. Forcing the process will only create stress and anxiety which will worsen any imbalance you already feel.

Allow yourself as much time as you need, and relish the deep relaxation. The length of the session is less important than the depth of relaxation that is achieved during the session.

Cleansing Crystals

Before and after each session, we must be sure to cleanse our crystals. As I mentioned earlier, crystals tend to soak up both negative and positive energies. We can cleanse the negative energies and purify our stones after and before each session to maximize their effectiveness.

Cleansing crystals is a simple process. We can easily do it by passing them under cold, running water, smudging them with sage smoke, or enveloping them in incense smoke.

USING CRYSTALS IN OUR DAILY LIVES

Along with being beautiful and useful in cleansing sessions, crystals are also functional in more practical ways. We can actually incorporate them into many of our daily routines and keep a little source of positive energy with us at all times.

- **Using crystals during meditation**: We've already covered the wonders of chakra meditation, but we can enhance both the effects of meditation and of our crystals by using them in tandem. Placing crystals around you or on chakra points during meditation can allow you to absorb even more energy and cleanse more efficiently.

- **Carry crystals with us**: Carrying crystals with you, whether it be in your pockets or as a piece of jewelry, can be a very handy and effective way of staying connected to a source of positive energy at all times. If you're looking to work on a specific chakra, wearing a necklace of one of that chakra's crystals will allow you to soak up that energy all day long. If you're particularly prone to anxiety during your day, wearing a crystal and helps you feel relaxed can help combat that.

- **Creating a crystal grid**: Crystal grids are a creative and aesthetically pleasing way of arranging your crystals in your house or garden. There are many sacred geometric patterns that mimic the shape of various chakras and sacred features of ancient medicine. By arranging our crystals into these grids, we can amplify their effects and introduce a hub of positive energy into our environment.

- **Create a crystal altar**: Similar to the crystal grid, we can create an altar inside of our living space. This altar will consist of incense, crystals, sacred idols, and even offerings to our chakras. We can meditate and perform crystal healing at this altar to increase our spiritual energy and our sensitivity to divine energy.

- **Use crystals in your home decor**: Using crystals in your home decor is one of the best ways of passively improving the vibe of your living space. Try incorporating the crystals that you need into wallhangings, lampshades, ornaments, plant pots, and even cutlery.

- **Use them while you sleep**: We can incorporate crystals into our bedroom too. Try placing a crystal on your headboard or under your pillow. You can also place crystals under the mattress, especially in areas where you want to cleanse specific chakras.

- **Use crystals in your self-care routine**: Lastly, using crystals in your self-care routine can be a fantastic, intimate way of treating yourself with positive energy and self-love. Try adding crystals into your bath and the water you use to wash your face. You can even place crystals in with your creams and skincare products to infuse them with positive energy.

Things You Need to Know

FAQ

We've been through so much in this book so far, and now that we're nearing the end, I'd hate to leave you with more questions than answers. So, let's try to address any outstanding questions in this FAQ. I hope that I can quell any remaining doubts you may have and finally set you on the path to enlightenment with all the knowledge you may ever need.

- **Do men and women have the same chakras?** Yes. All human beings have the same chakras regardless of sexuality, race, or origin. Although, our chakras themselves do have masculine and feminine qualities. The root, solar plexus, and throat chakras are masculine. The sacral, heart, and third eye chakras are feminine. The crown chakra does not have a gendered quality.

- **I've heard about lower and upper chakras, but what are they?** As we know, there are seven chakras. The central chakra is the heart. The three above that are sometimes called the upper chakras, and the three below that are sometimes known as the lower chakras.

- **Is it possible to feel my chakras?** Not in the sense that you could touch one, but often we do feel our chakras at work. Have you ever felt those butterflies in your stomach when you're with your partner? That's your sacral chakra. How about that nagging feeling in your head that you should do something? That's your third eye chakra.

- **Where can I get crystals?** You can find crystals on many online stores that ship across the USA and the world. You almost certainly have one in your state. Try to make sure your crystals are sourced from environmentally responsible suppliers if possible.

- **Where can I get essential oils?** Similarly to crystals, there are plenty of online stores that sell real essential oils. Make sure to check that the store you buy from sources their oils responsibly and have ethical business practices. Unfortunately, the essential oil market has a handful of MLMs (Pyramid Schemes) which operate with predatory practices, so make sure to do your research.

- **Am I crazy for believing this?** Definitely not! Society may have you believe that this is quackery and that none of it works. However, for thousands of years, millions of people have practiced these techniques and beliefs. Don't let an ignorant society stop you from reaching enlightenment.

Afterword

Finally, we reach the end of this book. We've gone from spiritual saplings desperately trying to grow up toward the sunlight to fully grown trees freely experiencing all the rays of the sun and the freedom that comes from being above the canopy of the forest. It has been quite a long journey, and we have covered a lot of information along the way. I only hope that I have given you the tools you need to take the remaining steps for yourself. Your chakras are in your own hands, as they always have been; the only difference now is that you have the knowledge to take care of them and reap their rewards.

Just remember: stay calm, focus on your goals, and never give up. With the knowledge you have learned here, you can change your life in so many ways. You have learned to love yourself and others more than ever before. You have learned to express yourself in ways you never even dreamed of. You have learned to cope with trauma in the healthiest way possible. With the knowledge of chakra healing, you have become self-sufficient in self-care. So, now you can take your knowledge out into the world and truly prosper.

References

American Heart Association. (2019, November 25). *Regular fasting could lead to longer, healthier life*. Www.Heart.org. https://www.heart.org/en/news/2019/11/25/regular-fasting-could-lead-to-longer-healthier-life

Chakras.net. (n.d.). *Shiva and Shakti*. Www.Chakras.net. Retrieved December 12, 2020, from https://www.chakras.net/yoga-principles/shiva-and-shakti

Cronkleton, E. (2018, May 15). *Aromatherapy Uses and Benefits*. Healthline; Healthline Media. https://www.healthline.com/health/what-is-aromatherapy

Empress Organics. (2017, May 5). *Balancing Your Chakras With Essential Oils*. Empress Organics. https://empressorganics.net/blogs/news/balancing-your-chakras-with-essential-oils

Fondin, M. (2015a, February 10). *Open Yourself to Love With the Fourth Chakra*. The Chopra Center. https://chopra.com/articles/open-yourself-to-love-with-the-fourth-chakra

Fondin, M. (2015b, April 23). *Speak Your Inner Truth With the Fifth Chakra*. Chopra. https://www.chopra.com/articles/speak-your-inner-truth-with-the-fifth-chakra

Fondin, M. (2015c, May 26). *Trust Your Intuition With the Sixth Chakra*. Chopra. https://www.chopra.com/articles/trust-your-intuition-with-the-sixth-chakra

Fondin, M. (2015d, June 4). *Connect to the Divine With the Seventh Chakra*. Chopra. https://www.chopra.com/articles/connect-to-the-divine-with-the-seventh-chakra

Fondin, M. (2020, October 7). *The Root Chakra: Muladhara*. Chopra. https://chopra.com/articles/the-root-chakra-muladhara

Frawley, D. (n.d.). *Opening the Chakras: New Myths & Old Truths*. Yogainternational.com. Retrieved December 12, 2020, from https://yogainternational.com/article/view/opening-the-chakras-new-myths-old-truths

Frawley, D. (2009). Inner Tantric Yoga: Working with the Universal Shakti: Secrets of Mantras, Deities and Meditation. In *Google Books*. Lotus Press. https://books.google.co.za/books?id=T6Vp_rTWk-AAC&pg=PA163&redir_esc=y#v=onepage&q&f=false

Hurst, K. (2017a, October 19). *Heart Chakra Healing For Beginners: How To Open Your Heart Chakra*. The Law Of Attraction. https://www.thelawofattraction.com/heart-Chakra-healing/

Hurst, K. (2017b, October 19). *Root Chakra Healing For Beginners: How To Open Your Root Chakra*. The Law Of Attraction. https://www.thelawofattraction.com/root-chakra-healing/

Hurst, K. (2017c, October 19). *Sacral Chakra Healing For Beginners: How To Open Your Sacral Chakra*. The Law Of Attraction. https://www.thelawofattraction.com/sacral-chakra-healing/

Hurst, K. (2017d, October 19). *Solar Plexus Chakra Healing: How To Open Your Solar Plexus Chakra*. The Law Of Attraction. https://www.thelawofattraction.com/solar-plexus-chakra-healing/

Hurst, K. (2017e, October 19). *Third Eye Chakra Healing For Beginners: How To Open Your Third Eye*. The Law Of Attraction. https://www.thelawofattraction.com/third-eye-chakra-healing/

Hurst, K. (2017f, October 19). *Throat Chakra Healing For Beginners: How To Open Your Throat Chakra*. The Law Of Attraction. https://www.thelawofattraction.com/throat-chakra-healing/

King, D. (2018, March 27). *Chakra Foods for Healing & Health - Blog*. Deborah King. https://deborahking.com/7-foods-to-heal-7-chakras/

Lindberg, S. (2020, August 24). *What Are Chakras? Meaning, Location, and How to Unblock Them.* Healthline. https://www.healthline.com/health/what-are-chakras

Lizzy. (2013a). *How To Select The Right Chakra Stone.* Chakras.Info. https://www.chakras.info/chakra-stones/

Lizzy. (2013b). *Know Your Sacral Chakra And How To Harness Its Power.* Chakras.Info. https://www.chakras.info/sacral-chakra/

Lizzy. (2013c). *Know Your Throat Chakra And How To Unlock Its Power.* Chakras.Info. https://www.chakras.info/throat-chakra/

Lizzy. (2019a). *7 Chakra Crash Course: A Beginner's Guide To Awakening Your Seven Chakras.* Chakras.Info. https://www.chakras.info/7-chakras/

Lizzy. (2019b, December 9). *3 Simple Yoga Poses To Activate Your Crown Chakra.* Chakras.Info. https://www.chakras.info/crown-chakra-yoga-poses/

Lizzy. (2020, April 9). *Know Your Crown Chakra And How To Tap Into Its Power.* Chakras.Info. https://www.chakras.info/crown-chakra/

McNally, R. (n.d.). *Reiki & The Chakras - Bring the Body into Balance & Harmony.* The Thirsty Soul. Retrieved December 12, 2020, from https://thethirstysoul.com/reiki/chakras-reiki/

Rosen, R. (2017, May 15). *Reclining Bound Angle Pose.* Yoga Journal. https://www.yogajournal.com/poses/reclining-bound-angle-pose

Shah, P. (2020, August 20). *A Primer of the Chakra System.* Chopra. https://www.chopra.com/articles/what-is-a-chakra

Singh Khalsa, K. P. (2016, September 9). *Chakra Massage.* MassageTherapy.com. https://www.massagetherapy.com/articles/chakra-massage

Spear, H. E. (2019, September 9). *What Is Color Therapy & How Can It Help Heal Our Chakras?* Mindbodygreen. https://www.mindbodygreen.com/articles/what-is-color-therapy-and-how-can-it-help-heal-our-chakras

Thorpe, M. (2020, October 27). *12 Science-Based Benefits of Meditation.* Healthline. https://www.healthline.com/nutrition/12-benefits-of-meditation

Tiffany. (2016, June 17). *Food and Chakra Pairing: Balancing and Healing Our Energy Centers Through Food.* Parsnips and Pastries. https://www.parsnipsandpastries.com/chakra-food-pairing-balancing-healing-energy-centers-food/

Tracy, J. (2019, September 18). *7 Chakras Healing Foods | Chakra Food Chart.* 7 Chakra Store. https://7chakrastore.com/blogs/news/healthy-chakras-chakra-healing-foods

Wisdom by Gurudev. (2016, July 18). *Music & Chakras.* Wisdom by Sri Sri Ravi Shankar. https://wisdom.srisriravishankar.org/music-chakras/

Yoga in Daily Life. (n.d.-a). *Bhujangasana*. Www.Yogaindailylife.org. Retrieved December 12, 2020, from https://www.yogaindailylife.org/system/en/level-5/bhujangasana

Yoga in Daily Life. (n.d.-b). *Chakrasana*. Www.Yogaindailylife.org. Retrieved December 12, 2020, from https://www.yogaindailylife.org/system/en/level-6/chakrasana

Yoga in Daily Life. (n.d.-c). *Setu Asana*. Www.Yogaindailylife.org. Retrieved December 12, 2020, from https://www.yogaindailylife.org/system/en/level-2/setu-asana

Yoga in Daily Life. (n.d.-d). *Shalabhasana*. Www.Yogaindailylife.org. Retrieved December 12, 2020, from https://www.yogaindailylife.org/system/en/level-5/shalabhasana

Yoga in Daily Life. (n.d.-e). *Yoga Mudra*. Www.Yogaindailylife.org. Retrieved December 12, 2020, from https://www.yogaindailylife.org/system/en/level-6/yoga-mudra

Yoga Journal. (2007a, August 28). *Boat Pose*. Yoga Journal. https://www.yogajournal.com/poses/full-boat-pose

Yoga Journal. (2007b, August 28). *Seated Forward Bend*. Yoga Journal. https://www.yogajournal.com/poses/seated-forward-bend

Yoga Journal. (2017a, April 12). *Plow Pose*. Yoga Journal. https://www.yogajournal.com/poses/plow-pose

Yoga Journal. (2017b, April 17). *Staff Pose*. Yoga Journal. https://www.yogajournal.com/poses/staff-pose

Yoga Journal. (2017c, May 16). *Supported Shoulderstand (Salamba Sarvangasana) - Yoga Journal*. Www.Yogajournal.com. https://www.yogajournal.com/poses/supported-shoulderstand

Yoga Journal. (2019a, January 7). *Bharadvaja's Twist*. Yoga Journal. https://www.yogajournal.com/poses/bharadvaja-s-twist#section_4

Yoga Journal. (2019b, January 7). *Big Toe Pose*. Yoga Journal. https://www.yogajournal.com/poses/big-toe-pose

Yoga Journal. (2019c, January 7). *Bound Angle Pose (Baddha Konasana) - Yoga Journal*. https://www.yogajournal.com/poses/bound-angle-pose

Yoga Journal. (2019d, January 7). *Camel Pose*.

https://www.yogajournal.com/poses/camel-pose

Yoga Journal. (2019e, January 7). *Child's Pose*. Yoga Journal. https://www.yogajournal.com/poses/child-s-pose

Yoga Journal. (2019f, January 7). *Cow Face Pose*. Yoga Journal. https://www.yogajournal.com/poses/cow-face-pose

Yoga Journal. (2019g, January 7). *Eagle Pose*. Yoga Journal. https://www.yogajournal.com/poses/eagle-pose

Yoga Journal. (2019h, January 7). *Firefly Pose*. Yoga Journal. https://www.yogajournal.com/poses/firefly-pose

Yoga Journal. (2019i, January 7). *Fish Pose*. Yoga Journal. https://www.yogajournal.com/poses/fish-pose

Yoga Journal. (2019j, January 7). *Hero Pose*. Yoga Journal. https://www.yogajournal.com/poses/hero-pose

Yugay, I. (2019, January 27). *How To Identify & Heal Blocked Chakras*. Mindvalley Blog. https://blog.mindvalley.com/symptoms-of-blocked-chakras/

Zoldan, R. J. (2020, June 22). *Your 7 chakras, explained—plus how to tell if they're blocked*. Well+Good. https://www.wellandgood.com/what-are-chakras/

THIRD EYE AWAKENING

A BEGINNER'S GUIDE TO OPENING YOUR THIRD EYE, EXPANDING YOUR MIND'S POWER, AND INCREASING YOUR AWARENESS WITH PRACTICAL GUIDED MEDITATION

Introduction

The third eye–what does opening the third eye mean to you exactly? The acquisition of power? Gaining new insight? Experiencing a new type of freedom? Personal and spiritual progression? We often filter new information through preconceived notions and previous experiences.

This is not necessarily a bad thing. I am not here to tell you that the way you have lived your life is wrong or right, and I am not writing this to explain to you how your choices in life have led you here or there. I am just here. I am just writing. I am a temporary stop in your life, offering you information that I hope will be helpful on your journey to wherever you are heading. What might this sliver of information be?

The idea that reality is not something someone else can describe to you, but rather something you construct from your perception through senses, experiences, information, and beliefs. This idea changes from person to person, as we use our senses differently and experience life in many different ways.

Your reality will be considerably different than that of someone born blind or deaf, as they do not have those senses to construct a reality around them the way we would—which is not to disparage these people at all. Rather, it is similar to the different realities constructed by those who have awakened their third eye and those not. The various groups understand and experience their realities even though they may be living in the same time, space, and culture.

In this book, we will discuss a few topics surrounding the third eye and its awakening; however, the techniques and methods that can work for me, or someone else, might not work for you. . The reality you are currently perceiving is not the reality that I perceive, it is not the reality that your friend perceives, and it is not the reality that your neighbor perceives. Similar to how you might try and explain color to someone who was born blind, it is quite difficult to explain what you may perceive with your third eye without experiencing it for yourself.

It is so important to have an open mind when dealing with new information so that we do not simply assign it a tag before storing it somewhere in our memory, but rather contemplate the new information in great detail. Accepting or rejecting it can only come after. This is the best way to deal with any new information you come across, especially information surrounding personal and spiritual growth, as it can dramatically change how you construct and live your life.

Unfortunately, there is a lot of information out there these days, and processing it all properly can be painstakingly slow and tedious, which is why I am writing this book. The third eye has been described in many texts throughout history and has been a popular topic of discussion.

I believe this is due to a restriction placed on our way of life. We do not really have any options on how we want to live our lives in these modern times as everything seems to be pre-decided for us. From birth, humans are taught a very specific set of socially acceptable beliefs, behavioral patterns, rules, and structures.

Now, this might be for better or worse, but it leaves us with very little free space in which we can construct our own life path. The third eye became a popular topic due to the insight it might provide us in this constricted reality, due to the freedom we might experience from awakening it, the power we might control after awakening it, and the personal and spiritual growth we might obtain during the process.

Is this what you believe?

In the first few chapters of this book, I will provide you with some information on the history of the third eye, compiled from research I have done on my journey. Eastern belief systems and traditions are very extensive when it comes to personal and spiritual growth, whereas Western belief systems tend to focus on a very specific set of rules to be followed, or else one might have to face whatever consequences are listed in their texts.

This does not mean Western belief systems are inherently bad. In fact, many of them have helped my understanding of spiritual growth. But there is an inherent problem that people who've grown up under Western religion experience; they find it difficult to understand what most Eastern traditions try to convey, as most of them are not strictly speaking a religion as Westerners perceive them to be.

This is something that philosopher Alan Watts understood deeply, as he tried to project the meaning behind Eastern traditions to the Western people in a way they might find more suitable to digest.

Why am I telling you this? Because going forward, there are concepts I wish you to look at—not from your own point of view, but rather from an angle you have never looked at them before.

Not to fret, however, as we will go through some familiar topics parallel to traditional beliefs, such as what the world of science has labeled factual in their endeavors to understand the reality surrounding the third eye. Understanding this will give a foundation on which you can build your new-found library of knowledge, as some people find it difficult to accept new information without a scientific point of view. Being logical can be both positive and negative. When you are stuck looking at something simply based upon your physical senses, it can be a good thing to take a step back just to see what your intuition tells you.

New information can light the way to new possibilities, like how history has depicted spiritual journeys and how modern times require them. There are many things on the road to opening your third eye; it's just a matter of whether you are willing to take the necessary steps.

There are some fundamentals, from meditation to relaxation, to more unorthodox methods like using crystals and oils, one must understand in order to move along this path, and we will be going over them, step by step. We will consume and absorb new information together, expanding our awareness of reality.

Walking hand in hand with awakening the third eye will be your chakras. Depending on your level of experience in this field, you might recognize the word, or you might not, but essentially the third eye is your 6th chakra. This brings us to the inherent issue of keeping your chakras balanced, and your energy paths flowing freely. I will do my best to help you to clear these paths, chakra by chakra, to show you your own potential for life.

I will help you to reach what many people believe to be the awakening of the third eye the best that I can. Now is the time to start, not yesterday and not tomorrow. As the philosopher, Alan Watts, once stated "The future is a concept, it doesn't exist. There is no such thing as tomorrow. There never will be, because time is now. That's one of the things we discover when we stop talking to ourselves and stop think-ing. We find there is only a present, only an eternal now."

Your Awakening Through History

This chapter will be information-dense, and there is a reason for that. When growing up, we learn how to speak and communicate through whatever language it is we are exposed to; we do this through intuition. We are exposed to a tremendous amount of experiences, expressions, emotions, and knowledge.

But, at a young age, we lack the brainpower to actually process all of this. Intuition acts as a temporary bypass for this, allowing us to feel and sense what intentions are projected through certain actions and words. Thus, we end up learning how to communicate not through the transmission of words, but rather through the extension of self intent.

We are not infants anymore but, if you are, and reading this, good for you! I digress. We lost that connection to the world around us as communication became a form of information transmission rather than intuition. So what would the best way be to regain the level of intuition we had when we were younger? Simply to shut down, to stop overthinking and broadcasting information, to stop getting hung-up on single thoughts, and let the information flow freely, entering your mind and moving along.

The reason this chapter is so dense is so that you may learn new things surrounding the third eye, and then simply move on to the process of actually awakening, having some practical knowledge to then fall back on should you feel the need.

More often than not, we struggle to see the full picture behind the intention, we simply try to deal with it at that moment. You may have stumbled upon this book because you are curious. Perhaps you are bored and just decided to read something different. Others might be obsessed with the idea that there must be more out there, and opening the third eye will help them to see behind the curtain.

Unfortunately, we need context as human beings, as life forms. If you are obsessed with the intention of seeing behind the picture, you will keep missing the full picture in front of you. This chapter is here so we can gather all the information, process it, contemplate it, accept it, or reject it, and only then can we begin to understand the third eye and its awakening.

So, let's begin with what we have forgotten.

THAT WHICH IS LOST CAN ALWAYS BE FOUND

As times change, so do the concepts of reality we live by, so it is not unheard of for religions to take shape and morph into whatever it is the current age requires from them. This is, to say the least, a chilling thought. What this means is that there are traditions that change through the times, so let's take a look at the old and unchanged information, starting with religion in relation to the third eye.

Hinduism

Hinduism is a worldwide recognized religion, so most people have heard about it before. For those of you who haven't, let me give you a quick breakdown of some of the details.

Hinduism is quite old, and by quite old, I mean the oldest religion according to most scholars. It is also the third-largest religion, right behind Christianity and Islam. Unlike the two aforementioned, Hinduism does not have a specific founder, almost as if it just started to exist. It differs from the others in another major way as well. It's almost like a compilation of multiple philosophies and traditions, resulting in a very unique study experience.

One of the concepts many Westerners have difficulty understanding is that it can be compared to a way of life more than an actual religion, with some amazing stories and lessons in between. One of the main belief systems that exists within Hinduism is samsara, the cycle of life, death, and reincarnation, which makes it easier to understand how the religion functions as a whole.

Hindus do have a set of core beliefs which, to me, are significantly more interesting than those of other religions. Truth, to Hindus, is eternal, the essential essence of the universe. Another of their beliefs is that one must always strive to do the right thing; this is known as 'Dharma', a word which has no translation to English. Some of these core beliefs come from the ancient scriptures known as 'The Vedas.' These scriptures contain revelations to ancient sages, and are with no end, meaning they will remain even after the cycle of life finished.

There are many gods and goddesses worshipped in the Hindu faith, the most complex and intricate god being Shiva, commonly known as 'the destroyer,' but also as 'the restorer.' Now, there are three central gods in the Hindu triumvirate: Brahma, believed to be the creator; Vishnu, believed to be the preserver of that which was created; and then Shiva, that which destroys in order to make way for new creation.

While Shiva might sound like a malevolent god, he is, in fact, good and evil combined. Hindus do not believe this destruction to be despotic or random, but rather constructive, so as to shatter illusions and destroy imperfections on the way forward.

This is one of the reasons why he is regarded as the most complicated of the three, as is apparent in his appearance as well. Shiva is depicted with the sun as his right eye and the moon as his left, having a third eye in between the two on the forehead. This third eye is the key to his wisdom and knowledge on all things spiritual. When utilizing this key, he becomes able to see beyond that which presents itself on the surface as obvious, as if unlocking the door to truth itself. There is a general belief among certain sects of Hinduism that all which is ignorant or evil vanishes when his third eye is opened.

This line spoke to me personally and may resonate with you as well. The inherent idea that this might spark when first reading it is quite an intriguing one. If you are able to open your third eye, will you finally be able to expose yourself to your own ignorance of this reality, and see past it? Ironically, what I learned after that made it all the more frightening of an idea.

One of the teachings in Hinduism describes the tale of when Shiva was disturbed from his meditation and worship by the love god, Kama. In anger, Shiva opened his third eye and destroyed Kama, burning him to ashes. Long tale short, however, the love god was brought back to life when Parvati, the god of harmony intervened. Many Hindus still believe that should Shiva open his third eye again, all that we have come to know as the physical world will be destroyed. I encourage you to find the rest of the text and study it, as it holds tremendous moral value.

But this brings me back to my previous realization.

It is stated that all which is ignorant or evil is reduced to nothingness in front of the third eye, with the belief that the world as we know it would be destroyed through the opening of it. If we apply this to the awakening of our own third eye, the picture becomes all the more clear, literally. The ignorance surrounding us, the way we have been taught to live, the evil our society has spewed forth will be, in a sense, destroyed before us should we open our third eye.

The awakening of our third eye may not simply be just to become aware of our own ignorance in our own reality, but also the ignorance of others in their respective realities. This idea consumed me for quite some time. Is reality really that fragile? Are the lives that we have constructed around us truly so easily unraveled? As I stumbled forth on my journey with this newfound realization, I came to accept it. Life is, after all, what we make of it, so it is better to accept that which we cannot change and learn to live with it.

This idea is most likely not new, as depictions of Shiva have been found to be older than 10,000 BCE. This information was never lost, strictly speaking, but rather lost to the generations. We do not teach kids that which is unnecessary to make them functioning members of society; in fact, many parents do not teach their kids much at all, leaving it to schools and nannies as the parents are usually too busy working, trying to provide for the family.

To some, this is a conspiracy level train of thought, but do most parents these days even know what is being taught to their children? Let's leave that discussion for another time.

Buddhism

Buddhism is similar to Hinduism in the sense that it is more like a compilation of philosophies, beliefs, and teachings that provide its adherents with a kind of guide as to how to live their lives. Similarly, they do not believe in a specific god.

What many people do not know, however, is that it was founded by Siddhartha Gautama between the 4th and 6th century BCE in northern India, and only spread to other Asian countries later. This religion started to spread to the West in the 20th century and has been gaining traction since. I personally believe this is due to the fact that Buddhists do not believe in a god or deity, but rather focus on gaining self-enlightenment through experiencing nirvana, and no, not the band, but rather a state in which everything—pain, suffering, the self, desire, everything—falls away and is released from the cycle of life.

The Buddha is actually just 'The Enlightened One,'—not a god or prophet or any of that, just a guy who had his own experience of nirvana and taught others how to do the same. Buddhists also believe that every few decades, a new 'Enlightened one' is born. This person would be able to reach nirvana and add to the teachings of the previous one. This is why many scholars do not recognize it as an organized religion, but rather view it as a way of life.

Now, you may or may not have come across statues depicting the buddha, most of which depict him having a small third eye. Buddhists see the third eye as more of a symbol for spiritual awakening, with wisdom to follow soon after. This brings us back to what nirvana is, and how the journey of most Buddhist only ends when they reach it. Nirvana is the end goal.

Nirvana can be seen as the end goal for anyone; it is a state in which the mind is freed from all the delusions that might exist in this physical world. Awakening your third eye is a way of seeing reality for what it is; your judgment is no longer clouded by greed or jealousy, your hatred falls away and peace enters your mind. Remember, your reality is constructed by your senses, and it is through those senses you learn to hate, become greedy, and experience jealousy. Adding another sense, the third eye, cracks open your reality in a spiritual sense, adding wisdom to that mixture. So, at that point, you have the wisdom to recognize that you might be greedy, and move away from it. It is the same for all experiences and emotions. When you add a third perspective to it, you become enlightened to your own ego.

This is what I have come to understand from studying Buddhism. I encourage everyone to study it, as the scripts provide you with a moral understanding which our modern world desperately needs. I am not telling anyone to commit to this, but simply adding the teachings to your mental library can help in many ways.

Sikhism and Jainism

When you are lost, you try to find a map or a way to help you navigate to where you need to be; in a spiritual sense, you would find a religion that resonates with you, and could help guide you to where you want to go.

Sikhism and Jainism are two religions that not necessarily stemmed from Hinduism and Buddhism, but share similarities. They are, however, unique enough so they can be classified as separate religions rather than just sects of the aforementioned.

People have different beliefs, and this is apparent in Sikhism and Jainism. Sikhs believe that there must be a singular god or deity, shapeless and formless, but nonetheless there. This is more similar to Western religions; however, some of their teachings overlap with those of Hinduism and Buddhism.

The Jains believe that the path to spiritual purity is a path of nonviolence and wellbeing. They focus on the health of the universe, itself, through not harming any living creature, as each has a soul, with not one being more valuable than the other. They are strict vegetarians and also believe in reincarnation.

I mention these two, even though they have no direct connection to the awakening of the third eye, because we all believe in different things. We find the belief which suits us best and go with it. While this may offend some, I apologize. I do not mean it in a condescending way. I simply mean that no matter where you are from and what belief you have, you will find your own path on your spiritual journey.

Taoism(Daoism)

Taoism, or as some might refer to it, Daoism, originated in ancient China around 500 BCE. Taoism is the way of living in harmony and balance with animals, nature, and the universe or the Tao. They believe that spirit is immortal, and after physical death, the energy comprising that spirit will become one with the universe.

This belief system is rather hard to explain in a definite sense, but you can see it as a way of how energy flows. They do not believe in specific gods, but rather that there are gods who exist, simply as a part of the energy flow. Chi, or Qi, is the flow of energy that guides everything in the universe. This thought process struck me as quite fascinating when I first encountered it, and only more so when I learned about balance.

Quite a familiar concept in the world made popular through teachings and media alike, is the balance between Yin and Yang. This is more the idea of balancing the pairs present in the universe, much like with the flow of electricity, you get a positive and negative. The energy in the universe works the same, good and bad, hot and cold, light and dark, the key being to have balance.

This concept came to be from observing the natural world, which is the part that stuck with me the most. Everything has a natural balance. Interfering with the balance will force the universe to rebalance whatever it is that you may have disturbed.

This is ever-present in our daily lives, from completely destroying the balance in our own bodies through the amount of rest we get, the food we eat, and the work we do, to how we disturb the balance of our planet. We feel the balance trying to correct itself within us, be it through intuition or physical signs. We see the planet trying to bring balance back to itself as we keep fighting against it.

The flow of energy is ever-present, shaping and molding as we move along, but it will always return to how it once was. We live, we die, the energy gets returned. When in the process of awakening your third eye, you will have to learn to balance the energy within you. That is the reason I decided to discuss Taoism with you, as you cannot awaken if you have an unbalanced life.

There are many reasons why this may interfere with your third eye awakening, the most basic being physical. You may be sick, or your perception might be consumed with a specific emotion such as love, greed, or hate. Balance is the key, and we will discuss how to balance the energy flow within you later on. For now, it is interesting to see how the concept of energy flow translates into other religions, and you might draw wisdom from either one on your journey to your final destination.

Western Religions and Traditions.

In many Western beliefs, the third eye is seen as a gateway, a tool through which we can see things we normally would not. Now I know this is what we just saw in the more Eastern traditions, but what I mean here is more basic and physical. Most Western beliefs focus on clairvoyance or the sight of spirits, angels, and demons.

While this is not wrong, in my personal opinion, it is more elementary and binary than what the universe actually is. The universe is not simply good and evil, as energy can take many forms.

In Christianity, there is no direct mention of the third eye. However, there is mention of the mind's eye. In the book of Mathew, Jesus stated that "The light of the body is the eye, if therefore thine eye be single, thy whole body shall be full of light. But if thine eye be evil, thy whole body shall be full of darkness." Many interpret to mean that should you not focus on the single, God, you will not be full of light but rather darkness.

Now some Christians believe that the third eye is akin to the apple from the tree of knowledge in the garden of Eden, of which Adam and Eve partook. This idea stems from the belief that when the serpent convinced Eve to do this, she, in turn, convinced Adam; they gained knowledge of that which they should not have, becoming "like God."

This interpretation has led many to state that opening the third eye would grant you knowledge of that which you must not have, and so you would be cast down to hell. Unfortunately, most leaders and founders of Western organized religion demonized anything they did not understand, and anything they thought to be counterproductive to their religious beliefs was automatically labeled as wrong. This resulted in their adherents becoming afraid of trying something new, out of fear for being punished or ridiculed. I guess you could say they were successful in their plan?

Not all Christians believe this, however. As with any religion, you get people outside the religion with different interpretations, as well as christians with their own interpretations.

Hermeticism and Esotericism

Established as another compilation of religious and philo-sophical beliefs, based on elements taken from Christian and Jewish spiritualism and mysticism, mixed with occult beliefs from ancient Egypt, Hermeticism gave birth to a new form of esotericism in the modern era.

The result was quite a compelling and persuasive religion which intrigued Muslim scholars and Western intellectuals right at the dawn of the renaissance. The interesting part of Hermeticism is the way it explains how the universe is indeed orderly, operating on specific principles measurable through alchemical and scientific studies. This is seen through the writings of big thinkers of this time such as Isaac Newton and John Dee.

This religion offered a flexible and tolerant environment for believers of an all-present god, combined with the mysticism of Christianity, Buddhisms, Judaism, Paganism, Hinduism, and Islam. It brought forth the idea that all the great religions have in some way a mystical truth to them, and can be tied together at their core in an esoteric manner.

As you can imagine, the belief system surrounding such a grand encompassing religion is quite vast, so going into detail is a topic for a whole other book. What can be taken away from this is the birth of modern magick, from the formation of the Hermetic Order of the Golden Dawn.

The Golden Dawn, when it first came to be established, was open to both sexes and treated them equally, as opposed to others before it who catered to only one of the genders/sexes. Inside this order, the teaching of Qabbalah, a western esoteric tradition covering mysticism and the occult was shared, with these teachings came alchemy, the magic of Hermes, and forms of occult science. The order was very secretive, with the general public being left in the dark of its existence until Aleister Crowley broke the silence in 1905, after which information started pouring out.

* * *

Modern Magick

Modern magick is a tricky subject to discuss, as there can be so many different interpretations to it, with some of them being burdened by stigmas and controversy. This is in light of modern organized religion branding anything obscure as either satanic or evil. This is best explained through the story of Damian Echols and the story of the West Memphis Three.

The West Memphis Three is the story of three teenagers arrested in 1994 for the murders of three young boys in West Memphis. During the trials to follow, it was brought to light that the three teenagers had an interest in the occult, automatically labeling the murders as part of a satanic ritual. This was poor judgment, as the understanding surrounding occultism at the time was what organized religion allowed it to be, which was simply satanic.

The outcry for these three teenagers was heard all over America as the evidence was unreliable and the bias against them in court was substantial. During his time on death row, Damian was helped by a zen master and turned to magick, after which he was released due to DNA evidence, you can read all about it in his own book as well.

But what modern magick proposes is that everything you want in life, you can obtain through putting the right amount of energy into it, through the use of specific sigils and practices.

What does this have to do with the third eye? Well, it's what you make of it. If you gather enough information and apply your own experience to that, you will find an answer. Awakening your third eye is much like that, if you want it to happen, it will, but you need to be prepared. You need to understand the interpretation of many in order to construct a more true picture. You need to find what humanity once lost; namely, perspective.

THE MODERN FACTS

As we move forward in society, we have become more egocentric, resulting in what I like to call the human paradox. We are human, constructed from the very matter we try to understand, fueled by the energy abundant in our universe, with the paradox coming to fruition when we realize just that.

We are simply conscious energy inhabiting matter, energy that became self-aware due to the complexity of the arrangement of matter that is our bodies.

Does this take all the mystery out of reality? Does this mean we live in a logical universe? It means quite the opposite. The fact that we became conscious means that the energy out there has the potential to be conscious as well. It simply needs to meet the required arrangement or necessary stimuli and observation. How do we observe the natural universe? Through the use of our senses and tools to enhance those senses and measure the outcome of certain reactions, which led to us constructing an universal language that we can use in order to communicate what we have found and come to understand, a language we dubbed science.

I believe the third eye to be one of these senses, a sense we can use to observe reality in a way we have never been able to before, a way science, unfortunately, has not quite been able to quantify. However, science has been able to provide us with some facts in order to ground our reality. Through neurological, biological, and physiological science, we have recognized the third eye as the pineal gland.

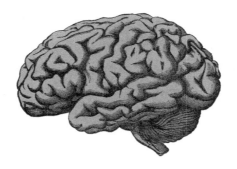

The Pineal Gland

Known as the pineal gland, or by some as the conarium, epiphysis cerebri, pineal organ, or pineal body, it is not necessarily a gland per say, however, it does account for the production and regulation of a hormone called melatonin. It is well noted that the function behind the pineal gland is not quite understood yet, the information around it is somewhat controversial except for some facts that have been established.

It is located in the middle of the brain, in an area known as the epithalamus, where the two hemispheres of the brain join. When looked at from the front, it is right about in the middle of your eyes, and from the side, around the area of your ear. As previously stated, it produces a hormone known as melatonin, which regulates your 24-hour sleep cycle, known as circadian rhythms. The full extent of what exactly melatonin does is still unknown, but we do know at least that it helps you to sleep.

Other chemicals produced by the pineal gland include serotonin, neurosteroids, and DMT. For those who are not familiar, DMT(Dimethyltryptamine) is a psychedelic compound found in the Banisteriopsis caapi, a jungle vine. The psychedelic 'trips' experienced by those who use DMT in a recreational setting, are explained to be reality shattering, almost as if you get the chance to look into the fabric of space-time, experiencing what exactly it is that makes the universe function.

The experiences vary, but most of the accounts leave the users with a profound sense of understanding. The parts of these stories that really stuck with me are the parts that seem almost identical from person to person, without them ever even knowing of each other's stories or experiences, and the most intriguing part is how some of these experiences match those experiences by monks and others who reach a certain level of enlightenment while meditating.

Simple food for thought, I guess.

Physically, the pineal gland is about the size of a pea, hence its name, and in most humans, it will calcify over time. This happens more or less due to not using it, I can't really tell you why it calcifies, but the conspiracy theorists would disagree, so I will leave that to your own deductions.

The interesting part about this gland is that it has a well developed eye-like structure in vertebrates (an animal with a spinal cord surrounded by cartilage or bone, which includes birds, fish, amphibians, reptiles, and mammals), especially in lower vertebrates. It does not function exactly like an eye though but rather a light receptor, which in some sense explains how it can detect day and night, in turn regulating your sleep patterns, but I do not believe that it is the only thing it detects, and neither do most scientists. The problem is, there is just not enough data.

WHY THIS MATTERS

So many people would read a book, looking for a quick answer to their question, especially when it comes to obscure topics. When it comes to the awakening of the third eye, there isn't just one answer, but many.

A mystic guru in northern India will explain it to you in a manner completely opposed to that of a modern-day magick practitioner. There are many ways to interpret the third eye and how to awaken it. Many believe you are born with it open, but due to you not using it, it closes, which is why they believe it calcifies.

The main reason I would like you to read over this chapter and contemplate what you have learned is to provide yourself with some perspective. You can even put this book down and go study some of the religions mentioned, inform your-self on other concepts of life and the flow of energy before continuing the process of awakening your third eye. If you do not wish to waste any more time studying up, or perhaps you already have, that's great, then we can start with the next step in your journey.

The Steps in Your Journey

I remember a time when I was but a child, my parents would drag me off to church on Sundays. I never really understood the significance of going to church or worshipping God, I doubt many kids do. Nonetheless, it becomes a habit, and the more you go, the more you begin to understand. Now, as I started to attend Sunday school, it became apparent to me that some of the adults teaching these classes were either forced to be there, themselves, or they were very devout followers of Christianity.

This created a divide in my small mind. You are either a follower or not and there is no in-between. At this age, I was not even aware that other religions existed, of course, that would be the goal of these teachers, making sure you do not stray on the 'wrong' path. I thought Christianity was the belief of all humans all over the world. This might sound ignorant, but I was only a child, and the only schools available were Christian schools. I only became aware of other religions, and the Darwinian theory of evolution, around the age of 10, when we moved.

This is where my journey began, I started realizing, WOW, there is a whole world out there full of different stories and beliefs I could learn. After talking to my mom about this, she, of course, freaked out. I was told never to dabble in anything and should never stray away from the path of God, otherwise, I would burn in hell for eternity. Long story short, I did not listen and started to explore. As a consequence, however, my mother started sending me to priests for guidance and therapy when I was around 14-years old. She thought it would help.

Eventually, I got fed up and moved away to live with my dad. Oh boy, was the culture different!

Why am I even telling you this, you ask? Well, to show you the effects your childhood can have on your spiritual journey and how you learn about spirituality, will change your perception of it forever. For quite some time, I had a problem with accepting the way Christians live. To me, it seemed like they live in fear their whole lives and this is true for many religions. Eventually, I learned more about it and met different types of Christians. I started getting the bigger picture and my spiritual reality changed.

We have all had a different journey. Not one is wrong, and not one is better than the other. What matters is that we realize we make of what we want. When it comes to awakening the third eye, you need to accept many beliefs. Now, there is a difference between accepting and devoting. I am not saying that, if you are a follower of one, you must convert to another, no. I am simply saying that you need to accept that they exist in a more profound way than simply knowing that they are there. This helps you to understand what you experience in more depth. You then have such a broad spectrum of understanding with which you can draw conclusions on that which you experience.

The steps in your journey matter—not because it's wrong or right—but because your experiences fuel the energy within. Now, this book is about the awakening itself, and seeing as I already gave you some information on religions and beliefs, let's not keep you waiting. I would suggest, however, either after or before continuing, to study up on at least a few other religions and beliefs, contemplate them, experience the stories, and open yourself up to the possibilities they present.

RELAX AND FOCUS ON YOURSELF

After evaluating your journey, and seeing what brought you here, it's time to relax. Yes, relaxing actually helps quite a lot when trying to awaken your third eye. This is due to the busy lives most people lead. We work almost every day of our lives, going through the monotony of modern society. It truly is soul-crushing, for me anyway, which is why I started to focus on breaking away from that, even if it was just for a few minutes a day.

Relaxing might mean something different to you than what it would mean to me. Some enjoy sitting with a friend and talk-ing, or going out to a bar or club and having a drink, others enjoy a sport-related activity or meditation, while some enjoy sitting alone playing a game on their computer, or watching TV. There are many different activities that help you relax and break away from stress, but for the moment, this is not the type of relaxing to which I am referring.

I am referring to simply sitting by yourself for a few minutes, even if you have a spouse or children. Simply explain to them that you want to switch off for a few minutes, being open to them about this can help you relax even more, and set their minds at ease as well. This gives you time to be alone, truly alone. For many people, this can be difficult, as they are either very social and cannot stand to sit alone in a quiet room for too long, like my partner, while some might not want to sit alone as they find themselves getting depressed. I, myself, am lucky in this regard, as I enjoy solitude more than I should, which makes it a good thing I have a social partner.

So what exactly do you do when you are alone? You do not have to start any hardcore meditation techniques just yet, especially if you are not used to it. Sitting alone provides you with a certain sense of clarity. No one is disturbing your thoughts; they are your own. Sitting like this, you can think of what you did that day, or maybe remember a fond memory. However, do not idle on that one thought or feeling.

Rather, let it flow on to the next one. Otherwise, it might cause you to overthink or become emotional. Imagine your thoughts like a river and your mind like a small canal. The thoughts and feelings flow into your mind and then flow out the other side.

This is the analogy I started envisioning when I first started to simply sit and see what exactly my mind would do if I just let it flow. Now, this will benefit you in a few different ways.

Stress Relief

Let's get the obvious out of the way. Stress is a big problem in our lives, and simply getting away from everything can help quite a bit. Use this time to forget what is stressing you out. This doesn't mean the problem will just disappear, but for those few minutes, you at least get to break away and return with a fresh mind, or even a new perspective. It might be very difficult for some, and easy for others, but remember it is your mind and you control the direction it takes, so try to move away from thoughts that might stress you out even if it's just for a few seconds.

Conserving Energy

No one is around to bother or drain energy from you, if you think about it, just being present in someone's company drains you emotionally and mentally. Depending on the conversation, you have to respond, you have to pay attention, perhaps you have to provide emotional support, but now it is just you. While this might sound cynical, there is nothing wrong with not wanting to deal with other people and their problems, at least for a few minutes.

Psychological Health

Nothing's there to distract you, no phone, no computer, no TV. All your attention can be turned to you. As your thoughts flow, you can analyze them almost from a third-person perspective, giving yourself a better understanding of your mental state. Are you sad? Are you happy? Are you stressed? Are your thoughts erratic? Why are you having those specific thoughts? Why those feelings? Is it even worth holding on to those feelings? This might sound strange, but it gives you a more profound understanding of yourself. We are focused on so many things during our lives, we sometimes lose ourselves in our own unique identities and the identities of others.

Physical Health

Seeing as you have a chance to focus on yourself, why not ask your body how it feels? Remember, we are not our bodies. We are our minds and, as such, we sometimes lose connection with our bodies, no matter how fit and healthy we might think we are. How do you ask your body though? It's not like you can just ask 'hey, how are you feeling?' Focus on a specific part of your body and feel what your nerves are experiencing. Let's start with a leg, beginning with your foot. Just focus on what it is feeling, what sensations you are experiencing, all the while trying to block stimulus from other parts of your body.

Let your mind cast a spotlight on a specific part, moving it up your leg slowly, with the rest left in the dark. You can move it along unto other parts until your whole body has been mentally inspected.

One day while doing this, I started to notice this gentle lingering pain I had in my knee. Long story short, it was due to a sports injury from my school days which I thought has healed long ago. I never noticed it before, and so I started paying more attention to what my body was telling me. We forget to do this sometimes, except for obvious injuries, or intense aches and pains we might experience.

This helped me to discover a lingering problem before it became a bigger one. We are so used to people telling us what is wrong with us, instead of asking our own bodies. I do not mean to disparage the doctors and medical professionals out there; if not for them, my knee would still be a problem, as I sought out a professional opinion and got the help I needed.

All I am saying is, your body is yours. Learn to listen to it, and understand it. Why does it matter? Well, remember how we talked about the flow of energy throughout the universe? And how there is a flow inside all of us? Knowing your body will help you begin to understand and feel the flow of energy inside you. This is crucial in awakening your third eye. How do you expect to open something if you can't feel it, right?

We will be discussing our inner flow of energy in a later chapter, but this is a good starting point for people who are new to this and going over the basics is a good way to stay on the top of it.

While on the subject of energy flow, let's take a quick look at something that might help you master it in the future.

* * *

KUNDALINI YOGA

Up to this point, you have tried just sitting and relaxing, as well as some breathing techniques. What comes next? For many, the journey of awakening their third eye is just a test of sorts, a way to validate their experiences. For others, it is more spiritual, and if you want to take it to the next level, Kundalini Yoga is a great place to start.

While some of you may have come across this term before, not everyone knows exactly what it is about, save for it being a type of yoga. Kundalini is described as your life force, an energy that lies right at the base of your spine, dormant until activated, at which point it is channeled upwards throughout your body and chakras.

A combination of physical and spiritual practices starts to get this energy flowing. Movement, complemented with breathing techniques and the chanting of specific mantras, leads to deep meditation. This process builds physical vitality and, in turn, helps the body to carry the new energy, leading the practitioner to a higher form of consciousness.

I am not going to go into detail here, as there will be a later chapter on guided meditation, but if you are interested in this type of yoga, I encourage going at your own pace. Many people write books and articles about awakening the third eye and kundalini yoga, but they never say that each person will experience it differently, and thus you need to take the time to understand your experiences and contemplate the results.

* * *

FOCUS ON YOUR DREAMS

What exactly does it mean to focus on your dreams? I am, of course, talking about your actual dreams that you have when you sleep, and not your aspirations in life. One of the things western media and culture depicts correctly about the third eye, is that dreams play a major role in its awakening.

In the previous chapter, we discussed how the third eye, or pineal gland, provides the body with melatonin, a hormone that regulates sleep. While our knowledge of this small part of the brain leaves much to be desired, I can tell you from personal experience that this is an integral part of awakening your third eye, a part you will need to focus on intimately.

When I first began focusing on the awakening of my third eye, I started to have these strikingly vivid dreams. Now, what I mean by this is that the details populating these dreams were so vibrant and organic, it almost seemed as if I was living an entirely different life inside a whole new reality until, of course, I woke up. I never really had this level of clarity inside of my dreams before, and while it is a little difficult to describe to you exactly how real these dreams felt, what I can describe to you are the feelings I experienced when being ripped from those worlds to wake up back in bed.

There were mornings when I would wake up remembering entire lives and the emotion that came with them. I had such a deep connection with everything and everyone in those dreams, only to forget again throughout the day. While I have experienced dreams like this before, I have never experienced them at this level of intensity, or frequency of occurrence.

Many of you may have experienced dreams like this before, or not at all, but this is a clear sign of progress towards awakening the third eye. Some people believe our dreams hold the key to our past lives, or even future selves. I am not here to make those claims. I am simply here to help you understand your progress through your journey. So let's take a look at how we can further open ourselves to these experiences, refine our understanding around them, and eventually gain insight into our own subconscious minds.

The Dream Journal

While keeping a dream journal can be quite a daunting task, especially for those who lead distractingly busy lives, it is a step required to mastering control over your dreams, understanding them, and in turn understanding yourself, ultimately furthering your progress to awakening your third eye.

What exactly is a dream journal you ask? Well, it's quite self-explanatory, being a simple journal you use to write down what you remember from your dreams the night before. While many people enjoy writing exorbitantly colorful essays on what they had dreamt, wanting to capture every detail, it is not always practical. When starting out, try to dot down just the basics of the dream, main points, or summaries, and, as you get used to it, you may start elaborating a bit.

Starting out

Here are the main steps for you to go over when writing a dream journal.

First - Get an actual journal. It doesn't have to be expensive, but getting something you like does help to get you into it. This depends on the person, but you can record your sessions rather as well. As someone with terrible handwriting, I know the pains of going through something I wrote ten days ago and having no idea what I am even reading. Typing it is fine as well, but you must remember, whichever way you decide to do it, it has to be easily accessible, as you need to do it as soon as you wake up, which brings me to the next point.

Second - Do it first thing in the morning, no excuses. The reason for this is quite obvious. In order for you to be able to write down lots of details, you need it fresh inside your head. Dreams are easy to forget, some people forget their dreams the moment they wake up, and others forget them even while writing it down or telling someone about it. So the best way to get the most detailed description would be for you to start writing, recording, or typing the moment you wake up.

Third - I know I said that a massive amount of detail is not necessary. This is true for when you are just starting out with your journal, but, as you get accustomed to the process, it will be beneficial to write down more details. This goes not just for the visual detail, but also the emotions that you experienced in the dream. It might be difficult, but it becomes easier the more you do it, enabling you to recall more and more detail. If writing is not your thing, you can even draw the specific moments that stood out for you.

Fourth - Write it down as if you are experiencing your dream in the present moment. This helps you to recall in more detail and makes the writing style a bit more simple.

Those are the basic points to get you started. Keeping a dream journal can be quite an interesting and enjoyable hobby, and can benefit you not just with awakening your third eye, but with processing emotions and fueling your creative side as well.

* * *

THESE STEPS ARE YOUR OWN

In the end, as with most spiritual journeys, only you can take the steps necessary to reach your end goal. Whether or not you know what that end goal is, you need to trust in yourself, trust in your intuition, and trust that the steps you are taking will lead you there one day.

Many people put their trust in religion, priests, gurus, spiritual guides, books(ironically), and the internet, but that is simply just the beginning. You have to take all the information you can, and form your own path, making each step your own, customizing your journey to suit your needs.

Balance is Everything

Having a balanced life is a noble goal to strive towards. Keeping a balanced life, however, is more difficult than one might believe. When talking about awakening the third eye, it might sound as simple as just opening your eyes. Unfortunately, however, it takes a great deal of time, effort, dedication, motivation, and a balance between all of them.

In the earlier chapters, we touched on the subject of chakras. In this chapter, we will elaborate on what exactly the chakras are, what they have to do with awakening the third eye, and how we can maintain a balance between them in order to improve our lives.

THE CHAKRAS

Chakras, or the chakra energy system, is known to most who dabble in any kind of meditation, yoga, spiritual journeys, or even just internet research. But most of this information is quite shallow in the sense that you might know what the chakras are, but know little about what exactly they represent.

The word chakra originates from Sanskrit. Sanskrit is believed to be the oldest human language, dating back thousands of years BCE. Translated from Sanskrit, chakra actually just means wheel.

You see, contrary to what many people believe, the chakras are not a pool or flow of energy, but rather a serpentine ever-turning wheel, similar to a cog in a machine. When you do not maintain these cogs regularly, one might fail or break, causing the whole system to stop functioning the way that it should.

Originating from India, chakras were first mentioned in an ancient text known as the 'Vedas'. The Vedas, being the oldest texts in Hinduism, reference the seven chakras, however, there is mention of another chakra system very similar in Buddhist texts as well, for now, we will be focusing on the seven chakra system, as it encompasses a more profound journey as a whole.

If you want to stop and think for a moment whether or not chakras are, in fact, real, I would not mind inviting you to do so. Many people get stuck on the idea that the chakras were simply a way to understand the body at a time when there really wasn't much of another way, a time before modern medicine as we understand it now. I am going to emphasize that this system has been in place for thousands of years, being molded and shaped to perfection. While it might have changed due to this, the root still remains, I can guarantee that when you start work on your chakras, you will feel a difference.

When I first started doing some research on this chakra system, I was quite skeptical. Who wouldn't be? We are raised and taught by a system that leaves little to no space for anything that is not beneficial to itself. However sad this might be, it is true, and it is up to the individual to stray from this predetermined path in order to find something they are not entirely sure of, something new, something challenging. If you do not challenge yourself, you cannot expect to change.

Now you might be starting to get the idea behind why the chakras are so important to awakening the third eye, especially since the 6th chakra is synonymous with the third eye. Maintaining the chakras can be a difficult process, or it can be a truly enlightening one, this all depends on the person, and exactly how willing you are to accept certain aspects of yourself rather than rejecting or denying them.

First off, there are a total of seven chakras. We will be going through them individually to see what exactly each represents, the energy they promote, and what might influence them negatively.

After we understand what these wheels represent, their locations, and what might block them, we can start taking a look at how we can resolve these issues, clearing your chakras one by one in order to keep your energy balanced. There are a number of ways this can be done, and chakras might not simply be blocked, but can also be either overactive or underactive. These states can be detected and dealt with, but for now, let us begin with your first chakra.

1st. The Root Chakra (Muladhara)

So as the name suggests, this is the base and root of all other chakras, with the approximate location being the pelvic floor and base of your spine, including the first three vertebrae.

You can think of this chakra as your foundation, hence the name root, on which you will be building your spiritual house, so to speak. This chakra is represented by the color red and is usually associated with the element of earth. In the most basic term, the root chakra is responsible for grounding you to the earth connecting your energy with everything around you.

From a more modern perspective, this chakra regulates everything regarding your personal sense of security and your day-to-day survival. This is connected to what essentially keeps you alive in your daily endeavors as well, such as the food and water you consume, the shelter you occupy, and your general physical safety. Essentially, when these needs are met appropriately, you do not really worry about them, leaving your root intact.

What a Blocked Root Chakra Might Lead To

When your root is blocked, there are a few problems that might occur, emotionally and physically. First, when this chakra is blocked, you might experience extreme anxiety, fearful nightmares, or you might feel a sense of panic to the point of severe panic attacks.

All these negative feelings can seep into your daily life, infecting your thoughts and decisions, leading you down a path simply out of fear.

This chakra is also connected to some physical issues you might be experiencing, such as internal problems with your colon and bladder, or elimination in general, and with your lower back all the way down your legs to your feet. Other experiences relating to a problematic root chakra might be that you have trouble concentrating due to worrying about your survival and well-being, general paranoia, and low energy levels.

Overactive and Underactive

Many people experience either an overactive or underactive root chakra, due to it being first in line, hardwired into your survival instincts. An overactive root chakra will lead to anxiety due to the fact that it produces fear. This fear may manifest in stress or nightmares. From a physical aspect, it might give you problems with digestion and more severely, prostate problems in males and ovarian cysts in females.

When the root is underactive, it is usually due to your basic survival needs being met from a young age on a daily basis. This might lead you to be known as a 'daydreamer.' You have nothing or had nothing to stress about previously, so your mind wanders, leading to problems in concentration as well. These problems might not be life-threatening; however, they will disrupt the balance in your system, leading to an unbalanced life.

Unblocking and Balancing

Each chakra has methods suited to them for unblocking and maintaining balance. Unblocking the root chakra is quite easy and fairly straight forward. While it may be straightforward, it will have a truly profound impact on your daily life, resulting in a higher level of self-confidence, leaving you relaxed and ready to face life.

Let's take a look at a basic meditation technique that might help you unblock and balance your root.

- With your shoulders pulled back and your spine straight, try relaxing all of your muscles as you sit and close your eyes, breathing deeply while doing this. Remember to inhale through your nose, pulling in air to the deepest part of your body, then exhaling through the mouth.

- Focus on the location of the root chakra, try to imagine a red dot the size of a golf ball at the tip of your tailbone.
- As you keep your posture and breathe deeply, try to visualize this wheel glowing every time you inhale. With each breath, it becomes more bright from the center outward. As this glowing expands and consumes the whole wheel, try to feel the warm and relaxing sensation that it brings with it. Revel in this sensation for a few minutes. Keep breathing as if you are pulling in energy to fuel this sensation.
- After a few minutes of sustaining this feeling, you may open your eyes. Do not get up yet. Simply sit and feel the energy dissipate as it's getting absorbed up into your spine. When you feel ready, you may get up.

After doing this every day for a week, you will feel the energy inside you build up as your self-confidence rises and your fear becomes transparent to you.

There are some yoga poses specifically designed for balancing the root chakra, such as the basic 'balasana.' In this position, you lie face down, resting on your legs and body, lift your arms up and point them forward as you keep your head between them face to the floor. Other positions include the malasana squats, the wide-legged forward fold, and the mountain pose.

There are certain affirmations you can repeat either out loud or simply in your head while performing these poses, before or after the meditation session, or even during the day. While you may construct your own affirmations, here are a few examples of what you might want to use.

"I have a healthy body, a healthy mind, and an abundant life."

"I am anchored to the earth and supported by the universe."

"I feel my root chakra opening, and I feel myself stabilizing."

"I am secure and happy"

"I am stable, grounded and relaxed"

Other ways of keeping your root chakra balanced include a healthy diet of protein-rich foods, red fruits and vegetables which usually carry lots of vitamin-C, and earthy vegetables such as beetroot and potatoes.

If you feel disconnected from your root chakra, try and take a walk out in nature, go for a swim, or simply relaxing in the sun will help as well.

* * *

2nd. The Sacral Chakra (Svadhisthana)

The second chakra is quite an interesting one, the Sanskrit Svadhisthana, which translates to 'the place of the self.' When you take out your ID card, what do you see? Do you see someone you recognize? Or perhaps someone you simply knew long ago? The sacral chakra is all about your personal identity as an individual, and what exactly you do with that individuality.

When you think about it, what exactly is your identity? What is it constructed of? It's basically how you react emotionally to specific situations out in the world. It's how you use your creative energy. It's your imagination, your passion, and also your sexuality. Yes, the sacral chakra also deals with your sexual energy.

Located right below your navel, this chakra is represented by the color orange and is usually associated with the element water. Many people who suffer from a low sex drive have a problem with the energy flow coming from the sacral chakra. They also tend to feel bored and uninspired.

What a Blocked Sacral Chakra can Lead To.

Similar to other chakras, when this one is blocked, you will feel emotionally and sometimes physically out of sync. As mentioned, if you suffer from a low sex drive, you might have to look into getting the energy flowing from your creative source, the sacral chakra. When blocked, you will most likely give great resistance to change, be easily offended, be more susceptible to depression, and addiction will become more prominent. This is not simply an addiction to drugs and alcohol, but also spending habits, eating, and gambling. In general, if you find yourself increasingly more attracted to things that are not spiritually nourishing, your sacral chakra is having problems.

Physical signs of this chakra having issues might include a sudden worsening of allergies, loss of libido, and bladder discomfort.

Unfortunately, it is difficult to pinpoint what may cause this chakra to become unbalanced. However, common examples include sudden big changes, rejection from a partner or crush, or physical changes to your reproductive health.

Overactive and Underactive

An overactive sacral chakra is the result of indulging in a lustful and gluttonous lifestyle. Living a pleasurable life is not wrong, in itself. However, everything requires balance. Sometimes, it can do you some good to abstain from certain activities.

An underactive sacral chakra will be the cause of focusing your life on practical matters, such as work and responsibilities, without taking a minute to enjoy what you have achieved. In today's life, many people are all about work and no play, but balance is the key.

Unblocking and Balancing

When starting work on your sacral chakra, you will notice changes in your creative flow, as inspiration seems to find you easier and more quickly than before. Keeping this chakra balanced can be as easy as asking yourself if what you are doing is good for you in a more profound and spiritual sense.

But of course, not everyone can clear and balance their chakras that easily, so let's take a look at a basic meditation technique to unblock your sacral chakra.

- First, find a quiet and comfortable place where you can sit straight up relaxing your limbs.
- Take a few deep breaths, coming in through the nose and out through the mouth, as if recycling the energy around you.
- Start to focus on the area where your sacral chakra is

located, visualizing an orange water wheel, slowly spinning on its axis.

- The element associated with this chakra is water, so imagine an orange glow in the center of this wheel becoming more bright with every breath, as the water wheel turns. Visualize it taking water and spreading it throughout your body, feel the water bring a warm sensation over you.

- You can do this until your whole body feels saturated with the warm water, five to 10 minutes should be enough. You may open your eyes and sit in place for a few seconds as you feel the water providing your body with nourishment.

Doing this meditation daily will help to strengthen your creative flow, and may increase your libido as well. However, it is always a good idea to have a checkup done of your reproductive organs should you be concerned.

There are some yoga poses that you can try to further your progress as well, with Dvipada Pitham known as the best position for unblocking the sacral chakra. In this position, you lie down on your back, lifting your hips up in the air, supporting yourself with your legs and shoulders, lift your arms up and over your head at the same time. Other positions include the pigeon pose, the goddess pose, and the warrior 2 pose.

As with all sessions, there are certain affirmations you can repeat either out loud or simply in your head while performing these poses, before or after the meditation session, or even during the day. Here are a few examples.

"I am confident that what I offer the world is enough."

"It is safe to express my sexual self in fun, creative and healthy ways."

"I know I can embrace change and make the best of my future."

"I am full of inspiration and the potential for creation."

"My body is vibrant, and I am comfortable inside it."

A healthy diet containing oranges, seeds for example pumpkin seeds, hemp seeds, poppy seeds, and sunflower seeds, and then also coconuts will help balance your sacral chakra. A good supply of water, as well as a good flavourful tea during the day, will help in flushing any toxins from your body.

If you seem to feel disconnected from your sacral chakra, try to express your creative self through any form of art, no matter how good or bad you might be at it.

3rd. The Solar Plexus Chakra (Manipura)

Have you ever been in a situation where you know you do not belong there? That gut feeling you get when something just doesn't feel right, well, that is due to your solar plexus chakra, translated as 'lustrous gem' from Sanskrit.

Similar to your 2nd chakra, this one is connected to your level of self-confidence, but less in a creative and more in a social way. This is where you will find your inner power and confidence in your wisdom. Ultimately, it is the source of your true willpower, ruling over your self-esteem. Physically, it can be seen as regulating your metabolism and digestive tract.

It is located right above your navel, extending up to your ribcage, and is represented by the color yellow. The element of fire is associated with this chakra, hence the name solar plexus, providing you with a fiery passion for life.

What a Blocked Solar Plexus Chakra Might Lead To

When your 3rd chakra is blocked, emotional issues might follow. Starting off, you might feel insecure about your life or that your accomplishments are small or insignificant when compared to others when this is not necessarily true.

There are a few things that can influence the state of your solar plexus because it regulates your willpower. When you believe you have failed, your chakra will be impacted greatly, causing your willpower to dwindle. When we experience certain feelings or a sense of low self-worth during our childhood, it may cause our 3rd chakras to become completely blocked, needing extra care and attention in order to open it again. If this is true for you, I would recommend seeking professional help.

Physical issues might occur as well, seeing as it regulates your digestion and metabolism. This will result in discomfort in your gut, problems with digestion, and sometimes even feeling gassy or bloated.

Overactive and Underactive

An overactive solar plexus will lead to uncontrollable anger as the fire rages within you, this is usually accompanied by a lack of empathy and compassion. A more severe result of your chakra being overactive is complications with some of your organs, such as liver and kidney problems, inflammation in the appendix can occur as well.

When your solar plexus is underactive, you may feel timid and insecure. This can happen for a few reasons, but is usually a result of your personal power being taken away— or at least the illusion of that.

Unblocking and Balancing

Working on your solar plexus will help you reconnect with your more empathetic side, bringing to life new compassion for others. An easy way of balancing this chakra is by letting go of your anger and making sure you help others in their time of need.

Here is a meditation guide for you, if you feel it necessary.

- As with other sessions, start with a few minutes of basic breathing, in through the nose and out through your mouth.
- Start to focus on where this chakra is located, right above the navel.
- Visualize a burning sun, a bright yellow star roaring with fire, it does not burn you, it just fills you with soothing heat.
- As you breathe, you can visualize this sun inside you glow as you breathe in, and dissipate the energy inside you as you breathe out.
- You can do this for a few minutes, the sun glowing brightly with every breath, and the energy inside you

warming you up while it soothes and consumes any anger you might feel.

- When you feel ready, you can open your eyes and finish your session

Doing this will help you to dissipate your anger, as well as contain your rampant ego while providing power to your inner will.

If you want to try a yoga position, the child's pose is usually recommended. Kneel down on a pillow or rolled-up blanket while sitting on your heels, make sure your knees are hip-width apart. Lean forward as if praying so your chest presses down between your thighs. Other positions you can try are the boat pose and the warrior 3 pose.

Affirmations you can include with these sessions are as follows:

"We do not need to be in control of everything."

"I release myself from negative past experiences and emotions."

"The only thing I need to control is how I respond to situations."

"I am at peace and exude confidence."

"I feel motivated to pursue life."

Your solar plexus deals with digestion and metabolism, and as such, it is always a good thing to include carbohydrates in your diet, supplying you with a steady and constant supply of energy. Many people also recommend drinking chamomile tea, as it settles your stomach while soothing your chakra.

If your solar plexus feels drained, try to focus on your talents; this will restore confidence and bring balance to your will.

4th. The Heart Chakra (Anahata)

As many people expect, this chakra is deeply and intimately connected to your ability to love, as well as most emotions stemming from that, such as compassion and kindness. As such, anything that negatively impacts your feelings of love, such as a breakup or rejection, will leave your heart chakra unbalanced. This leaves this chakra quite easily explained, as well as easily understood.

Physically, the chakra is located right in the center of your chest, encompassing your heart, lungs, and thymus gland. Represented by the color green, and associated with the element of air, this chakra is known as the bridge between your lower and higher chakras.

What a Blocked Heart Chakra Might Cause.

When this chakra is blocked, you might find it difficult to trust people, this can easily happen after a breakup or emotional trauma. This can lead to a major imbalance in your emotional state, resulting in anger, jealousy, and hatred.

As simple as the heart chakra is, it can be quite disruptive, should it be blocked. It is recommended by many gurus that you should start work on it rather sooner than later after a breakup. A blocked heart chakra will lead to a difficulty in understanding your own emotions as they spiral out of control, more often than not hurting those around you, more so than yourself.

Physically, you might experience deep pain in your chest and that exact pain is related to heartbreak caused by a loved one. A high heart rate and heartburn is also associated with issues surrounding this chakra.

Overactive and Underactive

When overactive, you might find yourself being too loving towards others, leading to poor choices. You might find yourself placing the needs of others before your own, and you might become codependent in your relationships with others.

An underactive heart chakra will make it hard for you to become close to new people, leaving you disconnected from your emotions.

Unblocking and Balancing

Easily understood, but difficult to maintain, the heart chakra is a sensitive area for many people, as they find it very hard to deal with the emotions they might experience when trying to unblock this chakra.

You can start by simply trying to balance your chakra by loving yourself. Focus on your own emotions and affirm that you are worth the time and effort, taking a relaxing bath, or simply treating yourself to something nice will bring warmth back into your heart.

There is of course a meditation session focused on the heart chakra for people having difficulties processing their emotions.

- It is important to find a comfortable place where you feel safe and will not be disturbed, as you will most likely feel vulnerable during this session.
- Start with basic breathing as you inhale through the nose and exhale through the mouth, try to relax more and more with every breath
- After a few minutes, start visualizing energy being pulled up from your root all the way up your spine into your heart.
- As you breathe, the feel the energy becoming more and more dense, surrounding your heart chakra, glowing a bright and vibrant green color.
- The bright glow represents your love, not just for others but yourself as well. Start focusing on that love. Focus on the love you may have lost in the past,

love that may have caused you heartbreak, but do not hold onto it, let it dissipate as the energy provides you with the strength to release it back into the world.

- Next, you can start focusing on loved ones lost, close family members or lovers took away by fate, feel their love for you radiate in your heart, and remember that even though they might not be here anymore, their memory will always be in your heart as their love soothes you.

- At this point, you will be able to accept what happened in the past and let it go, as there will always be love in your future because you are worth that love.

- As your emotions calm down, you may take a few deep breaths and open your eyes, feel the warmth in your chest, and when you are ready you can end your session.

All forms of yoga are beneficial to your heart chakra; however, backbends, the reverse plank, and upward-facing dog are preferred poses. There are some affirmations you can repeat to yourself as well, for example:

"I love myself unconditionally, and offer the same love to others."

"I forgive others, and I forgive myself."

"My heart is free from all the wounds of the past."

Keep in mind that these affirmations can be changed in any way you wish. You can construct your own that are more suited to you and your emotions.

A simple, rounded, wholesome home-cooked meal is all that is needed to provide you with a warm and loving feeling inside your chest, as any healthy diet is suited to your heart chakra.

When you feel your emotional energy is drained and your heart chakra is empty, simply show yourself some love, remind yourself that you are worthy of your own love and the love from others.

5th. The Throat Chakra (Vishuddha)

This chakra is located in the throat, as the name suggests, and translated from Sanskirt it's 'very pure'. What this chakra regulates most of all is your speech, but not in the sense you might think. Speech is a part of you, a way of communicating. The throat chakra regulates your true speech, the way you convey yourself to others, and express your emotions.

Many people have issues when it comes to telling the world how they truly feel, and others sometimes do not know when to stay quiet, these are all aspects regulated by this chakra. This chakra is also known as one of the first truly spiritual chakras, as it affects your ability to express your true intentions. Fear of being judged by others may also be the result of an unbalanced throat chakra.

Physically, it can have an effect on your neck and inner throat and will be influenced through situations where you are under verbal pressure, such as job interviews or bad arguments. It is represented by the color blue and is associated with the element of ether.

What a Blocked Throat Chakra can Lead to.

The throat chakra is fairly simple to understand, as it regulates speech, which is a fairly common thing. When this chakra is blocked, you have difficulty expressing your true self, leaving you feeling unknown, as if people around you do not know who you actually are. Your feelings are left unheard, which may affect your other chakras.

Physically, a stiff neck and sore throat can be the result of your throat chakra becoming blocked.

Overactive and Underactive.

When someone suffers from an overactive throat chakra, they tend to interrupt others or speak quite loudly. This usually happens due to them feeling unheard throughout their life. It may lead to people finding you annoying as you just do not seem to stop talking.

Physically, it can result in a sore throat.

An underactive throat chakra is usually experienced when you are rather shy and retract from social events. This may lead to energy being sent back down to your 3rd chakra as you fail to express yourself, resulting in digestive issues.

• • •

Unblocking and Balancing.

When we think about balancing the 5th chakra, it is quite easy, and as simple as thinking before you speak. This moment of clarity before blurting out an inappropriate remark, or expressing your true emotion will save you from an awkward social environment or an aggressive retaliation. The Buddha once said, "Think whether what you are about to say is either true, necessary or kind."

Let us take a look at a meditation technique for the throat chakra.

- Start with the usual breathing, in through the nose and out through the mouth, a relaxed setting is the best option.
- Relax as you breathe, clearing your throat gently.
- Visualize a small ball of blue light in the center of your throat, feel the blue light shining through.
- As you breathe, imagine the blue light soothing your throat, almost as if you are drinking an ice-cold glass of water. Imagine the energy opening your throat, removing any feelings of insecurity about your true self.
- As you become accustomed to the idea of expressing who you truly are, and how you might be affecting others through your words, you can start feeling the energy in your throat spread through your body.
- Take a few deep breaths before ending your session.

There are a few yoga poses that can benefit your throat chakra, such as the baby cobra pose, shoulder stand, supported fish pose, and the plow pose.

Considering how you speak and how you express yourself, you can construct some affirmations to use during the day. These affirmations are for your voice, so standing in front of a mirror and saying them out loud, as you watch your lips move, is the best way to perform them, here are some examples include:

"My voice is important in this world."

"I honor my true voice, and I let it speak."

"Others hear my voice."

"I speak my true thoughts with ease."

"Let go of doubt about the word I 'should' have said."

The only items to include in your diet in order to help your throat chakra stay balanced, are fruits found in trees. One of the most effective items however is blueberries. Adding a variety of strong spices to your meals is also a great option,

Just because there is no one around to hear you speak, does not mean you cannot express your true self, when you feel your throat chakra is unbalanced, you can stand in a room and speak out loud, expressing your emotions and thoughts.

* * *

6th. The Third Eye Chakra (Ajna)

Here we have arrived at the third eye, or as translated from Sanskrit, 'beyond wisdom'. This chakra is by far one of the most referenced in popular culture and media, due to its relation with mysticism and clairvoyance.

While so many people reference it, not all of them quite understand what it represents. The third eye governs your intuition, providing you with a sense to see the bigger picture through wisdom. It is also your connection to the universe, which is why tapping into it can provide great wisdom.

As discussed in previous chapters, its location is right on the forehead between your eyes. It is represented by the color purple and is associated with the element of extrasensory perception. Before the times of physical examination, humans knew exactly where it was located and realized that it presented us with a sense beyond what we could perceive physically.

. . .

What Happens When The Third Eye Becomes Blocked

Many people struggle to find their way in life, following what others tell them to without listening to what their intuition is trying to tell them. This is not necessarily because they do not have any intuition, but simply because the third eye is blocked. They cannot hear it.

Some of you might end up feeling like you are serving a broader purpose. You might even seem to be unable to acquire new skills in life. This will leave you exhausted, due to your mind working overtime trying to figure out what is going on. You start to become indecisive, have trouble sleeping, and clumsy.

As complicated as the third eye might seem, it is a fairly straightforward chakra. Unfortunately, it is one of the most sensitive when it comes to balance. The third eye will become unstable when the other chakras in your body are not balanced, leading to severe headaches, lightheadedness, and dizziness.

Overactive and Underactive

While having an overactive 6th chakra is not very likely, as we are usually so rooted in our physical reality, it is possible. When suffering from an overactive third eye, you are most likely plagued with paranormal experiences and premonition dreams.

An underactive third eye is the most likely. This will result in you being disconnected from your own intuitive progression. You will constantly try to figure things out in a logical manner, and become completely oblivious to your own spiritual progression and well being.

Unblocking and Balancing

The balancing of your third eye starts with your root chakra and, from there, works through all of the rest. Trying to keep the third eye balanced is as simple as reminding yourself that you are human. We can get obsessed with the idea of opening it but we are still just humans, and focusing on that can sometimes provide you with the balance you need.

Going somewhere like a beach, forest, or just your garden, you can stick your bare feet in the sand or dirt while reminding yourself that you are simply human, and accepting that you have limits.

Let's have a quick look at a basic meditation session for unblocking and balancing your third eye, as we will take a more detailed look in a later chapter.

- Find a place isolated from other humans, be it a room or in nature. The night time works best. The normal breathing technique applies.
- After taking a few breaths, start to focus on the center of your forehead and visualize a small hole in your skin, emitting a bright purple light.

- As you breathe, the light becomes brighter and brighter. Visualize a black hole in front of you and imagine falling into it while being led by this light. The light is warm and spreads energy throughout your body.
- As you absorb this energy, all your negative thoughts are being pushed out with your breath, and following is a faint whisper of your inner self.
- As you sit, you can see in front of you without actually opening your eyes, just visualize it, illuminate it with the light coming from the energy inside.
- When you feel like the image is complete, open your eyes. If the image is not as you saw, close your eyes and start from the beginning.
- You can finish your session with a few deep breaths, visualizing the small hole in your forehead closing up.

There are no specific yoga poses for this chakra. However, the kundalini yoga sessions will help to regulate the energy within. As for affirmations, there are a few examples but, I choose not to give them to you, as this is a chakra focused around intuition. I would like you to come up with your own. Just listen to your inner self. Many people suggest consuming foods rich in omega-3 when you have trouble connecting with your third eye, the best option being salmon, sardines, and walnuts.

If you seem unable to connect with your third eye, you will have to dedicate a larger amount of time to quiet meditation. During these sessions, you can focus on interpreting signals that seem to come from outside of your body. Doing this in nature is the best option.

7th. The Crown Chakra (Sahasrara)

The final chakra in your body is known as the crown chakra. One of the more subtle chakras to work with, translated from Sanskrit it is 'thousand petals', usually depicted as a thousand petal lotus.

As stated, it is quite a subtle chakra, and explaining the type of energy it transmits is difficult. Luckily, there is a modern way to interpret it. When you think of magnetism, there are usually two poles, with the opposite attracting and the same poles repulsing. You can imagine the crown to be a pole from a magnet and the conscious universe another. There are many references to our higher selves, our true selves which command our physical selves. This magnet is our connection to that higher self.

If the energy flow is not aligned, you will be pushed away from your higher consciousness, and if it is too strong, you will be crushed. Consciousness is everywhere; it is the universe, so maintaining a balance between you and it, is the ultimate goal in becoming your higher self.

The chakra is located right at the top of your head, hence the name crown, and is represented by a violet/white color. The element representing it is thought, which is why it plays such a large role in connecting you to different states of consciousness.

When The Crown is Blocked

When this chakra is blocked, you might start to feel disconnected from the world, as if you do not really have a place in it, which can lead to emotional distress and depression. The crown is not normally in an open state, although it does open and close every now and then, you need to make a conscious effort in order to keep it unblocked. This is rather difficult, and usually takes a tremendous amount of effort.

Physically, if your crown is unwell, you will experience chronic headaches coupled with poor or loss of your sense of direction. There is a wide range of things that can lead to it becoming blocked, but the most common is when there is a big change in your life, such as a change in career or identity.

Overactive and Underactive

This chakra deals with consciousness as a whole, and as such, cannot become overactive, consciousness is infinite and never-ending, just like the universe itself. You might start to experience a sense of arrogance and greed should the energy start flowing freely, but it will usually start balancing itself out.

While subtle, this chakra can become underactive, resulting in a loss of purpose and fulfillment. This will lead to confusion during your life and can cause a compulsive need to oversleep.

Unblocking and Balancing

Balancing your crown is as simple as focusing on your conscious thought. When you think, make decisions, or work towards your goals, you are making conscious life choices, feeding your purpose. This creates balance with your spiritual and human connection.

Meditating on your crown chakra is quite difficult, and can take years to master, as it delves deep into the consciousness of the universe, itself. But there are techniques for a basic session.

- As with all the other sessions, get comfortable and start with basic breathing, in through your nose and out through your mouth, relaxing as you do so.
- As you sit with your legs crossed, place your hands in your lap with your palms facing upwards. This acts almost like an energy receiver.
- Visualize a lotus flower right on the crown of your

head, as you breathe in deeply, feel it opening up, emitting a bright violet light from within.

- As the light grows stronger, feel the energy shoot up your spine into your crown, as the light emits straight up into the sky.
- Breathing deeply, let your consciousness explore, feel your body become warm as the energy flows through you.
- Keep focusing on these sensations and keep your senses tuned to the universe, you will feel a strange and subtle connection between you and everything in existence, this might only be for a second, but the moment it happens, you will know.
- When you are ready, you can open your eyes, take in what you experienced, and end your session.

The connection you form with the universe over time becomes more and more distinct, this can take years, however.

The position you are seated in is a yoga position itself, known as the seated lotus.

There are a few affirmations you can repeat to yourself during these sessions, however, due to the subtle nature of the crown, the effects may be minimal.

"I am constantly connected to my highest self."

"I know my own spiritual truth."

"I am at one with the world around me."

Many people suggest drinking herbal teas and consuming ginger in order to balance this chakra, however, personally, I never noticed a difference. Dealing with the unique nature of the crown, is not a physical experience but rather a spiritual one, more so than any other chakra, even the third eye. Of course, a healthy diet is very important when dealing with any of your chakras, so keep that in mind when you decide what you are consuming.

The true nature of consciousness has eluded us all, spiritual and scientific minds alike, leaving us to make our own deductions from our experiences.

When you try to compound your crown energy, it is more an effort of the collective chakras rather than the singular, as they all need to be in a constant state of balance in order for the crown to be activated. Meditation is not necessarily the key, but at least a step in the right direction for your journey.

MAINTAIN THE BALANCE

By now, you should start to comprehend the importance of balance in every aspect of your life. The seven chakras are a map, a path to walk in order to maintain the balance within yourself, in your life, and in your spiritual journey.

The chakras make it easy, almost like a cheat sheet to an exam.

There are seven days in your week, and seven chakras. The math is simple. If you can muster the discipline and resolve in order to dedicate each day to a specific chakra, taking a few minutes of your time, you are guaranteed to dramatically improve your life emotionally, spiritually, and physically.

The benefits surely outweigh the effort needed, right?

Awakening the third eye is more than just a singular objective. It is a lesson, something small you gain along the path to finding your true self.

While this book is about awakening your third eye, I cannot understate the importance of maintaining the balance, otherwise, you will not be able to interpret what you find, even when your third eye has awakened.

Research, Tools, and Practice

When we walk our own path, it can be quite difficult to find the right steps, and even when we eventually find the steps, they do not seem to resonate with us. It is very important that we make our spiritual journeys as authentic to ourselves as possible, and not follow in the steps of someone else.

While we can obviously learn from others, be it from their mistakes or the information and help they provide us, we can only take what we are given and form something on our own.

In this chapter, I will provide you with some helpful tips on a few things that might help you on your journey. I want to provide you with this before the guided meditations for your third eye, so that you may be ready.

BREATHWORK

What exactly is breathwork? Well, as the name suggests, breathwork is a collection of breathing exercises, practices, and techniques people all around the world use in order to improve physical and mental health, as well as spiritual health.

Why does it matter? Controlling your breathing is a key step in awakening your third eye, through helping you gain control over your body, making it easier in the future to interpret the flow of energy.

As stated, it is a collection, so there are many different ways breathwork can be performed, from the ancient techniques monks have used over the centuries to modern practises established recently. Some of these can be done while meditating or simply when you are taking those few minutes for yourself. Let's take a look at some of these methods so you can try a few, at which point you can decide if these practises suit your journey.

Shamanic Breathwork

Shamanic breathwork is more like a ceremony to attend rather than something to do on the fly, but nonetheless, it can be beneficial to you on your spiritual journey. This ceremony is designed to bring you back to yourself.

It begins with the cleansing of the area itself. This can be done through various rituals such as burning or smudging of sage while prayers are made. This provides the ceremony with sacred space in which people can start with rhythmic breathing exercises. These rhythms are specifically made to tune into your energy flow and consciousness, altering your mental state.

You can find a local shaman from which you can learn and attend these ceremonies, as they can be different each time.

Vivation

Vivation is a more modern example. Similar to how you can simply sit and focus on yourself, vivation takes it to the next level as a physically pleasurable breathing and meditation practice. With most of its roots set with Indian Kriya and Tantric Yoga, it expanded by modernizing the techniques.

It focuses on your inner self and body, listening to it and getting attuned to it. Through this process, you will focus on your emotions and how to move past them. There are really quite a few elements in this process, which can be categorized into five main sections.

Circular breathing, complete relaxation, awareness in detail, integration into ecstasy, and doing whatever you do, as will-ingness is enough. Each of these sections has a few elements to them, so if this does sound like something you need, it wouldn't hurt to try and learn.

. . .

Transformational Breath

This method of breathwork is a great example of what breath-work can do for your physical body. This breathwork is unfortunately restricted to those who pay for the courses, and as such, I cannot divulge any specific techniques, but what I can tell you are the proven benefits.

Essentially, this method does increase the oxygenation throughout the body while stimulating circulation. This results in the alleviation of headaches, stress, and respiratory problems. It has also proven useful in treating addictions. Anything that helps you on your spiritual journey can be worth investing in, it's simply up to you, what is it you want to do?

Holotropic Breathwork

A powerful approach to personal development can be found in Holotropic breathwork. The process itself is rather simple, as it relies on the inner self and the psyche of each person, while the breathing techniques are used. Usually, a person would lie down on their back, while accelerated breathing is used in sync with evocative music, triggering an altered state of consciousness.

During these sessions, you experience a profound internal experience, which can help you on your journey. This is quite useful when trying to get rid of some lingering psychological or emotional trauma, but of course, it is always better to consult professionals.

Other

There are many forms of breathwork out there. These are simply the more popular ones people have come to try. While breathwork is helpful, it may not be for you, or the specific techniques you find during your research might not suit you. At that point, you are welcome to construct your own breathwork practice, one that fits your spiritual journey better.

TOOLS FOR BALANCING YOUR CHAKRAS

Although we have already gone over your chakras, there are a few things I did not mention. This is due to the fact that they can be considered extras, information not necessarily useful to everyone, however, it might be useful to those struggling to align a specific chakra, or possibly all of them.

There are unique stones, crystals, and gems in the world that resonate with the energy produced by specific chakras, similar to how they are associated with specific colors and elements. These materials might help you connect and unblock the energy flow in the chakras you struggle with.

The Root chakra:

Associated with the color red, it's not wrong to presume that red gems would resonate with this chakra.

Red Carnelian - This stone is generally associated with strength and bravery. Seeing as the root is responsible for your connection to earthly energy, the red color sometimes mixed with orange hues is perfect, as it connects you to the deep energy core of the earth.

Blood Stone - While the stone itself is mostly green, it has red spots inside of it, resembling the sight of splattered blood on a rock, hence the name. While this might sound eerie or malignant, it in fact pushes away negative energy, providing you with confidence.

Obsidian - A natural volcanic glass, this gem might be black, but it is said to protect you from harm. It might help you feel safe as you find your root.

Red Jasper - Known as a stone of empowerment and balance, it will help you find your resolve when trying to connect to your root chakra.

The Sacral Chakra:

Linked with the color orange, there are a few gems and stones to help you with the 2nd chakra.

Moonstone - While not inherently orange, a peach-colored moonstone does exist, which is known to reduce worrying thoughts.

Citrine - Bearing a golden yellow color, this stone boosts your self-esteem, which might help people who suffer from low confidence and jealous feelings due to a blocked 2nd chakra.

Orange Calcite - Known as a stone that energizes your lower chakras, it is particularly effective towards unblocking your 2nd chakra, as it helps with creative resonance.

Carnelian - Presenting itself as a glassy, semi-precious stone, it is known by the name the singer's stone. This resonates well with your creative spirit, especially for those vocally talented.

The Solar Plexus Chakra:

Brandishing a yellow color, there aren't many gems or stones for this chakra, but there are two known effective ones.

Amber - These fossilized tree resin gems are known to help with mental clarity and confidence, so when you are stuck on decisions, this will help.

Yellow Tourmaline - Being a fairly rare gem, you might have difficulty finding one, but when you do, you will become aware of its detoxifying effects immediately, as it repels negative energy.

The Heart Chakra:

Known to be depicted with the color green, there are quite a few gems and stones to help soothe your heart.

Green Calcite - Another form of calcite, in this color, it is known to absorb negative energy, and provides you with a sense of compassion when you need it.

Green Aventurine - This gemstone is a quartz, and is known as the comforter, or heart healer. That discretion is fairly self-explanatory, but they are also known to protect against emotional imbalance.

Jade - A well known and easily recognizable gemstone, these are notorious for bringing balance to your emotions, especially when dealing with loss. This might be just what you need to help you through a difficult time.

Rose Quartz - Whilst not green, this gemstone does benefit the heart chakra by regaining balance through difficult times.

The Throat Chakra:

Being represented by the color blue, there are quite a few options for you should you be struggling with this chakra.

Lapis Lazuli - Having an intense color of blue, this stone is known as the stone of truth, which will help you speak through your true self when you are having trouble expressing your intentions.

Amazonite - Bearing turquoise, this stone protects against negative energy, especially when you suffer from a fear of being judged by others.

Aquamarine - One of the more well-known crystals that resonate with the throat chakra, it helps you to accept your true self and the expression of that self.

The Third Eye:

Third eye crystals are known to help during meditation, especially when clasping one in your hand during your session.

Amethyst - Famous for its beauty, it helps with third eye related headaches and provides wisdom to those who let it.

Black Obsidian - This gem provides a balance between your emotional responses and logical cognition, which is the epitome of wisdom.

Purple Fluorite - This gem sharpens the user's intuition greatly, which makes it one of the best pairings for the third eye chakra.

The Crown Chakra:

Due to the nature of this chakra, clear crystals are best suited to help you resonate with it.

Quartz - Plain clear quartz is known to help resonate with your spirituality.

Selenite - Also a fairly clear crystal, it helps you unblock not only your crown but also your third eye, providing clarity and purpose.

Sugilite - This crystal is not clear, but it provides you with a grounding experience, should you feel lost in your own consciousness.

* * *

OILS, HERBS, SPICES, AND INCENSE

There are many substances in the world that can help you with not only awakening your third eye but revitalizing your health and enhancing your meditation sessions, as well. Some people are not open to the idea of using incense and oils. I, myself, do not really use incense, as I find the scent very distracting, no matter the ingredients. There are, of course, many people who prefer incense to be lit before a meditation session.

Each of these substances can benefit you in more than one way, but it is important to know the right substance for any specific session. For now, we will focus on three main substances.

Oils

Oils can be used in quite a few different ways. However, the most prominent is through anointment. In many religions, oils are used in sacred rituals to anoint a person or object, by rubbing or pouring the oil over them. This process can take anything from a few seconds to hours, depending on the ceremony taking place. The objectives of these rituals usually range between providing spiritual fortification, physical revitalization, or simple blessings.

Here is a list containing some of the more well-known oils and their uses.

Purifying: As the name suggests, oils in this category are known for their purifying effects, such as removing foul odors, cleaning the physical object or person, or the cleansing of negative energy.

- Hyssop
- Myrrh
- Atlas Cedarwood
- Virginian Cedarwood
- Juniper Berry

Enlightenment: Oils in this category are known for their ability to help individuals to reach states of enlightenment during meditation and daily activities.

- Cypress
- Rosemary
- Frankincense
- Sandalwood
- Palo Santo

Grounding: Usually, people use this category of oils when they are trying to connect with nature in order to balance their energy flow.

- Spikenard
- Vetiver
- Patchouli
- Galbanum
- Myrrh

Spirituality: People often use these oils for anointment and connecting with their spiritual selves, as well as meditation.

- Cinnamon
- Clove
- Lavender
- Scotch Pine
- Ginger

Herbs and Spices

While many of us consume herbs and spices almost on a daily basis, we never stop to think what the benefits or other uses might be. We usually focus on the extra flavor it provides our culinary exploits, but herbs and spices can be used in other ways as well. For example, one of the more popular rituals to clear out negative energy is to burn sage.

Here is a list of herbs and their respective categorical uses.

Health: The herbs in this category provide simple health benefits when consumed.

- Peppermint - Especially useful for treating irritable bowel syndrome, which can impair your three lower chakras.
- Turmeric - Containing compounds that act as anti-inflammatory medicine, it can be used after long sessions of movement meditation.
- Ginger - Commonly used to reduce or eliminate the nausea that can occur after a deep meditation session.

Medicinal: While healthy herbs and spices can provide basic treatments, medicinal herbs are usually included in more potent brews for physical and spiritual treatments.

- Gingko - This herb is known to treat dementia and Alzheimers. It can be consumed as a tea in order to boost brain function in order to awaken your third eye and open your crown chakra.

- Echinacea - Known to boost immunity against viruses, it is usually used in a form of tea or juice to treat the flu. Perfect for when you need a boost in your root chakra.
- Chamomile - When suffering from intense stress, chamomile can calm you down enough to induce proper meditation.

Spirituality: This category of herbs and spices are used when dealing with spiritual rituals or meditation, perfect for assisting in the awakening of your third eye.

- Sage - Used for cleansing an area of negative energy. Some people like to burn a bit of sage in the room in which they meditate so that negative energy will not interfere with the session.
- Rose Petals - Used in a bath, rose petals help clear out your heart chakra. This will assist in your overall balance of energy.
- Rosemary - The herb, itself, can be used for protection against negative energy, which might come in handy during a deep and emotional meditation session.

Incense

While many people have heard about incense, not all of them understand the complete idea behind it. Basic incense is made by mixing substances together and binding them with flammable material in order to sustain the burning process. There are three main or basic forms of incense that most people use: stick, coil, and cone.

Burning incense is about more than just having a good aroma present, however. It can be part of a sacred ritual, a ceremony to show respect, a cleansing endeavor, and of course, just for the enjoyment of the aroma.

As I mentioned earlier, I don't particularly like burning incense. But here are a few incense ingredients that I have found useful, and might prove useful to you.

- Amber - This is best used when meditating on your third eye, as it amplifies truth-seeking and wisdom.
- Dragon's Blood - Here is one of the more rare and extremely expensive ingredients used in incense. While it is difficult to find authentic dragon's blood incense (it is a type of tree resin), the effects are energizing and might be what you need to open your energy flow.
- Frankincense - Fairly cheap compared to other incense ingredients, this one can help with any basic meditation. If you find your meditation space needs a bit of refreshment, you can burn this.

Oils, herbs, spices, and incense can be used in many different ways. Meditation towards a specific goal might be reinforced with the use of any substance. Yoga might become more intense with the correct combination of scents.

Aromatherapy is known to unlock various aspects of the self.

The uses of oils, herbs, spices, and incense are endless. All will depend on how you wish to apply them to your journey. Or, you may simply ignore them, altogether.

PSYCHEDELICS

Psychedelics are a very interesting subject, and a much-debated topic when it comes to spiritual progression. While these types of substances and their use for spiritual journeys need a whole book of their own, we will simply touch on them lightly here.

Many people in these modern times have their journeys kick-started through their first psychedelic experience, as it kind of opens the door for you and shoves you right into the thick of it, just to pull you out again. As the popularity of these substances has risen tremendously in the last few years, it is always a good idea to tread lightly, as one experience is never the same as the other.

When discussing the third eye and its awakening, psyche-delics are usually one of the first things to pop up, and right-fully so, as when a curtain is pulled back with such vigor, and seeing what's behind it with such vibrance, it is not easy to simply forget. Nonetheless, we can fall deep into those discussions. For now, let's take a look at a few popular psychedelic substances used in ancient and modern spiritual practices.

· · ·

Ayahuasca

Ayahuasca is presented to you in the form of a brew or tea, made from vines and leaves of specific plants, although there may be other herbs mixed in as well. First used many years ago as a spiritual and religious rite by Amazonian tribes, it has gained popularity since. The active compound in this brew is DMT, which produces a strong psychedelic reaction, akin to opening the third eye and seeing past reality itself.

DMT/Changa

Changa is a mixture of herbs and a crystalized form of DMT, which can be smoked. When inhaled a few times, the experience is almost immediate and quite intense. Although the hallucinogenic experience only lasts for a few minutes, the profound insight gained through this is enlightening to many.

Psilocybin

This psychedelic compound is found mostly in fungus or mushrooms, which is usually referred to as magic mushrooms. The experience can last for hours and can change your perception of reality forever, or maybe just give you a little insight into your life. While many people use these mushrooms as part of spiritual meditation, others simply consume them for the fun and happy experience it can provide.

· · ·

LSD

LSD, or acid, is known as a manufactured substance rather than one that has been cultivated. As such, many frown upon its usage for traditional spiritual journeys, rather than sticking to naturally grown substances. While the experience is quite vivid, most people just consume it for a fun time.

Cannabis

While not hallucinogenic, some 'highs' felt when smoking this herb can lead to profound realizations. The herb is used in many shamanistic rituals around the world and helps the user connect with their inner energy. Meditation while using cannabis can enhance your experience tenfold.

MICRODOSING AND MEDITATION

After covering some psychedelic substances, it would be quite pointless if I did not cover microdosing as well. But first, what is microdosing?

For those of you who are unfamiliar with the term, microdosing is self-explanatory in a way, as it involves using very small amounts of a psychedelic drug. Microdosing became quite popular right after the rise in popularity of psychedelics in general. Dosing yourself with a sub-hallucinogenic amount of say, LSD or psilocybin, results in many beneficial outcomes.

Some studies have concluded that the effects of microdosing can result in an overall improved mood, less anxiety, improved meditative practice, mental focus, a less taxing exercise experience, improved eating habits, and improved sleeping patterns.

All these benefits are good and well, but we are going to focus on how it can enable you to awaken your third eye. The inherent idea behind microdosing is to change your state of consciousness by taking small doses. This will dramatically improve any meditation session, and assist in dealing with emotion and opening the flow of energy between your chakras.

Changing your state of consciousness and level of focus will improve the level of energy flow and control over it throughout your body, especially when practiced properly.

If you are interested in microdosing, here is a regimen you can follow. I tried it for a while, it can help you get out of the rut you might be stuck in, and ultimately further your journey of awakening your third eye.

Microdose Regimen

There is a kind of agreed-upon regimen to follow, which will enhance the benefits and reduce any negative effects. In general, a microdose is taken once every three days. Even though this might sound ineffective, it actually works out perfectly. When taking a dose on the first day, the psychedelics itself is gone within just a few hours, but the effects it provides remain for another two days. After those two days, you can take the next dose.

A dose usually consists of either a few micrograms of magic mushrooms (usually ground into a powder form) or, a small piece of an LSD stamp. For a more accurate measurement, it is usually calculated at either one-twentieth or one-tenth of a basic recreational dose.

You have to take the dose in the morning, however, preferably before 10 a.m. You can continue with your day as you normally would. You can follow this dosage guide for a month, after which you will have noticed a difference in your spiritual perception and general mood.

In regards to awakening the third eye, I can recommend this to anyone who is having difficulty on their journey. When you become more focused on your spiritual journey, you will start to realize just how easy it is to stray from the path that you are walking.

Microdosing can be a temporary tool, something to use in order to bring you back onto your own path. Like using a telescope to peer into the vastness of space, you can use psychedelics to gaze into consciousness, allowing your third eye to use it as a catalyst to something more profound.

PRACTISE

While I do not encourage the use of psychedelic substances without guidance, it is hard to deny their impact on your spiritual journey through life and may be just what you need in order to find the steps which could lead you to awaken your third eye.

Finding methods that work for you is the key, and putting them into practice daily is what will bring you to the ultimate conclusion of your spiritual journey, with awakening your third eye to be simply a by-product of something more grandiose.

A Guide For Your Journey

Many of us are unable to find our way without any help. While some might seek out guidance from a guru or master, others do not always have the opportunity to do that. Luckily, there are many books and texts scattered all over the world, with the internet making research into these subjects that much easier.

In this chapter I will attempt to guide you as best I can. There are many meditation techniques, developed for many different reasons, most of them can be used any way you adapt them, which makes meditation the key to awakening your third eye.

POPULAR TECHNIQUES

While everyone is different, set methods for meditation are a proven benefit to anyone who chooses to use them, so let's start with some of the basics, after which you may adapt them to your personal needs. We will handle these techniques with the objective of awakening the third eye.

Mindfulness Meditation

One of the first techniques used when starting out with meditation is the most basic and easy method, simply known as being mindful. It does not matter what you are doing during your day. Being mindful when doing these things instead of just going through the motions of routine can help you become fully focused in your life.

This is a simple method of meditation that I found useful for getting used to the act of meditating. As for awakening the third eye, you can think of this as the first step that leads you closer to it.

- Start off with setting aside the time every day, finding a quiet spot where you will not be disturbed. If this is not possible, it's ok. But it is preferred. You can sit either with your legs crossed on the floor or cushion, on a chair, bench, or sofa, it doesn't really matter.

- Be sure to straighten your upper body, but do not become stiff. Find that perfect relaxed feeling without falling over.
- While it is not necessary to close your eyes, you may do so if it's more comfortable.
- Start to focus on your breathing. Feel the breath come in, and leave your body, your chest expanding and retracting. After doing this for a few minutes, your mind will automatically start to wander off. This is normal. Simply let your thoughts wander and then return to focusing on your breath after a few seconds.
- If you feel an itch or an uncomfortable sensation, do not automatically respond to scratch or adjust your position, pause for a second and make a conscious decision to move or scratch. This is what being mindful is about: acting instead of reacting.
- As your thoughts wander, try not to engage with them, Simply let them be and move on, focusing on your breath when you can. You may set a timer before the session or when you are ready, you can decide to end the session.

Before simply getting up, however, pay attention to that moment, the sounds around you, your emotions and physical sensations. At this point, decide how the rest of your day will be, and then continue.

* * *

Spiritual Meditation

Simply put, spiritual meditation is being mindful of something greater and deeper than your own ego. The self is something we get stuck on. Focusing on our individuality may sometimes result in losing the connection we have with our spirit.

This takes time, however, so be patient.

When looking at this meditation in terms of awakening your third eye, your spiritual sense is what needs to be improved for you to make use of your third eye in the first place, bringing you a step closer to the eventual awakening.

The steps required for this method are very similar to mindful meditation, so you can use that as a baseline. However, instead of simply being mindful, there are a few other things you need to focus on during a spiritual meditation session.

- First, start off with all the basics of mindful meditation, getting comfortable, and focusing on your breathing for a few minutes.
- When you start to feel immersed in relaxation, you can focus on any grudges you might be holding. While this may seem contradictory to spiritual progression, it's not what you think. The point of this is to collect all those grudges together, understand why they are there, and then simply wave them

goodbye. While this might be difficult for a plethora of reasons, forgiveness is one of the first steps in spiritual progression.

- The next step is to open yourself to new possibilities. This can be done by simply accepting the fact that we are all human, creatures here on earth connected to all other creatures. While we are small and insignificant in the grand scheme of the universe, we still exist. Rather than getting stuck on the idea of self-importance, open yourself to the idea that your individuality might be holding you back from experiencing true freedom.

- The final step is to accept yourself. While this might seem difficult after just going through the previous step, you are still an individual. But many of us have made ourselves into something we are not. In this step, take a moment to search for your true self. If you are a different person depending on your environment, such as home or the workplace, it might be time to commit to finding out who you really are.

While these steps can be quite difficult to take, you can take them each in due course. You do not have to take all of them in a single session. In fact, that would be impossible, which is why this meditation takes time. In the end, however, awakening your third eye will bring to light everything you have discovered through these sessions, providing you with the wisdom to use those discoveries together.

* * *

Mantra Meditation

Mantras are known as words or phrases which you can repeat during meditations, be this through speaking, chanting, whispering, or simply repeating it inside your head. This method can be useful in many ways, but for the purpose of awakening the third eye, it can help further your progress substantially.

While almost any word or phrase can be used as a mantra, it is important to note your intentions during these sessions, as that is what you will be focusing on while repeating your mantra.

Seeing as the focus is on awakening the third eye, I will construct a quick mantra for you as an example.

"I see my wisdom"

The intent behind this is to see into the abyss, reaching in to find my wisdom.

- First, construct a mantra for your intention, or use the example given for practice. Understanding your intention before beginning to construct a new mantra is important, as you do not want to sit and repeat something that is not connected with your true intention. It is important to remember this intention throughout the session.

- Similar to the previous methods, get comfortable and relax. Focus on your breathing for a few minutes while reminding yourself of your intentions for this session.
- Start repeating your mantra. Chanting, speaking, or thinking is fine. However, anything out loud is the best option. Do not expect anything supernatural to happen. Simply remember your intention while repeating your mantra. After many sessions, you may be in a trancelike state, altering your consciousness, at which point you might find exactly what you intended.
- You may continue for as long as you'd like, for a few minutes or even a few hours, so long as you repeat your mantras and remember your intention behind them. These mantras give your mind a sort of anchor to keep it from drifting off, which is why mantras are so effective.
- As your session ends, breathe deeply and speak your mantra, feeling your intention vibrate through your body as energy.

Finding a teacher to help with these more complex meditations is a good idea, as they are able to personalize your experience, almost like a tailor making a suit just for you.

* * *

Visualization Meditation

This method of meditation is well known for its use in reaching one's goals. Whether these goals are material, physical, spiritual, or emotional, it is a great practice to get you focused on what you are striving for.

Many people struggle with calming their minds, while others find it easy. Visualization is a method in which you can sort of bypass the thought process by simply focusing on a specific collection of thoughts, forming a kind of image in the process. Some people are more visual thinkers than others, which is why this method exists.

This method takes advantage of your active mind and bustling imagination in order to construct your goals in a visual manner that you can focus on. When using this for awakening the third eye, you can visualize an actual eye where the 6th chakra is located, opening it in order to peer into yourself or out to the universe.

- Starting off, find a quiet place to sit with no distractions. An active mind is a distraction, in itself; No need to add to that. I prefer a low light area for this method, even going so far as sitting in a dark room at night, but not everyone is comfortable with doing that.
- As with most sessions, the basics apply, starting with basic breathing and becoming as relaxed as possible. Try visualizing the air filling your lungs as you breathe.

- When relaxed, you can start visualizing whichever goal it is you wish to achieve; in this context, it is awakening the third eye. There are many ways you can visualize this, the easiest being simply to see yourself opening your third eye. Many try to visualize their third eye to see within themselves, trying to find the wisdom within, while others try to see outward, imagining the universe as visible and as vibrant as can be.

- You may continue this session as long as you wish, depending on what exactly it is you are visualizing your focus might start to dwindle, at which time it is a good idea to end the session.

- As the session ends, with one focused on the third eye, visualize it closing back up, this is to symbolize that you do not want your energy to be flowing out. Otherwise, you might get a headache later during the day.

Visualizing is quite a strong form of meditation, and while many do not realize it, they are using it every day during their lives. The simple thought of visualizing your goals is a basic form of this meditation method, and when employed with great focus, the benefits can be tremendous.

Movement Meditation

While movement meditation is quite different from other forms of meditation, it does not mean it is any less useful or enlightening. As the name suggests, you are in a constant state of movement during the session.

This form of meditation is especially useful to those who find it seemingly impossible to simply sit still and focus or relax. While any movement can be coupled with meditation, there are specific movements that have been developed in order to increase the potential benefits of this method, one of these techniques is known as tai chi.

These movements are designed to take advantage of the natural flow of energy within our bodies while focusing the mind through meditation. This is beneficial to the process of awakening the third eye, as you can energize your chakras and in turn, gain control over your 6th chakra more easily.

As stated, any movement works, even jogging. What makes this method effective is how you pay attention to your body and thoughts throughout the process, so here are a few pointers.

- When you move, you have to pay attention to your body, not simply make it move, but feel your muscles expand and contract, the warmth and blood circulation. Focus on your breath and heart rate. Try to visualize how the energy is flowing inside of you as you move, and how you want to put that energy to use.

- Be attentive to what your body is trying to tell you during these sessions. Whether certain areas are stiff and others seem to move with ease, allow your body to express itself, be it through pain, pleasure, pressure, or lack thereof. This is useful for realizing which parts of your body need more attention.
- During these sessions, you can either repeat mantras, visualize, or be mindful, but remember to focus on your body. The best way to do this is to think of it, not like your body, but just a body you are controlling in this world.
- Getting advice from personal trainers or dietitians can be a good idea, especially if you feel the flow of energy inside you is off.

ADVANCED TECHNIQUES

While the techniques above can be described as basic meditation techniques, it does not mean that they are easy to master. Practitioners all around the world might spend years mastering those techniques. However, it will all depend on the practitioner. Mastering a meditation technique does not simply mean learning to 'do it well,' but rather coming to understand the experience in a more profound sense. Those basic techniques can come in more advanced forms, as well.

In this part of the chapter, I would like to expose you to some of the more advanced meditation techniques. These techniques are well known, but there are only a few people who actively try to understand the inherent ideas and processes behind them in a more profound and spiritual sense.

That is what separates those who are advanced from those at more basic levels.

I would advise everyone to at least try the basic methods before moving on to these techniques. This is not because you might fail or perform the methods incorrectly. The issue presents itself through an individual's experience in any practice, method, or technique.

The basics prepare your conscious experience through your physical body, similar to how movement meditation teaches you to move with intent. You become accustomed to your emotions, your thoughts, and even physical ailments during basic meditation. This, in turn, will prepare you for the raw surge of energy experienced in the more advanced techniques. Interpreting these experiences will, of course, be up to you.

The basics are there to ease your conscious and subconscious mind into what might be a complete overhaul of your reality, while the advanced methods will crack open your shell, exposing you to reality.

Tonglen Meditation

We have all heard the tales of Tibetan monks and their achievements in and through meditation. While some of these things are true and other exaggerated, the fact remains that their meditation techniques work.

A very popular and quite strange method of meditation practiced by these monks is Tonglen meditation. When I say quite strange, I mean it in the sense of an experience to which one is not accustomed, or perhaps, has not yet experienced. Tonglen is known by many as 'giving and taking' or 'sending and receiving.' A method used to take in the pain and suffering from others with the inhale, and with every exhale we wish them relief.

That is what makes this meditation method a bit more advanced, getting used to something we as humans are often not so used to, compassion for others.

The idea behind this meditation is to rid yourself of selfishness, providing you with a more profound sense of reality. This is similar to how Christians will congregate in mass prayer to benefit others.

As this form of meditation is repeated, you will become more aware of your resistance or confusion to what this reality offers. You will start to understand your own suffering and that of others, sharing it together so that you can help each other.

The official Tonglen meditation has four main steps. While it can be adapted to suit the practitioner, we will focus on only the four steps.

* * *

Bodhicitta:

In the first step, start to relax and clear your mind. If you truly want to achieve the advanced level of this meditation, you will have to reach bodhicitta. A state of enlightenment where you exude compassion. In this state, you have to try and detach yourself from existence as an individual.

* * *

Visualization:

As you remain in this state, you can start with visualization. As you breathe in, try to visualize the person you are focusing on. If there is no person, you can simply visualize the negative energy in the air. Feel yourself breathing all this negative and heavy energy into yourself, be it from a person or the ambiance. As you exhale, try to visualize yourself radiating light, releasing positive energy. Do this until you sync each breath with negative in and positive out, continuing for a few minutes with absorbing and releasing.

The Catalyst:

At this point, you can start focusing on your own pain and suffering. While Tonglen is practiced for others, you can use your own despair as a catalyst to feel the pain of others in a similar situation. Do this while still performing the absorption of negative energy and the release of positive energy.

• • •

Compassion:

In the final step, you have to expand on your state of compassion. I do mean expand literally here, like extending a helping hand to someone. Expand your awareness of others who are suffering. If you lost a loved one, extend your compassion to others in the same situation. If you are practicing Tonglen for another person, extend that compassion to others in a similar situation to that person.

This method of meditation can extend the reach of compassion infinitely. As you practice, you will notice an increase in your general compassion for others. In regards to the third eye, this form of meditation increases your understanding of reality by linking your energy with others.

When achieving bodhicitta and remaining in that state for longer periods of time, your sense of emptiness increases. This provides you with the experience to interpret a wider variety of energy when your third eye is awakened.

Microcosmic Orbit Meditation

The first question many people have when it comes to this method of meditation is usually: What is the microcosmic orbit?

This method is descended from ancient Taoist teachings. As discussed in the first chapter, Taoism is focused on the flow of energy throughout the universe. Everything in this universe, in the cosmos, has energy moving in circles. Similar to how protons and neutrons form a nucleus around which electrons spin to form an atom, so do the planets move around stars and the stars around the center of the galaxy. All the energy has a delicate equipoise, like yin and yang.

What makes this method so advanced is the way that it helps us to understand the universe through ourselves. As part of this universe, our energy is in constant circulation, so we must learn to keep the energy within ourselves balanced and circulating.

The end goal of this meditation is to balance the energy which, in turn, will help you with stress and anxiety. But with energy flowing through you more efficiently, you can awaken your third eye more easily.

- Start by sitting down in a chair. You will have to sit upright, with your feet flat on the floor.
- Focus on each breath and start getting a feel of your spine and the crown of your head—just be aware of them.
- After a few minutes, start visualizing with each inhale, energy rising up from your root through the spine, settling on the crown. As you exhale, feel the energy flow down the front of your body back to your root. Do this with each breath, focusing on the sensations that your body presents to you.
- When your mind starts to wander, simply remind

yourself to focus on breathing again. You can visualize your chakras as checkpoints through which the energy must travel.

- As you go through this session, you will start feeling energized and focused. Keep cultivating that feeling for a few minutes. You may keep the session going for as long as you want.
- When ending the session, focus all the energy you have absorbed down into your lower abdomen. Bring your hands over the area as if holding it there and focus on it. You are now essentially storing the new energy for the rest of your day.
- You can open your eyes and stand up, leaving any negative energy behind.

This method of meditation will assist you in awakening your third eye quicker, but it will help in many more ways as well. When practicing this method, you are revitalizing yourself. This will benefit your body and inner self.

Identity Shift Meditation

As with the previous method of meditation, this one focuses on your place in the universe. However, it works in a completely different way by focusing on perspective rather than energy flow.

- Start out by finding a comfortable spot. You may either sit or lie down.
- As you relax and keep breathing steadily, you can start to focus on your mind. There is a mantra that comes with this step which you can repeat out loud or just to yourself. 'I am not the mind; the mind is in me.'
- As you repeat this mantra, start feeling your mind, try to explore every part of it.
- Next is the mantra 'I am not in the body; the body is me.' While repeating this mantra, focus your awareness over the rest of your body and its sensations.
- 'I am not in this building; the building is in me.' This will be the next mantra, repeat it as you expand your awareness to the outside world. Envelop your room and the rest of the building.
- This awareness will be expanding gradually until you reach the edges of the planet. You may construct a mantra for each stage depending on how detailed you want it to be, and how far you want to go. City, country, planet, solar system, and galaxy are all within you.

When concluding your session, be sure to let the newfound awareness settle inside you. This method of meditation can be very useful when trying to awaken your third eye. The awareness gained will help understand and interpret your awakening.

* * *

Kundalini Yoga

We went over Kundalini yoga in one of the earlier chapters. Shakti is the dormant energy at your root, which can be awakened through various poses, chants, and breathing techniques. There is another side to it, however, which led to some people claiming that Kundalini yoga was dangerous.

Kundalini yoga is best done when a trusted teacher or guide is present. As it might not be dangerous when performed correctly, however, when taught incorrectly, it can be a frightening experience. This is due to the nature of the method, as it brings up raw emotion. While you may be content at the conclusion of the session, you may also end up frustrated due to practicing for months with no progress to show for it. Another more severe outcome will lead to emotional and/or psychotic breakdowns.

There is another reason it is listed as advanced, besides what was mentioned above. If you are prepared for the session, through previous meditation experience of any kind, and through a proper mindset, it can be done without a guide. Previous experience will help you to mitigate and process the surges of energy and emotions throughout the session, leading to a less severe or even a successful outcome.

The master teachers can prepare you for these sessions, so it is still the best option to seek one out. This is why I will share only some basic information, which will not result in any severe negative outcomes.

Session Structure

- Each session starts with an opening chant
- Next is a warm-up that consists of breathing exercises and some basic poses for stretching.
- The third stage is known as kriya. This is the more intense part as it can last how long you or the teacher wants it to. It consists of a combination of breathing exercises synchronized with a specific set of poses, mantras, and gestures.
- After kriya, you are allowed to relax your body in order to absorb the effects of the session.
- When ready, you are guided into a state of meditation. This session usually consists of expanding awareness and understanding of what you experienced.
- The session ends with a closing chant.

Here are some beginner poses you can try to prepare yourself:

- The Lotus pose
- The Cobra pose
- The Archer pose
- Spinal Flexing (cat and cow poses)

Kundalini yoga may take weeks or even years to yield any results, it all depends on the individual. There is a possibility of an immediate reaction, which can be either negative or positive. This process changes your level of consciousness completely, which can be life-changing, and dangerous. However, it makes awakening the third eye a much more profound experience.

Tai Chi

While popularly known as a Chinese martial art, it is a form of movement meditation. This method is advanced due to the sheer amount of movement techniques, however, it is considered as having the safest forms of movement techniques. Due to the precision of the movements, it is best practiced with a master. The movements were established through the ten principles of Tai chi.

1. Straightening the head.
2. Having the correct position of the chest and back.
3. Remain relaxed with no tension.
4. Movement comes from the center.
5. Harmony between the upper and lower body.
6. Do everything in motion or everything in stillness.
7. Movement is continuous.
8. One leg is heavy and one is light.
9. Breathe in harmony with your movements.
10. The mind is leading the body.

The ten principles are there to guide you through the thirteen postures. These postures consist of eight hand positions and five leg positions. The movement results in a form of self-defense martial art with smooth meditation.

Hand Positions:

1. Peng - Ward off.

2. Lu - Deflect.
3. Chi - Apply force.
4. An - Press weight into.
5. Cai - Twist.
6. Lie - Split.
7. Zhou - Strike.
8. Kao - Body strike.

Each position is precise and should therefore not be practiced without any guidance.

Leg Positions:

1. Jin- Advance.
2. Tui– Withdraw.
3. Ku– Left.
4. Pan– Right.
5. Central equilibrium.

These positions are usually taught with a mantra, 'the body follows steps to move and steps follow the body to change.'

Tai Chi is one of the most popular techniques when trying to maintain balance in your life while wanting to exercise as well. This provides someone looking to awaken their third eye with something useful. Not everyone is capable of sitting and meditating for extended periods of time, which makes tai chi the perfect option.

* * *

A PERSONAL GUIDE

We all have stories to tell in this world. Some might be more useful than others, but the fact remains that there surely is no shortage of stories. I will share a personal tale of mine, an experience I had during a magic mushroom trip. I hope this story might help enhance your understanding of reality, as the experience certainly changed mine.

At the tender age of nineteen, some close friends and I went to a small abandoned piece of land, a place we knew we could set up camp and not be disturbed. As we arrived, we unpacked and immediately consumed a few grams of mushrooms each. We decided on playing some background music to set the tone of the trip.

We talked about all kinds of things, however, as the night progressed we started calming down and splitting up. Not that we did not want to talk, but at that point, we knew we were in for quite the ride. During the infancy of my experience, I decided on simply sitting down and absorbing everything around me.

As I closed my eyes, I implemented a form of meditation where I intensely focused on my breathing. During this experience, it almost felt like I was breathing energy into my body and then back out. As I breathed in, I felt everything around me, the grassy scent entering my nose, a cold breeze from behind, and the smoldering heat from a small dying fire about four feet to my right. As I breathed out, I could feel everything slipping away again.

At this point, I started thinking about how most of what we perceive is simply input from our senses. Most of what we do are just reactions to that input, we rarely decide to do something consciously and with intent. At least for me, at the age of nineteen, this realization changed my perception of reality. I decided at that moment that every day thereafter, I will wake up and make a conscious decision on how my day will go.

The rest of the night went as expected. We all gathered together again and started talking about our experiences. We laughed at some of them and debated others but, in the end, we all just had a good time and left the next day.

After discussing this experience with a few friends later that year, a man came forward from the group, a friend of a friend. He, from his own experiences and experimentation, passed unto me a method for meditation, which will focus the mind in a similar way to that of my previous experience. I accepted this method graciously and evolved it according to my own interpretations, and experiences.

This led me to awaken my third eye for the first time.

While this awakening was more akin to an eye blinking rather than opening, lasting for a second, I caught a glimpse of truth. I hope you can take this method and form a technique that suits you personally.

Find a place to relax and be alone. This method works better at night but can be done during the day as well. Whether you decide on sitting somewhere in your home or outside in nature, be sure it is dark. If you decide to do this during the day, try to avoid direct sunlight. I'm advising this due to the acute light sensitivity you will develop after the session, it only lasts for a few minutes.

- Sit down and relax, try to be as comfortable as possible, as this session can last more than an hour.
- Focus on your breathing as with all other methods. Start to imagine your body being filled with more and more energy as you inhale deeply and exhale slowly. Do this for a few minutes.
- At this point, you can try to focus on your heartbeat. Try to consciously make it beat slower while slowly breathing in and out.
- You will start to feel your heartbeat like a wave throughout your body, feel every breath of energy ride that wave to the tips of your nervous system.
- After a few minutes, you can start focusing on the center of your forehead.
- Visualize a small black sphere in the center of your vision while keeping your eyes closed.
- Focus on that sphere for a few minutes, after which you can visualize it growing, almost as if it is coming closer from a distance.
- As it comes closer, feel its presence envelop you, as if you are standing in front of a massive black hole.

- As you are consumed, focus on the center of the sphere, visualize a small light like a star shining, approaching you slowly.
- Try to perceive that wave inside you grow stronger with every beat while the light approaches.
- As the light reaches you, visualize it small, like a grain of sand, letting it gently touch your forehead.
- As this happens, feel the energy inside you connect with it, feel the surge of power from your root chakra shoot up your spine and synchronize with that light.
- Focus on what you experience at that moment, as it will disappear quickly.
- You will notice that your heart rate most likely increased dramatically at this point. Try to calm it.
- I usually recommend ending the session after calming down, but you may try to spark that connection again by starting the process over.
- This is where light sensitivity comes into play. Even when your eyes are closed, you will sense that any light shining toward you is immensely magnified. Do not open your eyes at this point.
- Focus all the energy inside your third eye back into your root, as if you are slowly closing your third eye. You will feel the sensitivity start to dissipate as you direct the energy flow. You might still be a little sensitive to light for a few minutes after, but that will go away as well.

This method, when adjusted to your own body and experiences, will give you a glimpse of true reality. The point of synchronicity between you, the universe, and energy, is what you have to achieve. While this might happen for just a split second, the goal is to practice to turn that split second into more. The microdosing methods mentioned in the previous chapter can greatly increase the effectiveness of the session, should you become stuck.

If the tale I shared improved your understanding, or the method I described helped further your own goals, I am glad. If neither of them helped whatsoever, well it does happen. We might be two completely different people, after all, so do not be dispirited, as your awakening is simply waiting for you on your own path.

GUIDE YOURSELF

The only person in this world that knows what is best for you is you. While getting help from others is a good idea, and guidance might be necessary, other people's advice and methods can only bring you so far.

These meditation methods and techniques I have found to be quite useful, but when you start to play around with the idea that you can construct your own methods, only then are you truly awakening your potential.

How is This Beneficial?

There are usually two questions on almost anyone's mind when presented with the idea of awakening their third eye.

'Is it real?' and 'How does it benefit me?'

For now, let's focus on the latter question.

A few years back, when my spiritual journey was only in its infancy, I started to doubt what I was doing. At this point in my life, I was still fairly young, and one of my friends suggested we go out to the countryside as a group and enjoy some time away from everything. We decided to stay with a long-time friend who had moved to his parents' old farm. When we arrived, I was made aware that we would be provided with a choice, we could either relax by the main house, or go out to an open spot and experience magic mushrooms for the first time. I, of course, chose the latter.

While I'm not going to go into the details, I had quite a profound experience, an experience that reassured me that I was on the right track, and stays with me still. I decided to further my spiritual progression and soon came to realize the true benefits it provided.

Health

While you would not expect that a journey into awakening your third eye would be beneficial to your physical health, your expectations change as you become closer to that goal. When first starting out, you go through the process of clearing your chakras, at which point you realize your physical and dietary habits may not be the most life-sustaining.

I am a firm believer that you do not need to wave goodbye to meat, junk food, and sugary treats. While they might be unhealthy and addictive, there is nothing in this world that comes close to simply enjoying a good old fashioned junk food fueled movie night. There are people that would disagree, of course, but giving in to earthly pleasures is only human.

The spiritual journey is about finding your true self, and I enjoy a good pizza. It's my soul food, and so I encourage everyone to not just throw away something you once enjoyed, unless you are afflicted by a specific condition of course.

Becoming aware of your health during your journey is a part of that journey, you learn to listen to your body and any ailments it might want you to become aware of, be it dietary or physical. This becomes apparent when first starting to meditate, as you learn things about your body you never knew before, or perhaps forgotten about.

Spiritual and Emotional Benefits

Obviously, there are some spiritual and emotional benefits to awakening your third eye, as well as the journey to get there.

As you progress from starting to basic meditation, you gradually become more attuned to yourself. While this sounds simple, many people today have lost themselves to life. We are constantly distracted and busy, leaving little time for our emotional and spiritual wellbeing. During your journey, you realize certain things about your emotional state, traumas that you have buried deep and wanted to leave forgotten.

While that might sound like a terrible experience, dealing with emotional turmoil is a part of life. Accepting that, you are able to move forward, realizing that it might have been affecting you all your life. You might be able to sleep better, be more confident, or even trust and love again.

Becoming more open-minded is certainly another benefit of the entire journey. As you become more aware of the different ways people perceive the world around them, you come to realize that the way you look at life might be a bit closed-minded. When this happens, you might discover things you enjoy, things you either never knew existed, or things you were simply not interested in trying.

At the same time, you might come to realize that you only thought you enjoyed doing something because friends or family enjoyed it, changing your way of life for the better, as it is okay not to enjoy doing things that others do.

Many people expect the awakening of their third eye to be a specific moment in time, a measurable happening, but it's not. Yes, a time does come when you experience a very specific sense of clarity, but if that is all you are looking for, you will not reach it, as you cannot reach something up high without building the ladder to get there.

* * *

Shattering Your Reality

There is no doubt that one of the main reasons you started reading this book is because you heard the tales of how the third eye may allow you to see into true reality. Luckily for you, it is possible.

Unfortunately, however, it is not that easy. Have you ever tried looking for something around the house and ending up never finding it? Then, a few days later, you find it as if it just appeared out of thin air. Certain aspects of awakening the third eye are very similar to that experience. When you start to focus on it too much, it ends up unobtainable, and then one day, it happens, and oh boy does it happen.

At this point, the reality around you becomes completely different, you look at things in a way you have never been able to see them before. Now, I don't mean the fabric of time-space seems to change as you view it, but rather that you see beyond that fabric, and see the needle and the threads.

This experience is very similar to what people call an 'ego death.' While ego death is mostly caused by a "breakthrough" when using psychedelics, this experience can be obtained through awakening your third eye. Ego death can be described as a loss of self-identity or the death of the self. This means that what you perceive as your subjective self dies.

This might sound alarming but, the moment you realize exactly what and who you are, without any influence from your ego, you become more than what you used to be. You gain profound wisdom on your personal identity. Your identity is always changing, molded according to whatever situations to which you are exposed. With that taken away, your core is revealed.

This revelation presents a problem to people who are emotionally or mentally unstable, but can be the solution as well. When they are exposed to this broken version of themselves, it can either mend the broken parts, or shatter the remaining pieces even further.

Remember, we all perceive reality differently. Once your perception changes, it can never revert to what it once was.

For this reason, you have to be careful not to peer into the abyss for too long.

* * *

General Life Improvements

While many of us want some profound change in our lives, sometimes all that is needed is a light touch, a small nudge in the right direction.

When on your journey to awakening your third eye, you come to realize a great deal, things that help you in everyday life. How to deal with your emotions, how to deal with other people's emotions, simple relaxation, stress relief—all these things culminate into a collection of life-changing improvements that we need in order to survive our daily routines.

Faq

We all have questions in life. Some of these questions may be easy to answer, while others might need a complicated explanation, and some cannot be answered at all.

This part of the book is dedicated to some of these questions, which I will try and answer for you to the best of my knowledge. I will split the questions up into segments that mirror the chapters of the book, with a final category dedicated to general questions.

Is there a point in studying other religions?

While this question is rather simple, the answer may not be as easy to understand. When you study a new subject, you gather information which you can apply throughout your life, similar to how you would apply math to simple situations like, counting your change.

It is my belief that studying other religions provides you with more knowledge which you can apply in a large variety of ways. Some of this new information may not be of use to you practically, but rather spiritually and emotionally. When we only learn about one religion, we tend to get a bit close-minded, confrontational, and biased when it comes to other cultures and religions.

You can be a devout believer of one religion, but still study others.

If I am Christian, is opening my third eye wrong?

While many followers of Christianity believe they will be punished for dabbling in this subject matter, it is simply not true.

Is magick and its use to awaken the third eye satanic?

There is a yes and no answer to this question, as magick itself is not inherently satanic. However, there are ways of using and studying magick known as going down the left-handed path, which can be considered satanic.

I am very busy and only get a few minutes to myself a day, how can I relax?

You can relax while you work. Just take a few seconds to breathe and collect your thoughts. While it's not that effective, it gives you a moment of clarity.

Will kundalini yoga help me awaken my third eye?

Kundalini yoga has many uses, and it will definitely help with awakening your third eye, as it stimulates the dormant energy within you.

Can I ask for outside help if I am not sure how to continue on my journey?

Of course! There are many gurus and masters out there, and professional psychologists will provide you with some insight as well. Just make sure to whomever you go, that they are reliable.

I have tried everything but I am unable to feel any of my chakras. What do I do?

Sometimes it can be difficult to tap into our spiritual energy, especially when we lived most of our lives ignoring it. In this case, I would suggest sitting with either a shaman or guru in order to get personalized guided sessions.

Can I skip the other chakras and focus on my third eye alone?

While you can do this, and actually achieve the awakening, it is highly unlikely, as the energy flow in your body needs to pass through all the previous chakras in order to get to the 6th, but anything is possible!

Where can I get these gemstones and crystals, how do I know they are not counterfeit?

There are many places that sell these stones and crystals, and unfortunately, there are those who will try to take advantage of the market. The best option is obviously to go to a shop in person, as you can feel the gems and crystals in real-time, and there is usually someone knowledgeable to assist you. Not everyone lives near a store that sells these items though, at which point you will have to order online. Simply do your research and consult trusted sources. Eventually, you will be able to confirm a legitimate site to order from.

Are there other things that help? I've heard incense, oils, and herbs can help cultivate energy?

This is true. There are oils that correspond to certain energies and incenses that help with specific moods and energy flows.

Are group breathwork sessions worth it?

It all depends on you. Are you comfortable in these sessions? Are the people providing guidance helpful? It won't help to try if you feel it's necessary, and you can always just walk away should you decide it's not for you.

Are psychedelics worth it?

I would say yes to this, even if you try them just once. There are always risks involved with anything we do in life. However, we must decide for ourselves if the risks are worth it. In my personal experience, I would say your spiritual journey is not complete with at least trying any psychedelic substance at least once.

Why am I struggling so much to meditate? I can't focus at all!

Meditation is not for everyone, although you can try different methods. You can try to get into a relaxed state even before your meditation session, at which point you can try to relax even further. Burning incense might help as well, although personally I never liked incense that much.

Will Tai Chi help with awakening my third eye?

While tai chi has many benefits, one of them is controlling your inner energy or chi. Similar to how chakras balance your energy, tai chi will help you to interpret the flow of energy around and inside you, making it easier to awaken the third eye.

• • •

Can I create my own meditation method?

Yes! If you feel the meditation methods you have tried do not work for you, try creating your own through mixing and matching, or giving birth to a whole new method altogether!

How do I know it's working, and that it is beneficial?

Well, this is a difficult question to answer, as everyone has different experiences. To be honest, you know when you know. The benefits would become tangible quite quickly as you notice an improvement in your mental state, as well as your spiritual progression.

As for 'if it is working', that will be up to you, did you get what you want out of your experiences? As simple as that.

Afterword

To reach a complete conclusion, you will have to experience your own spiritual journey. No one will be able to provide you with a worthy conclusion. All I can hope for is that the information I have presented you with might help you in some or another way.

There are many more books out there to read, many more practices to experiment with, and so much more experience to gain. Keep in mind, and I know I have said this a lot during this book, but the path to awakening your third eye is not a simple one, and it is not a short one. There is much to accomplish in order to awaken it, and even then, your journey only begins its next stage.

I have been working on my own journey through life, just as we all stumble in the darkness to find a flashlight, we are all human, looking for meaning in this life. The third eye can be a flashlight, and in the darkest of times in our lives, we can use that flashlight to find the way we are meant to go.

Although you might bump your toe into a chair or corner, do not give up, you will find it.

References

7 chakras: What is a chakra? How to balance chakras for beginners. (2017, September 28). The Law Of Attraction. https://www.thelawofattraction.com/7-chakras/

Buddhism - The life of the Buddha. (2019). In Encyclopædia Britannica. https://www.britannica.com/topic/Buddhism/The-life-of-the-Buddha

Emerson, C. H. (2019). Pineal gland | Definition, location, function, & disorders. In Encyclopædia Britannica. https://www.britannica.com/science/pineal-gland

Feeling out of sorts? Here's how to balance your chakras. (2020, January 4). Well+Good. https://www.wellandgood.com/chakra-balancing/

Iqbal, M. (2013, July 21). The 'third eye' connection. The Hindu. https://www.thehindu.com/sci-tech/health/the-third-eye-connection/article4932128.ece

Lizzy. (2019). 7 Chakra Crash Course: A Beginner's Guide To Awakening Your Seven Chakras. Chakras.Info. https://www.chakras.info/7-chakras/

Penzu. (n.d.). Penzu. https://penzu.com/dream-journal

Pineal gland function: Definition and circadian rhythm. (n.d.). www.medicalnewstoday.com. https://www.medicalnewstoday.com/articles/319882#understanding-circadian-rhythms

Shamanic breathwork. (n.d.). Venus Rising. https://www.shamanicbreathwork.org/shamanic-breathwork

Society, N. G. (2020, August 31). Taoism. National Geographic Society. https://www.nationalgeographic.org/encyclopedia/taoism/

Team, M. (2018, December 12). What are the different types of meditation? Forms, benefits & technique. Mindworks. https://mindworks.org/blog/different-types-meditation-technique/

The Third Eye in Hinduism & Buddhism -. (n.d.). www.lotussculpture.com. https://www.lotussculpture.com/blog/third-eye-hinduism-buddhism/

Umakant Premanand Shah, & Dundas, P. (2017). Jainism | religion. In Encyclopædia Britannica. https://www.britannica.com / topic / Jainism

Vivation International—breathwork, meditation, empowerment. (n.d.). Www.Vivation.com. http:/ / vivation.com /

William Hewat McLeod. (2019). Sikhism | History, doctrines,
practice,   &   literature.   In   Encyclopædia   Britannica.
https:/ / www.britannica.com / topic / Sikhism

IMAGES USED:

https:/ / pixabay.com / photos / sri-lanka-buddha-statue-
religion-1024347 /

https:/ / pixabay.com / photos / india-god-shiva-religion-
3882101 /

https:/ / pixabay.com / photos / zen-yin-yang-spirituality-
harmony-5533487 /

https:/ / pixabay.com / illustrations / crown-chakra-energy-chi-
spiritual-2533113 /

https:/ / pixabay.com / illustrations / solar-chakra-chi-energy-
spiritual-2533097 /

https:/ / pixabay.com / illustrations / sacral-chakra-energy-chi-
spiritual-2533094 /

https:/ / pixabay.com / illustrations / root-chakra-energy-chi-
spiritual-2533091 /

https:/ / pixabay.com / illustrations / throat-chakra-chi-energy-
spiritual-2533108 /

https://pixabay.com/illustrations/brow-chakra-energy-chi-spiritual-2533110/

https://pixabay.com/illustrations/heart-chakra-energy-chi-spiritual-2533104/

https://pixabay.com/photos/spiritualism-awakening-meditation-4552237/

https://pixabay.com/illustrations/pentagram-magic-occult-mystic-1740380/

https://pixabay.com/illustrations/brain-anatomy-human-science-health-512758/

https://pixabay.com/photos/notebook-book-leather-leather-cover-420011/

https://pixabay.com/photos/sand-footsteps-footprints-beach-768783/

https://pixabay.com/photos/hand-holding-chakra-stones-gems-3759354/

https://pixabay.com/photos/fantasy-eyes-forest-aesthetic-face-2824304/

https://pixabay.com/photos/zen-garden-meditation-monk-stones-2040340/

https://pixabay.com/photos/meditation-meditating-hands-1794292/

https://pixabay.com/photos/meditate-lake-mood-4882027/

REIKI FOR BEGINNERS

YOUR GUIDE TO REIKI HEALING AND REIKI MEDITATION WITH USEFUL TECHNIQUES TO INCREASE YOUR ENERGY AND CLEANSING YOUR AURA

Introduction

"If you want to find the secrets of the universe, think in terms of energy, frequency, and vibration." –Nikola Tesla

Imagine for a moment that you are exhausted. You have just had a long day following a night of little sleep because you had to work late into the evening. In the next five minutes, a meeting will start. You do not have enough energy to walk to the boardroom, let alone concentrate on the content of the meeting or maintain an appearance of vivacity. What do you do? There is no way you could get out of the meeting. Perhaps you could get coffee, but you have lost count of the number of coffees you have already had, and after each cup, you feel more feeble—more drained.

Perhaps instead you could just grab a cup of water. Yet, sincerely, you do not even have the strength for that. You need something that can get you out of your seat first. So, what do you do? Your face collapses into the palms of your hands. You breathe deeply as they are cupping your face. If you press deeply into your palms, it's possible the blood vessels in your eyes will make an imprint into your fingers, making you feel as if you are looking at a galaxy. It is just your blood vessels, but this impression seems outer-worldly.

For two minutes, you continue in this state, lying with your head cupped in your palms, breathing in your hands, and watching the galaxy continually shapeshift. Before the five minutes elapses, you are on your feet walking downstairs to the boardroom, not perfect, but not completely defeated, either. Some revival has occurred. If you are conscious enough, you make a mental note to take a quick headrest during the meeting—if you can get away with it.

This headrest forms the basics of how Reiki works (Reiki Self-Treatment: Procedure Details, 2019). Though you may have taken breaks cupping your face in your hands in the past, you may have not realized that what you were doing was a Reiki hand position. As your hands support your face, you feel the warmth and energy from them. The hands are channels of energy. Thus, when you relax your face into them, the energy between your face and hands flow. This leaves you feeling relaxed and revitalized.

Moreover, this collapse of your head into your hands is an unconscious reaction. You do not decide to rest your face into your hands, but as your lack of energy plummets, you give in and let your head fall. Five minutes later, you feel better and more prepared to go about your day. In this sense, Reiki is an unconscious, primordial form of healing. As a reflex, you rely on it when all other reserves have failed.

If two minutes of Reiki can give you enough energy to overcome debilitating exhaustion, can you imagine what half an hour each day could do?

THE CRISIS IN ENERGY

In the contemporary world, we have a crisis in energy. The recent rise in the number of burnout cases and unprecedented levels of stress and anxiety show that modern people are severely lacking energy (Elflein, 2016). The insane levels of competition to obtain skills and well-paying jobs does not do anything to help rejuvenate people. However, while there is a general consensus that stress and burnout is a major present-day problem, not everyone agrees on the roots of this issue.

Yet, what is burnout other than a crisis in energy? The clue is in the name. Even the word stress suggests the fundamental nature of something being too much or too overwhelming for an individual to handle. In other words, the person experiencing the stress does not have the vitality to manage the problem, thus feeling crushed in the process.

If there is not enough energy or flow, there is often an undesired consequence. This is true at every level. Consider, for example, if a certain body part does not get enough oxygen or blood flow. That body part will become gangrenous, and if not removed, the disease will spread. Additionally, many accidents have been caused simply by exhaustion or sleep deprivation. If people do not rejuvenate sufficiently, they make mistakes or cannot respond appropriately to situations, thereby creating even worse problems.

On a more social level, if two people meet, and they are experiencing very different energy levels, it will be hard for them to endure one another's company. This is rather unfortunate as the two individuals may have much in common, but their varying energy levels provide them with no firm platform on which to begin the relationship.

You may doubt this to be the case. However, consider situations when you are very tired and very low on energy. If a colleague or acquaintance suddenly enters your space as bubbly and enthusiastic as a firecracker, you might tense up like a hedgehog; or your blood might begin to boil slightly, and you will think there is something wrong with you. You will have no idea whatsoever as to why you suddenly felt tense or irritated.

On the other hand, if you have very high energy levels and someone you know has very low levels (and might be feeding off yours), you might feel drained speaking to them. These people are colloquially referred to as "energy vampires" (DiGiulio, 2018). Even though you would like to be kind or empathetic to them, when talking to these individuals, you will realize that energy is a very precious resource.

This is the crux of it. Energy is a resource, and lacking this precious resource can result in very costly mistakes. With plenty of it, energy can be a catalyst for many successful ventures, beautiful friendships, and simply general well-being. With that said, humans have a complicated relationship with energy.

Think of physical activity. Many people exercise to increase their energy levels and promote healthier sleeping patterns. Since exercise requires a great deal of energy to perform in the first place, the immediate reaction is for people to feel very tired afterward. Yet, hours later, their energy levels remain consistent, and they are able to sleep far better.

According to Mathew Walker, sleep is a crucial ingredient in maintaining one's concentration and diligence. While sleeping, you also burn calories, creating potential energy. That is why sometimes when you wake up in the middle of the night, you'll notice that you've worked up a sweat. Ironically, at the same time, doing passive activities such as binge-watching Netflix may result in a decrease of energy. Even though watching TV is ultimately relaxing, you are not burning very many calories (DiGiulio, 2018). Thus, potential energy is not being created.

It all comes down to energy. To say that there is an energy crisis in our modern world is an understatement, and calling it burnout or stress does not get to the root of the problem. However, naming it a disaster in energy gets to the bottom of the issue.

Unfortunately, one of the biggest issues getting in the way of solving this problem is living in a material world and having a material mindset. Though mentalities are changing with the expansion of psychology and psychotherapy, as well as the surge in popularity of mindfulness and mediation, many people believe that problems have a material nature. However, this is not often the case.

For example, while major financial difficulties cause people much pain and suffering, giving them an abundance of wealth will not end their problems. A clear example of this is the fact that 70% of lottery winners go bankrupt after a short length of time (Lottery Winners Who Blew the Lot, 2020). Getting rich overnight did not solve their problems, and actually, years later, they faced even worse circumstances; their financial prosperity caused rifts in their relationships with their loved ones.

Living in a material reality means we also concentrate on the visual aspects of the world and pay little attention to other senses, such as how a situation feels. We know how we feel when we are deprived of sleep, urgently seeking coffee for a boost. Later in the day, when we need a bit of a spike again, we might suddenly notice a bar of chocolate and gobble it up, waiting for the next boost. We see the chocolate and we see the coffee, but we do not try to feel what our body is telling us.

This is a huge issue with the material world. Coffee and chocolate, which come with a daily price tag, are very visually transfixing. Our body craves energy, but these two things are simply quick fixes. If we want to solve the crisis in energy, we need to take a step back and really get to the origin of the issue.

* * *

MIND, BODY, AND SOUL

When initially dealing with an energy crisis, we have to consider the exact nature of energy. Where does it come from? Where do we feel energy?

On a purely physiological level, our bodies obtain energy from mitochondria in our cells. Mitochondria use calories, oxygen, and other nutrients to power cellular processes. In other words, the mitochondrion in each cell generates power for our whole body (Mitochondria, 2014).

However, we are hardly conscious of the millions of biochemical reactions happening in the millions of cells in our bodies. The experience of vitality occurs chiefly in a psychological manner. Thus, though we acquire energy from cellular processes, our psychological awareness is the only true way we have contact with our energy.

For instance, when you deal with stress and burnout, you are struggling with an obstacle to your mental vitality. In the case of stress or anxiety, often extremely paralyzing thoughts and worries tend to override your mind, making you feel unable to deal with a problem. The problem or problems (as stress and anxiety tend to occur when many issues are occurring simultaneously) seem overwhelming—much bigger and greater than you can handle. It goes without saying that psychologically, one feels hopeless and paralyzed not simply because of the existence of the problems, but because they do not believe they have enough strength to overcome the simultaneously occurring issues.

Lastly, as many of the world's societies have moved away from religious ideologies and adopted more secular visions, the concept of the existence of a soul or spirit has been overlooked. Admittedly, a trend is developing among New Age philosophers and thinkers such as Sam Harris to focus on spiritual aspects. In this way, a modern resurrection of spirituality is gaining ground. This revisiting of spirituality has been responsible for the discovery of new ideas and approaches to well-being such as the rise in the practices of meditation, mindfulness, and energy healing. As the trend shows, attaining happiness and healing from physical and psychological issues essentially has a spiritual tendency.

As we often overlook the importance of spirituality and its connection to energy, consider the word "inspiration" and the phrase "human spirit". Both contain the root "spirit". Sometimes, we tend to confuse the words "mind" or "psyche" with the word "spirit". However, the spirit needs to be distinguished from the notion of mind. Modern thinkers such as Robin Sharma have made this very distinction.

Sharma made this very profound statement: "The mind is a wonderful servant, but a terrible master". This indicates that people are not their minds. As opposed to the mind, the spirit can be characterized by its ability to overcome negative thoughts, destructive patterns and mindsets, and harmful biochemistry and perspectives. This is often why when people firmly decide to change the course of their lives, they are able to rid themselves of bad habits, harmful lifestyle choices, and self-destructive attitudes. Thus, having a healthy spirit is key in making necessary and also unprecedented changes to our lives. This importance should never be understated.

This is where Reiki comes in. Reiki focuses on energy healing in all three areas—our bodies, minds, and souls. One is not superior to any other; they are all integral to our vitality. Vivacity in one often entails strength in another. It is for this reason that any serious form of healing has to consider recovery for all three. Reiki is one of the few forms of therapy that does just this. This is why Reiki is not only holistic, but essential.

WHY REIKI?

Reiki may seem like a counterintuitive approach to dealing with physiological and psychological issues, but sometimes things appear counterintuitive because they are deeply intuitive; thus, we are no longer conscious of them.

For example, when you suddenly become very stressed, tense, or annoyed, one of your first reactions is to sigh deeply. Sighing is an involuntary reaction to negative feelings. It is also an indication that someone is experiencing stress, tension, or irritation. Unconsciously, what you are doing is trying to expel negative energy. Additionally, you are also trying to inhale fresh air to increase the flow of oxygen; and that new, fresh air makes you feel more invigorated.

This is what people are doing in a more extreme manner when they exercise. They are trying to optimize flow and reinvigorate themselves with more oxygen (and fresh air), creating better blood flow and increasing energy. Like reiki, exercise is also almost counterintuitive. Every day, people need to encourage and push themselves to exercise, but the goals remain the same: optimize flow and promote a surge in energy.

We looked at another example earlier. When you rest your face into your hands, you are instinctively searching for energy. As children, we may have gotten into the habit of doing this, but now we have become unaware of how this act automatically revives us.

In the modern world, we have grown out of touch with our intuition, so much so that intuitive practices seem absurd or ridiculous. Some of us do not even believe a soul exists, yet we are on a continuous search for inspiration and motivation. It is only now, when we are facing alarming rates of suicide (Suicide Statistics, 2020), depression, burnout, and stress (Elflein, 2016), that spiritual healing and the revitalization of energy do not appear all that ridiculous.

Reiki for Beginners is a guide to help you start your journey with the life-changing practice of Reiki. It intends to introduce you to the three levels of Reiki: Shoden, Okuden, and Shinpiden. While taking you through each of the levels, this guide aims to help you master energy healing using Reiki. Furthermore, it will help you understand the history and theoretical aspects of this practice while assisting you to master the various hand positions, Reiki levels, and meditation so that you can begin healing yourself.

Although this manual is not meant to be an exhaustive study on Reiki, it does intend to take you through the three levels to help you extend this therapy to your loved ones and others in your community. As there is an energy crisis in our modern dog-eat-dog world, enhancing one's energy can be likened to a spiritual wealth—one that is very much lacking but that is very much in demand.

What Is Reiki?

"Even though the body appears to be material, it is not. In the deeper reality, your body is a field of energy, transformation, and intelligence." –Deepak Chopra

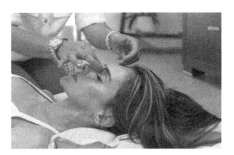

UNDERSTANDING REIKI

Essentially, Reiki is healing with energy. It is an alternative and holistic form of healing that relies on meditation, hand positions, and increasing one's flow and energy to soothe physical ailments, provide mental wellness, and increase spiritual vivacity.

To first understand Reiki, you can study its etymology. Reiki is a Japanese word. If you break it down into its two roots, you get *rei* and *ki*. *Rei* means "universal" while *ki* translates to "life energy" (Newman, 2017). Thus, Reiki is a practice that tries to provide healing through increasing the flow of energy to areas of the body or mind. Alex Bennet provides more insight into understanding the term ki.

The Japanese word *kti*, from which the word "Reiki" is formed, is the essential life force—the energy and warmth radiated by the living body, human or animal. Everything that is alive contains and radiates ki; when ki departs the living organism, life has departed (Newman, 2017).

As mentioned in the introduction, if the flow of blood or oxygen to a specific body part is disrupted, first this body part will not be able to function, then gradually it will die. This is not only true on a physical level, but in mental and spiritual dimensions as well. For example, when you are overwhelmed by angry and bitter thoughts, you do not stop being angry and bitter, but instead become even more so. It takes perspective and calming thoughts to dispel such negativity.

This echoes Martin Luther King's famous quote, "Darkness cannot drive out darkness; only light can do that. Hate cannot drive out hate; only love can do that" (King, 1963, p. 37). King's statement is not only virtuous but also logical. In a physical dimension, this also happens to be logical. If your foot is not receiving blood, what you do is increase the blood flow to it so it can heal; you do not continue to prevent blood flow.

Reiki incorporates this logic into its practice. If you are tired, weak, or suffering from physical pain, you need to optimize energy flow to a specific area. The same occurs with ki, or life energy. Bennet helps to elucidate this point: "Since ki nourishes the organs and cells of the body, supporting them in their vital functions, the disruption of ki brings about illness" (p. 2). Since humans are primarily composed of energy, Reiki can help not only physical impairments, but those of a metaphysical nature as well.

Having said this, mastering Reiki is simple, but it is not easy. It necessitates learning mediation, practicing various hand positions, and understanding the nature of energy. Currently, there are only about a thousand Reiki masters worldwide (Reiki, 2019). While the practice offers numerous physical and psychological benefits, it is technically a discipline. This guide aims to familiarize you with Reiki and help you begin your journey in learning this discipline.

ORIGINS OF REIKI

When people first study Reiki, they come across the name Mikao Usui. Although Mikao Usui is formally responsible for founding this alternative form of therapy, Reiki takes its roots from much older philosophies and bodies of knowledge. In this sense, Mikao Usui's role can be described as formalizing Reiki into more cohesive and integrated healing methods based on ancient teachings. Therefore, anyone who wishes to begin a comprehensive and well-informed study of Reiki needs to begin with Buddhist Qigong.

Buddhist Qigong is a subdivision of Buddhism that developed four thousand years ago in China. As the spiritual philosophy is so ancient, it is arguably older than Buddhism, deriving from ancient Chinese philosophy, way of life, medicine, and tradition. Nevertheless, after Buddha's fame became recognized and spread throughout Asia, Buddhist Qigong rose as a subculture of Buddhism.

One of the hallmarks of Buddha's life that greatly influenced Buddhist Qigong, leading to its creation, was Buddha's talent for healing his followers and others who he encountered. In general, the Buddhist way of life concentrates on healing through various methods, namely meditation, improving one's karma and leading to exploration of the layers of the mind and of Reiki.

C. Pierce Salguero supports this point with the following comment:

Practical tools for mental and physical healing—including but not limited to meditation—were adapted and elaborated across virtually all of Asia for most of Buddhism's history, and indeed have often played a major role in the popularization of the religion in its new host cultures (Paging Dr. Dharma, 2016).

As Buddhism became recognized for its ability to restore people's good health through its practices, many people across the continent of Asia were attracted to its success. In our modern world, it can be difficult to acknowledge what kind of impact Buddha's work would have had. In ancient times, medicine was largely primordial, and people back then suffered greatly from disease, lack of basic sanitation, and poverty. Consequently, the healing by Buddha's practices was a necessity many people could not do without.

Having said that, Qigong and subsequently Buddhist Qigong are derived from traditional Chinese medicine, which continues to be practiced in the contemporary world, as well as from other philosophies such as Confucianism and Daoism (Qigong, 2020).

When Buddha's influence became more prevalent in Asia, traditional Qigong and Buddhism developed a set of practices that would create the practice of Reiki. What distinguished Buddhist Qigong from other divisions of Qigong was its concentration on mind and spirit as the basis of healing (How to Tell, Buddhist or Taoist or Confucian Qigong, 2017).

Like with other forms of Buddhism such as Theravada, Mahāyāna, and Vajrayāna, during Buddha's lifetime and long after his death, Buddhist Qigong became widespread in influencing the way of life in Asia. It was in Japan where Mikao Usui formalized Reiki from the age-old customs of Qigong and established it as practice.

As stated earlier, while Mikao Usui is recognized as the founder of Reiki, this is rather misleading as it suggests that the technique of Reiki did not exist before him. Usui's own words imply something of a similar nature: "Reiki does not belong to one person or one community, but it is the spiritual heritage of all humanity (Who Is Mikao Usui And The 3 Things You Have To Know About Him, 2020).

What Mikao Usui can be credited with is mastering Reiki, refining it, formalizing it into a structured practice, and sharing this with the world.

Mikao Usui

Mikao Usui was born in 1865. When he was four years old, he began living in a monastery studying Tendai, a division of Mahayana Buddhism. During Usui's time at the monastery, he became interested in world religions, psychology, and medicine (Who Is Mikao Usui And The 3 Things You Have To Know About Him, 2020, para 3). Naturally, it was his training in psychology and medicine that initiated Usui's path in energy healing.

The Richard Ellis School of Reiki offers insight into Usui's calling. It was during 1888 that he contracted cholera as an epidemic swept through Kyoto. He had a profound near-death experience during which he received visions of Mahavairocana Buddha and received direct instructions from him. This was a pivotal experience for Usui that caused him to make a major reassessment of his life. He developed a keen interest in the esoteric science of healing as taught by Buddha, and he developed the compassionate wish that he might learn these methods in order to benefit mankind (The History of Reiki 1865 - 1926, 2011, para 5).

Therefore, it was Usui's own close encounter with death that encouraged him to seek alternative healing techniques. The following few years, Usui devoted his time to pursue medical knowledge, causing him to diverge from Tendai. Usui soon became attracted to Shingon Buddhism, a division of the religion that solely concentrates on Tibetan Buddhism and the scriptures of Buddha himself (The History of Reiki 1865 - 1926, 2011). It was Usui's time in a Shingon monastery in

Kyoto that facilitated his proficiency in energy healing and the establishment of energy healing as a practice.

The period between the late nineteenth and early twentieth century in Japan was a particularly catastrophic time. There were several epidemics that occurred, including another cholera outbreak, this time spanning twenty years. Also, in 1923, an earthquake took place causing a great deal of destruction to Japan and Yokohama (Who Is Mikao Usui And The 3 Things You Have To Know About Him, 2020, para 26).

Though these catastrophes severely impacted the Japanese people, Usui became dedicated to his people. He used Buddhist learning, his own experience overcoming cholera, meditation, healing through physical touch, and energy to help the Japanese nation. According to Reiki Scoop, Usui passed on Reiki teachings to roughly 2,000 people and assisted 13 individuals in becoming Reiki masters (Who Is Mikao Usui And The 3 Things You Have To Know About Him, 2020, para 32).

Hawayo Takata

Mikao Usui can be credited with creating a national awareness of Reiki, but it was Hawayo Takata who exported this practice to the world—first to the USA and later to the rest of the globe.

Takata's journey with Reiki began when she first received healing from Chujiro Hayashi's Reiki clinic. Chujiro Hayashi was a maritime officer who studied under Usui, eventually opening up his own clinic in Japan. At the time, Takata was suffering from a bladder disease from which she was told she would die. It was at Hayashi's clinic where Takata was able to fight her disease. Amazed by her own complete recovery, in 1936, Takata decided to learn the art of Reiki (Bennet, p. 4).

After training for two years, Takata journeyed back to her motherland of Hawaii and opened numerous of her own clinics, training others to be practitioners. From that point onward, Reiki became an international practice (Bennet, p. 4).

Reiki and Modern Popularity

It could be argued that the contemporary world is undergoing a kind of reformation or a revisit of ancient pools of wisdom. Eastern traditions, religions, and philosophies are growing in popularity all over the Western world. Suddenly, everyone seems to have an interest in yoga, mindfulness, and Vipassanā meditation (Kisner, 2020, para 2).

The core belief systems of Daoism and Buddhism have become very valuable exports to the West. They have also become digital. It is a unique meeting point for ancient customs and modern civilization. Reiki is one such practice that has surged in use.

Some reasons for the increase in Reiki's interest include contemporary issues such as burnout, stress, depression, and anxiety. Furthermore, as Reiki offers a holistic approach, many people are drawn to its ability to provide a remedy for physical ailments, but at the same time, aid people in finding mental endurance and energy. In a very secular world, we are discovering daily that many problems are not simply material but spiritual in nature. Thus, Reiki is a reasonable alternative as it concentrates on spiritual cleansing.

Jordan Kisner's article in *The Atlantic* gives more insight into the rising demand for Reiki:

Disillusionment with established medicine has been mounting for decades, fueled by the rising costs and more depersonalized care that have gone hand in hand with stunning technological advances and treatment breakthroughs. Eastern medicine and holistic healing models provided attractive alternatives to what critics in the late 1960s called the 'medical industrial complex', and by the new millennium extramedical "wellness" had become big business (Kisner, 2020, para 19).

Reiki has come a long way. While it may have begun a hundred years ago in a remote area in Japan, its export to Western countries has allowed numerous patients to receive the treatment while allowing scientists to study the results of the therapy. Scientific data has seen positive results on patients receiving Reiki treatment weekly (Reiki popularity growing, 2015). As there has been much success, many people are now turning to Reiki to help them manage everything from chronic pain to insomnia and fatigue. In recent years, the practice's surge in popularity has now been fueled by

YouTube videos and blogs. Consequently, Reiki has been given a new life.

Every day, individuals in remote areas can learn this art without leaving their homes. As YouTube videos, blogs, and books are written about the practice, the more universal healing can be obtained. Not only do the prospects of Reiki look promising, but perhaps we can expect general wellness to spread and become a global phenomenon.

REIKI MEDITATION

Meditation constitutes one of the core components of Reiki healing. As Reiki is developed from Buddhist tradition, meditation is a significant feature of the practice. Meditation is an umbrella term for various kinds of mind training and spiritual cleaning. Reiki meditation is one variety. While every form of meditation has its own goals, the objective of Reiki revolves around energy. As the core of Reiki healing rests on the concepts of rei and ki, central to Reiki meditation is experiencing specifically the universe's energy.

This is not accomplished easily. Ramya Achanta provides more insight into the process of learning Reiki meditation when saying, "It involves symbols and mantras to facilitate your meditation experience" (Reiki Meditation – How To Do And What Are Its Benefits?, 2017, para 4). The symbols Achanta refers to are explained in the various levels of Reiki, while the mantras alluded to are the five Reiki principles. As we cover Level I, we will name these five principles as the next chapters are more concerned with the application of Reiki.

Reiki meditation also varies in structure compared to other meditation practices. For example, mindfulness meditation often entails the repetitive technique of clearing one's head of their thoughts. It can be described as a kind of tug-of-war between one's concentration and one's rebellious mind. On the other hand, Reiki meditation follows the process of cleansing, channeling energy to the chakras, healing through hand positions, and ending the session (Achanta, 2017).

In this sense, Reiki meditation differs from other kinds of meditation such as Zen and Vipassanā as it integrates the application of hand positions into the session. Thus, the practice is composed of two parts. In the next chapters, we will look at how to put this into practice.

Reiki meditation also varies from other kinds of meditation because it can be performed by an individual on themselves or by a person on another individual. Typically, meditation aims for individuals to have no contact of any kind—verbal or physical—with another person.

Yet, as the hands have so much healing power, this kind of contact is welcomed in Reiki, for it is through one's hands that one can transfer energy and open the chakras. Andrea Ferretti discusses in the article "A Beginner's Guide to the Chakras" how various yoga positions incorporate hand positions to open the chakras to help release tension and overcome physical pain.

SIGNS REIKI IS FOR YOU

Many people get involved in a kind of "pharmaceutical web". Adam Rostocki calls this the "pharmaceutical trap". First, it begins with something like insomnia. You treat your insomnia with zolpidem but are unaware of the side effects. Although you may read about the side effects in the pamphlet, you are still likely to continue medicating your insomnia with zolpidem. At the same time, your anxiety is likely to increase.

You become worried that you cannot sleep or are becoming dependent on a drug to induce sleep. As a result, you are now suffering from anxiety. If your anxiety becomes too unbearable, you may have to get treatment for it or seek professional therapy. Additionally, long-term use of any drug impacts your other organs, so while solving a problem now is necessary, other long-term ailments will surface.

Sadly, your insomnia goes untreated. You may have medicated your insomnia, but you have not actually solved the issue. Insomnia may sound harmless, yet current data shows there is a sleep crisis. The Good Body reports that "about 30% of American adults have symptoms of insomnia" (Insomnia Statistics, 2018, para 2).

While you may not be struggling with insomnia specifically, there could be other issues that may be preventing you from living a fuller life. These ailments can be physically or mentally related. However, often people do not receive Reiki treatment as they are not aware of the signs. Below are some issues that Reiki healing can help with.

- Fatigue: Reiki improves flow throughout the body, so if you are suffering from constant extreme exhaustion, this could be an issue with the flow of energy throughout your body. A certain chakra may be blocked or there might be tension preventing the stream of energy from reaching certain areas, thereby depriving you of energy (5 Signs That A Reiki Cleanse Would Benefit You, 2019, para 4).
- Stress: As mentioned in the introduction, stress is a feeling of not being able to handle certain pressure or a crisis. It is not solely the pressure or disaster that is the problem but rather that you do not have the strength to get through it. Once again, it may be due to an issue with energy circulation. To manage stress, Reiki can help you get the necessary strength which, in turn, balances your emotions (5 Signs That A Reiki Cleanse Would Benefit You, 2019, para 6).
- Inability to concentrate: While an inability to concentrate implies fatigue, it could also hint at an emotional imbalance. As with stress and fatigue, Reiki aims to discover the source of imbalance and redirect the flow of energy to that area. Since fatigue can be likened to an absence of energy, the inability to concentrate can suggest an imbalance. Something you are not aware of is pulling your concentration all the time. Crystal Palace

Osteopaths refers to these things as "emotional disturbance[s]" (5 Signs That A Reiki Cleanse Would Benefit You, 2019, para 7). With Reiki, you can discover the source of the emotional disturbance and what is usurping all your energy. Once you get to the bottom of it, you can redirect energy to other areas, such as your mental attunement, to assist with concentration.

- Depression: Depression bears some similarity to stress. While stress makes an individual feel overwhelmed and incapacitated so that they experience worry and anxiety, depression causes feelings of nihilism and submission. This is due to the individual's lack of physical strength and emotional resilience, all originating from insufficient energy. The key to healing a complex disorder such as depression is giving people resources—namely energy and confidence—to manage the crises and obstacles in their lives (5 Signs That A Reiki Cleanse Would Benefit You, 2019, para 8).

- Pain: Generally, pain is associated with tension. A specific body part might not be getting enough energy supply, causing an energy blockage. In the case of pain, generally the blockage will have been occurring over a long duration. If a specific area is causing you discomfort, Reiki sessions will target that area, supplying energy once more to provide relief (5 Signs That A Reiki Cleanse Would Benefit You, 2019, para 5).

The above are a few examples of how Reiki aids people around the world. It is commonplace for people to suffer from these ailments or disorders globally; however, few people will ever realize that the source of their problem is insufficient energy flow. In fact, as scientists have discovered that humans and all life forms are composed of energy, it is no wonder that inadequate energy supply can have devastating impacts on our spirit, mental alertness, and physical forms.

Shoden: Usui Reiki Level I

❦

"Reiki gently brings our spiritual journey into focus and increases the natural flow of events and patterns of manifestation in our lives." –Linda A. Rethwisch

SHODEN: USUI REIKI LEVEL I

Reiki is a three-tier practice. When starting your Reiki journey, you begin with Shoden, which is Japanese for "first teachings". There are three sections of Shoden, and in each segment you cover a unique Reiju. In Usui Reiki Level I, trainees and patients are introduced to the chakras and the concepts of Shizen Joka Ryoku, the body's natural cleansing system, and Byosen.

Reiju

A Reiju is a ritual or spiritual blessing usually received in one session. This "spiritual blessing" entails the Reiki practitioner creating a safe area around the patient, thereby allowing the patient's ki to flow. Though Reiju is a ritual, no physical performance occurs. Frans Stiene of The International House of Reiki gives more information on the nature of Reiju:

Mikao Usui was 'just sitting' as the Great Bright Light, encompassing the entire cosmos and being that space of open possibility. In that space, Usui could offer the Reiju as a healing, a blessing, an initiation, or all at the same time. In that space, the student could receive whatever he or she needed, at that moment in time. There was no need for ritual; only the ability of the person 'giving' the Reiju to be the Great Bright Light (Stiene, 2012, para 3).

During a Reiki session, a Reiju can be performed by the Reiki master to begin the process of healing. The Reiju primarily involves sitting in the presence of the master to experience the universe's energy. During this ritual, it is crucial for the patient to feel this universal energy as it allows their ki to flow (Reiju and Attunements, para 3).

However, if an individual is in a Reiki training session to be a Reiki practitioner, they would need to obtain a minimum number of Reiju. As there are three sections of Reiki Level I, the trainee would need to acquire three of the different spiritual offerings from the master. Furthermore, the trainee would have to keep learning to recognize and observe the universe's energy.

In your training to be a Reiki healer, it is essential to meditate on universal energy and life force. While meditating, try to experience how energy flows through your body when in a sitting position. Meditation is one of the key practices you can use to feel this life force. Therefore, it is essential to be in a completely silent environment which also has little activity. If there is too much movement in the area, you will be distracted from sensing your own innate energy flow.

Chakras

The notions of chakras and auras hardly need an introduction as these entities are well understood internationally. That said, no guide to Reiki would be complete without discussing the chakras and aura. When receiving a Reiki treatment, the master will concentrate on the chakras as these are the main energy openings. There are seven chakras that are aligned starting from the individual's crown down to the end of their spinal column.

In the list below, the seven chakras will be named, and a brief explanation will be given of each of their functions:

- Sahasrāra chakra: the crown chakra
- The Sahasrāra chakra is considered the "source of light" as it enhances your spiritual connection with a "higher being" (Sahasrāra Chakra, 2019, p. para 1). As this chakra links with our higher selves, in Buddhist and Hindu philosophies, it is the most important of all the chakras.
- Ajna chakra: the third eye chakra
- The Ajna chakra relates to rational or clear thinking, reflection on the internal and external world, and contemplation on one's self (Third Eye Chakra - Ajna).
- Vishuddha chakra: the throat chakra
- The Vishuddha chakra is associated with speech and communication. When unblocking this chakra, it enhances a person's ability to communicate honestly and openly with themselves and others. Transparent conversation with oneself is considered just as important as an honest conversation with the external world (Vishuddha Chakra: The Throat Center, 2020).
- Anahata chakra: the heart chakra
- The Anahata chakra is the heart chakra. It is associated with love, connection, warmth, and empathy. While this chakra is our core to extending kindness and compassion to others, if we are hurt by others in romantic relationships or carry the pain from negative social interactions, our heart chakra can become blocked. Thus, unblocking the Anahata

chakra is key to not only releasing such pain, but to helping us to build solid relationships again.

- Manipura chakra: the navel/solar plexus chakra
- The Manipura chakra is situated by the navel and solar plexus. On a physical level, it relates to digestion and metabolism, while metaphysically it is associated with our ambitions or intentions (Snyder, 2017).
- Svadhishthana chakra: the sacral chakra
- The Svadhisthana chakra is located by the lower pelvis. As it is close to the groin area, there is a distinct connection between the Svadhishthana chakra and intimacy. It is necessary to transfer energy to this chakra to assist with emotional balance in deep relationships and to provide healing to reproductive functions (Synder, 2017).
- Muladhara chakra: the primary/root chakra
- The Muladhara chakra is positioned by our perineum, the edge of our spines, after our coccyx. It is our primary chakra and associated with foundation and stability. For example, if you damage your coccyx, you will not be able to walk. Therefore, unblocking the Muladhara chakra is essential for performing all tasks.

If you intend to become a Reiki practitioner, it is crucial to always concentrate on clearing or opening the chakras. Many of the hand positions, which we will discuss in Chapter 5, provide healing to the patient, with each one focusing on a different area. An obvious example is one of a Buddhist monk sitting in the lotus position with his or her hands pressed together in front of their heart. The hands in this area allow the universal energy, ki, to be directed specifically to the Anahata chakra.

As a prospective healer, it is necessary to take time and give special care to each hand position for every one of these chakras as they are the foundations of an energy healer.

Shizen Joka Ryoku and Byosen

Shizen Joka Ryoku is the intrinsic function every body has to heal itself. This is not limited to animals only, like dogs or cats who lick their wounds to clean them; the human body also has this capability.

A clear illustration of this is when our white blood cells attack foreign and harmful pathogens that enter our systems. Unconsciously, our systems are alerted, and the white blood cells come to our defense. Another example is if something damaging goes straight into your eye; your eyeball immediately begins to water to flush out the foreign invader. While we all know such things thanks to biology lessons at school or university, we tend to forget about the body's innate healing system.

However, it is arguable that we do *not* forget. When many of us get sick, we do not seek a medical consultation with a doctor immediately since we know that if it is nothing too serious, our bodies will be able to overcome the ailment. Besides, since most issues are primarily blockages of energy, if we can direct our internal energy to our chakras or areas that are suffering from tension, even healing chronic illnesses is possible. We are simply relying on the body's natural healing function.

Another principle to Reiki Level I is Byosen Reikan Ho, the removal of toxins from the body. When preparing for their first attunement, Reiki masters ask patients to avoid consuming alcohol, caffeine, sugar or nicotine prior to the session. In order to completely cleanse oneself, it is essential that there are no harmful chemicals in the body as it will impair the healing (Reiki Attunement - The Process and Purpose). Additionally, the patient is encouraged to let go of negative thoughts such as resentment and bitterness as this too will negatively impact the attunement process (Reiki Attunement - The Process and Purpose).

While Reiki concentrates on opening the chakras and evenly distributing one's life force, Byosen Reikan Ho is concerned with removing negative energy and toxins. In Reiki Level I, trainees learn about Byosen Reikan Ho, but in Reiki Level II, prospective Reiki practitioners need to apply this knowledge of the first level. Thus, only a simple introduction of Byosen Reikan Ho is necessary. In the next chapter, we will look at the practical components of Byosen Reikan Ho.

* * *

SHODEN: PRINCIPLES

When a student begins their journey with Reiki, they are taught five mantras, or philosophies. These are referred to as the Reiki principles and students are expected to apply them to their lives every day. The five Reiki principles are as follows:

- Just for today, I will be grateful.
- Just for today, I will not anger.
- Just for today, I will not worry.
- Just for today, I will do my work honestly.
- Just for today, I will respect all life (Who Is Mikao Usui And The 3 Things You Have To Know About Him, 2020, para 33).

One should not simply repeat these principles but try to meditate on and embrace them throughout the day. By integrating these mottos, Reiki becomes similar to a way of life. Meditating on the five principles helps one to build a connection to their meaning and the gravity of each mantra.

As with mantras in general, there is power behind the words. For example, if you berate yourself, you are likely to use words such as "fool" or idiot" or call yourself stupid. When you say these words, they have an innate power or vibration. Unfortunately, the power in these words is likely to impact you negatively, making you feel weaker.

On the other hand, consider words such as "calm" and "transcend". They are powerful for different reasons. They too have intrinsic energy to them, and when you repeat them to yourself, you feel better and channel more positive vibrations.

The Reiki mantras above relate to the core purpose of the practice—they intend to restore one's energy and give one the strength to cope with trauma or catastrophes. If you analyze the first mantra "Just for today, I will be grateful", concentrating on the word "today" minimizes one anxiety and helps a person to condense their energy to what they can handle. On a separate note, much of Buddhism centers around being present for this helps the individual to focus on what is tangible and, consequently, in their power to really control.

When performing a Reiki healing session, the patient is asked to repeat the mantras. Try wording them so that you can feel the calming energy each one inspires. Furthermore, when saying them to yourself, note how you reserve your strength for today and relinquish control over tomorrow. In other words, you direct your energy to the day.

MODERN ADAPTION AND POPULARITY

As mentioned in the introduction, Reiki has become digitized. While it is possible to receive Reiki healing through a video or podcast—and many teachers have provided this service online—it is recommended during your first Reiki attunement sessions to opt for a physical session. However, as there are always limitations with distance and time, it is possible to go online for this service.

The same is true if you intend to become a Reiki healer. It is advisable to learn the practice through its physical application. In the presence of a Reiki practitioner, you can see all the various steps taken during a session. Similar to a healing session, there is Reiki Level I content uploaded by institutions such as the International School of Reiki. If you do feel face-to-face classes will be more useful, there are many schools offering the same service. Usually, these organizations offer training in Reiki I, II, and III, so they can be worthwhile.

SHODEN: LEVEL I AND ATTUNEMENT

As Shoden is the first level of Reiki, much of the training is devoted to learning about the origins of energy healing and understanding how Reiki works. Much of it is theoretical, and we covered this in the introduction. Furthermore, in Reiki Level I workshops, you also learn about chakras, the five Reiki principles, Shizen Joka Ryoku, and Byosen.

Once you are finished learning the theoretical background, you can have your first attunement. You will need to receive your attunement personally from a Reiki master. The Reiki master can begin the session with a Reiju to open the patient to the universal energy (What Is A Reiki Attunement And Why Is It Necessary To Get One, 2020, para 4). The master will sit in a deep meditative state, concentrating on getting the patient to experience the universal energy.

Stillness and silence are imperatives throughout the session. Next, the Reiki master may introduce the student to the five Reiki principles or the Reiki I symbols. The patient needs to focus on the power of these words when repeating them as they are not simply words, but carry innate vibrations helping to draw negative energy out.

Next, the healer will search the body for any points of tension or blocked chakras where the flow of energy has been stalled. Such areas might be physical, like a knot in the back where tension has been building up. There could also be a similar problem with the heart chakra, where energy is not flowing too well. The problems may be physical or emotional. Heart pain is associated with emotional suffering and physical ailments such as Mitral Valve Prolapse (MVP).

The Reiki healer will press their hands onto the areas showing tension or build-up, or just below or above the injured areas (What Is A Reiki Attunement And Why Is It Necessary To Get One, 2020, para 38). This is done to open the channel for energy to the area. Sometimes, the practitioner will also press down on the tense area. Remember, to prepare for your first attunement, you need to rid your body of all toxins, including caffeine, alcohol, negative emotions, bad habits like watching negative TV programs, and self-destructive thoughts (Reiki Attunement - The Process and Purpose). Throughout this part of the session, the patient will keep their eyes closed.

As Reiki masters have varying methods of performing a Reiki attunement, they differ in length. One session could be five to fifteen minutes in length. Some masters include a prayer and meditation as part of the session, so it might take longer (What Is A Reiki Attunement And Why Is It Necessary To Get One, 2020, para 40). It should be noted that before one can be a healer, they need to receive a Reiki attunement. This is to ensure that the universal energy can be transmitted from the practitioner to the patient.

After Attunement

After their first Reiki attunement, many people experience different reactions. Penny Quest describes some reactions patients have felt after this attunement:

After an attunement is over, students often describe the beautiful spiritual or mystical experiences they have received, such as "seeing" wonderful colors, visions, or past life experiences. Others report receiving personal messages or profound healing, sensing the presence of guides or angelic beings, or simply having a feeling of complete peace. Some people go through a real shift in their awareness immediately afterward, describing the sensation as almost like being reborn, so that they experience everything around them more intensely —colors are brighter, their sense of smell is enhanced, and sounds are sharper (Quest, 2003, para 1).

Thus, responses include heightened sensitivity, healing of pain and tension, increased tranquility, relief from stress, and spiritual visions. On the other hand, there can be adverse effects post-attunement. You may experience symptoms of physical cleansing and detoxification such as a runny nose, headaches, or diarrhea. The more toxic you are, the more symptoms you may notice. There is no need to be alarmed, though; the body is simply flushing out the toxins (What to Expect During and After a Reiki Attunement, 2020, para 2).

Furthermore, sensitivity is also increased. However, it should be noted that this is sensitivity to both positive and negative feelings and sensations. Thus, while you may laugh intensely and experience deep love for everything, you will also become more affected by light, colors, and touch. These are common after-effects. As some people have more toxins in their bodies, they will feel much more sensitive post-attunement.

21-DAY PURIFICATION

Generally, patients are required to go on a 21-day detox after an attunement process. There are several steps one needs to follow during the 21-day detox:

- Perform a self-cleansing on oneself for five minutes every day

(In Chapter 5, hand positions will be discussed, and you need to perform a self-healing on yourself selecting the most appropriate one).

- Regularly drink water, keeping yourself hydrated.
- Eat plenty of fruits and vegetables, and avoid processed foods.
- Try to meditate, or do yoga or movement meditation.
- Sleep about eight to nine hours every night.

The purpose of the 21-day purification is to continue the spiritual and physical cleansing of the body. It complements the attunement session with the master. As mentioned above, cleansing of any form does often involve adverse effects. Thus, if you do experience extreme sensitivity or headaches, it simply indicates your cleansing is effective.

REIKI LEVEL I

Reiki Level I is composed of learning the background of Reiki, learning what Reiki is, and understanding Byosen, Shizen Joka Ryoku, the five Reiki principles, and the chakras. If you are interested in becoming a Reiki healer, you will also be introduced to some hand positions that are used for energy healing. To move on to Reiki Level II, you will need to understand very well what Reiki is and how it works. Furthermore, the various theoretical concepts mentioned above such as Byosen and the chakras are covered in more detail in Reiki Level II, but theoretical comprehension of these notions is essential in Reiki Level I.

You will also need to have an attunement session with a Reiki master. Though only one attunement session is required, it is advisable to have additional ones to deepen your spiritual cleansing and promote the flow of your ki (Learning Reiki).

For patients, attunements offer deep cleansing. However, prospective practitioners require familiarity with the universal energy and need their own ki to flourish in their bodies before they can provide spiritual cleansing to another. The 21-day detox is equally important. During this period, it is essential to perform a self-healing treatment once a day. This is for both patients and future healers.

This chapter sought to introduce Reiki Level I to readers. It covered the basics common in this level. However, different institutions vary in their approaches. Some introduce Reiki symbols during Reiki Level I, while others do not. To comple-

SHODEN: USUI REIKI LEVEL I

ment your application of Reiki Level I, you will need to use the hand positions provided in Chapter 5.

Lastly, while Reiki Level II concentrates on more self-healing and healing others, if you would like to use this guide to simply heal yourself and not advance to Level II or III, that is perfectly acceptable. In this case, it is recommended that you go over hand positions next.

Okuden: Usui Reiki Level II

"All healing is first a healing of the heart." –Carl Townsend

OKUDEN: USUI REIKI LEVEL II

The second tier of Reiki is Okuden. In Japanese, Okuden means "inner teachings". While Shoden Level I focuses on theoretical backgrounds, Okuden explores some other concepts but also initiates the prospective healer with the practical process of healing. Similar to Shoden, there are also spiritual blessings (Reiju) and attunement sessions which are separate from your classes should you wish to become a Reiki practitioner. In Usui Reiki Level II, the training covers the drawing of Shirushi (the Reiki symbols), Seiheki Chiryo Ho, the development of intuition, the application of Byosen, and Jumon and mantras.

• • •

Reiju

Some training courses offer two spiritual blessings, but there are others that provide three. Once again, every Reiki center is different; some are more intensive and in-depth. In recent times, Reiki training for one level can be conducted over a day, so throughout that day, the Reiki teacher will transfer these Reiju to the students. For example, courses offered from Alternatively Better and Epona Equine Reiki Centre take place over a day.

In Shoden, the Reiju the Reiki healer transfers to the patient or student aims to introduce the universe's energy to the receiver. As passing the Reiki Level II grants the Reiki practitioner the ability to perform Reiki healings on others (Classes), the prospective healer needs to become deeply familiar with sensing the universe's energy.

Right now, It may seem daunting as a potential healer to read this, but it is recommended to have one's first Reiju and attunement in person with a Reiki master. As this is a spiritual sensation that occurs, there are no exact theoretical indicators. Having said that, since energy is being transferred to you, one of the indicators is a sense of revival or rejuvenation. This can occur in a spiritual, creative, physical, or even emotional form.

Nevertheless, it is difficult to explain to a person what happens after they receive Reiju. It should also be noted that after this spiritual blessing is given to you from the Reiki master, you have received it. The connection with the universe's energy is now within you, and you can transmit it to a loved one or patient.

* * *

SHIRUSHI: REIKI SYMBOLS

One of the aspects which embodies Reiki is an emphasis on visualizing and then drawing specific symbols. As mentioned earlier, Okuden means "inner teachings" in Japanese. What makes these teachings "inner" is that they are hidden (Reiki Level 2 | OKUDEN – What To Expect From It And Its Symbols, 2020, p. para 1). In other words, the notions of Reiki concentrate on entities that are characteristically internal. They are so internal, in fact, that they remain "hidden".

There are three to five core Shirushi. Some schools teach all five, while others focus on only three. James Deacon explains that it is possible that the Mikao Usui only used two symbols in the original Reiki training (More Concerning Reiju, 2005, p. para 2). It was probably when Hawayo Takata exported Reiki to the west that more symbols were incorporated. While there are varying numbers of symbols, it is specific to the institution. One possible explanation for this is that some courses span one day, two days, or six months. Thus, there is more time to learn about each symbol and practice visualizing and drawing it.

The Power of Symbols

Symbols are sources of power. While they are basic pictures (like hieroglyphics), each image is charged with not only meaning but energy. This might sound odd to you, but throughout the world, certain symbols have the power to create strong emotional reactions or oblige you to do something.

Symbols have meaning. Meaning is a part of their nature. Road signs are symbols with simple meanings. Some symbols have a deeper meaning. They are a powerful gate to the deeper and less conscious levels of human experience. Symbols evoke profound emotions and memories—at a very primal level of our being—often without our making rational or conscious connections. They fuel our imagination. They enable us to access aspects of our existence that cannot be gotten to in any other way (The Power of Symbols, 2017, para 5).

Consider pictograms of a water drop or the Christian cross. The water drop does not only represent water, but a source of life, a drinking hole, vitality, nature, and now, that your device is waterproof. Concerning the Christian cross, it takes influence from the Egyptian Ankh, and thus, has survived close to eight thousand years. The Christian cross has intrinsic meanings like the "key of life" (Ankh - Egyptian Symbol of Life, 2015), faith, managing the burden of life (the crucifixion), or believing in Christian values (Cross, 2020). The connotation is so entrenched with the pictogram that it is hard to remove the meaning from the symbol.

If someone from Italy wore a Christian cross, even those from distant lands such as China or Japan would be able to associate the meaning of the cross with Christian values. It is the same as a water drop. If you showed someone a picture of a drop of water in various countries around the world, people would be able to make similar inferences as to its meaning, such as the source of life, vitality, and nature.

Moreover, symbols are logos, too, or rather, there is no real difference between a logo and a symbol. Usually, logos are associated with brands, but the intention behind them and symbols remain the same—they represent a specific association as well as its products, services, and values.

Symbols are not simply pictures; they fuel our society. Traffic signs manage the coming and going of vehicles while pictograms of a basic design of three stairs indicate a fire escape and where to go in an emergency. Furthermore, symbols transcend time. Their power does not always end with the death of a civilization, as is the case with the Egyptian symbol of the ankh, which has survived the ancient Egyptian kingdom, continuing through Christianity 8,000 years later.

The Power of Reiki Symbols

Though the pictograms of Cho Ku Rei and Da Koo Mo are associated with Reiki, they derive from ancient traditions. In Reiki, Shirushi are considered sacred as they connect you with a hidden energy, only released on contemplation, visualization, and reproduction of the symbol. Reiki Scoop provides more insight into the nature of symbols: "Each of these symbols acts like a key that unlocks "hidden" energy. This is just a comparison, of course, but the idea stands. They connect to a certain energy, vibration, and manifestations of the universal life force" (Reiki Level 2 | OKUDEN – What To Expect From It And Its Symbols, 2020, p. para 45).

In Takata's Reiki teachings, the internal power within each Reiki symbol was explained. Each one holds a unique power concentrating on a specific source of energy. However, in general, each symbol revealed Reiki philosophy.

The Five Level II Shirushi

- Cho Ku Rei: the power symbol
- As it represents "universal energy", Cho Ku Rei is considered the primary symbol of Reiki. The "coil" in the symbol is seen to be the universal meditator (Price). Its intersection depicts the channel or path to that universal energy. Like with Reiju and the basic concepts of Reiki, channeling the universal energy is said to bring healing and cleansing (Reiki Level 2 | OKUDEN – What To Expect From It And Its Symbols, 2020). Thus, when visualized and drawn, the power symbol helps a person to make a connection with this universal energy, bringing about their healing and cleansing.
- Sei He Ki: the calming symbol
- According to Natasha Price, "Sei He Ki has been interpreted as meaning 'God and man become one' or alternatively 'the earth and sky meet', both referencing the connection between two elements, the conscious or mental body, and the subconscious or emotional body" (Price, Universal Symbols: The Calming Sei Hei Ki, 2019). In the pictogram itself, an interplay between two figures can be seen. While there is a split between the two, it should also be

noted that they complement and run parallel to one another. These two figures represent "man" and "divinity" or "body" and "spirit". In this sense, these two entities are in constant interaction with one another, but they also complement each other. In other words, they are dependent on one another. Reflection on Sei He Ki can help an individual first ponder on the necessity of balancing their emotions and mind, spirit, and body; however, it can also help the individual to attain this balance. Continuous meditation on this symbol assists a person in feeling tranquility with all the various aspects of their being aligned and stable.

- Hon Sha Ze Sho Nen: the distance symbol
- In Japanese, Hon Sha Ze Sho Nen means "no past, no present, no future" (Price, Universal Symbols: The Distant Healing Hon Sha Ze Sho Nen, 2019, p. para 1). Deep contemplation of this symbol allows an individual to transfer healing beyond time. In this sense, Reiki allows healing and cleansing to transcend time. Price provides more information on this process: "By using the Hon Sha Ze Sho Nen symbol, we become one with the energy which flows through us and across all time and space" (Price, Universal Symbols: The Distant Healing Hon Sha Ze Sho Nen, 2019).
- Shika Sei Ki: the heart-healing symbol
- In the previous chapter, we analyzed how if your heart chakra is blocked, you can experience

numerous issues. This can include emotional
problems such as loneliness, heartache, and
reluctance to love, or they can be physical in nature,
such as heart or chest pain. To complement opening
the heart chakra, you can meditate on, visualize, and
try to reproduce Shika Sei ki. Pinky Punjabi wrote the
following on healing through this symbol: "This
symbol is best used for heart-related diseases or also
for people undergoing emotional stress in life. [It is]
one of the most amazing symbols for anger-related
issues. This symbol eliminates negative energies from
the heart, giving way to unconditional love" (Punjabi,
2015).

- Shika So: the throat chakra symbol
- Shika So and Shika Sei Ki are usually learned in
  tandem as they both focus on deep emotional
  cleaning and healing. Reflection on Shika So relates
  specifically to difficulties in expression, throat pain,
  and thyroid issues. Unblocking the throat chakra can
  reduce tension in this area and aid with giving the
  individual relief from the above problems (Punjabi,
  2015).

When you are first introduced to the Reiki symbols, you will
learn what they are, how they function, and why it is essential to reproduce them, either through visualization or reproduction.

. . .

Visualizing

Visualization of the five Reiki symbols requires a lot of mental exertion. Though it can be exhausting to create an exact replica of an unfamiliar symbol, this process is key in uncovering the hidden power of the five Reiki symbols. Cho Ku Rei is an easy one to begin with.

First, imagine an infinite spiral that is intersected by an upside-down L. By reproducing this pictogram in your mind, you are creating a conscious association with the universal energy. Furthermore, when visualizing the spiral, concentrate on its infinite nature, and thus, its abundance. When you think of the upside-down L, recall how this is the universal energy's channel within you. It intersects at Sahasrara, your crown chakra, and continues down this path, traveling to every chakra.

During meditation or your 21-day cleansing, try to concentrate on picturing the five Reiki symbols. If you can only manage to focus on two or three, that is fine too. Remember that for many Reiki training programs, you are only required to learn three Reiki symbols.

As with Cho Ku Rei, while imagining a spiral and upside-down L, try to create associations with other images so that you can accurately envision the symbol. When you do manage to form a precise reproduction, visualize it for a couple of minutes so that you build a stronger link to it.

· · ·

Drawing

In Usui Reiki Level II sessions, time is allowed for students to draw these symbols. Websites such as Reiki Scoop teach their followers techniques for how to draw them accurately. If you think of the sacred symbols as a series of lines and circles, it can simplify the process of drawing them.

While drawing recreates tangible images, the physical process of reproducing these pictograms helps to cement them in your mind. It also allows the power of the Reiki symbols to enter a physical realm. You realize they are not only for mental well-being, but for physical relief as well.

Sei He Ki manages the complementary relationship of physical and emotional well-being. It is no simple feat to accomplish a balance between these two. Yet creating a tangible representation of Sei He Ki allows you to actively remember that this balance is a necessity.

The main objective of drawing Reiki symbols is to integrate them into the healing process itself. When you begin to use Reiki remedies to restore energy, drawing the symbols on areas inflicted with tension provides relief to these regions. For example, if you are struggling with loneliness, reproduce the image of Shika Sei Ki over your heart chakra to open it to the energy of the universe.

Not only is there the power of physical touch that provides healing to this area—perhaps your emotional dis-ease is also creating tension in the region of the heart chakra—it also reminds you of the love your highest being unconditionally bestows upon you and the abundance of love across the world.

While drawing this symbol on your heart chakra, remember the nature of love. There is no one person, nation, or society that has a monopoly over love. Love is universal. Like with this example of drawing Shika Sei Ki over the heart chakra, try to do the same with the other chakras.

You may not be suffering from feelings of loneliness or isolation, but perhaps you want to acquire the ability of free communication and meaningful expression. In this case, you can practice drawing Shika So over the throat.

SEIHEKI CHIRYO HO

Seiheki Chiryo Ho takes the initial spiritual cleansing received in Reiki Level I further. As with the spiritual detox in preparation of the attunement and for the 21 days after this healing, this concept tries to cement good habits and establish attainable goals for a person (Seiheki Chiryo Ho, 2006).

While Reiki primarily concentrates on healing through universal energy, it also endorses maintaining one's physical health. Reiki, in fact, seeks to balance emotional wellness and mental vitality with physical well-being. In other words, spiritual growth is not superior to physical vigor but rather equal to it. With this in mind, Reiki intends to improve the individual's well-being by encouraging good habits and establishing goals for its patients to obtain. For instance, many patients attend Reiki sessions to help them quit smoking (How Meditation and Reiki can help you stop smoking, 2020) or to assist them in finding direction in life (Fleming, 2018).

In the section on hand positions, we will look at the practice of implementing Seiheki Chiryo Ho so that you can begin to lead a life of good habits and clear direction.

DEVELOPMENT OF INTUITION

There are two misconceptions that should be clarified before discussing Reiki and its objective of developing an individual's intuition. First, many people believe that intuition informs them of when they are doing something wrong or protects them from something that will harm them. This is true, but intuition also tells us when something is right for us or will benefit us. The problem with this is that we think of the "gut instinct" as helping us to avoid adversity and negativity, as opposed to leading us to experiences of positivity. We do not typically believe it can direct us to opportunities or relationships.

Oftentimes, we pay attention to what our intuition says about people who have wrong intentions for us. Though we may not act on it, we still listen to what our instinct is saying to us. On the other hand, when we feel a very strong connection to someone, in order to save face, we might not encourage the relationship or shy away from establishing a further connection.

The second misconception about intuition is that it is unreasonable or illogical. When we discuss the various kinds of knowledge, we believe there are analytical and intuitive types. By saying that intuition is not logical implies that it is unreasonable or even wrong. In the introduction, we spoke about many processes that are so deeply ingrained in our habits and customs that we do not even recognize that they exist. For example, to feel a child's forehead is a form of being able to tell if they suffer from illness (Bennet).

If your mother or grandmother felt your forehead after you said you were feeling feverish, you would not think it nonsensical. It has been a reliable method of figuring out if a person has a fever since before we developed thermometers. Intuition is a reliance on ancient habits that have become instincts through centuries of practice. These instincts or this kind of knowledge is so ingrained that we need not reprocess it on every occasion.

In Reiki Level II, you reflect on the significance of sharpening your intuition as well as how to apply this intuition when becoming a practitioner. As with a fever, you use your hand to tell if someone is sick or not. While heat may be an indicator of infection or inflammation, if an area is also too cold, it is not receiving enough energy or blood flow. These are some of the signs you look out for as a Reiki healer.

It is also important to note that not all your instincts will be logical or reasonable. You may not have consciously figured the logic out. Therefore, developing your intuition remains a significant feature to improve if you want to be a Reiki healer.

APPLICATION OF BYOSEN

The instincts addressed in the previous section are relevant to applying Byosen. For Shoden, you study the notion of Byosen, and for Okuden, you learn how to practice it.

Toxins are harmful to our bodies. They cause a variety of health issues. A build-up of tar from smoking can prevent easy breathing and affect oxygen supply. Fat droplets in your blood cells can result in blood supply being lost to that area, which ultimately is responsible for heart attacks and gangrene.

When practicing Byosen, search the patient's body for any of these signs showing there may be a build-up of toxins, which include the following:

-The area is cold: This may indicate that there is not an even supply to the region.

-Lack of pulse: Once more, this implies a lack of an even supply.

-Heat: The area is above the general temperature of the body.

-Pain: If the healer touches the area, there is some sensitivity.

-Tingling: If the patient feels a pins-and-needles sensation, it may indicate toxins in the area (Petter, p. para 2).

The more serious the affliction, the more time is needed with the injured area. For example, if two or more of the above symptoms appear in that region, the higher the number of toxins. Or if one symptom is very advanced (e.g., if the temperature is dramatically higher than the rest of the body), then once again, you will want to spend more time healing that region (Petter).

When beginning the Byosen treatment, Petter describes the process: You place your hands on that area and feel the Byosen. If you feel a strong Byosen, such as level four or five, you know that something serious is happening there that needs possibly time-consuming attention. As you hold your hands on this area, you should pay attention to the peaks and valleys of the Byosen. It comes and goes in waves (Petter).

It should be noted that when practicing Byosen on someone, if the symptoms appear very advanced, it is strongly advised to seek assistance from a medical professional or Reiki master. As you are still in training and gaining experience in this form of healing, it is better to do this in more serious cases.

* * *

JUMON

In Usui Reiki Level I, the Reiki student was introduced to the five Reiki principles. There are some training programs which teach these principles, mantras, and Jumon at the same time. We will not go through the five Reiki principles again, but we will look at Jumon and mantras as well.

Mantras and Jumon are quite similar. James Deacon explains that mantras can be single words or phrases with an intelligible meaning. In other words, mantras are repeated words or phrases with a meaning understandable to the speaker. Jumon are also words or phrases, but they serve more as chants or incantations that focus much more on the sound and, as a result, the vibration of those sounds. Deacon explains that Jumon is "a mystic, spiritual or magical incantation—a 'spell'—a sacred phrase or invocation".

The Jumon used in Reiki have mixed origins. Some originate from Buddhism and Taoism, while others are from Shintoism. Over the years, their pronunciation has changed slightly.

Jumon for Usui Reiki Level II:

- *a ba ra ha kya*
- *watari no fune*
- *qu xie fu mei*

Similar to mantras, when saying these words, try to concentrate on the sound that is created by each syllable. The art is in repetition. First, pay attention to trying to reproduce each syllable. When you have mastered the individual sounds, then try to repeat the phrase several times, listening carefully to the sound of the sequence and the vibration it produces in your mouth, as well as after it leaves your mouth.

As opposed to mantras, where the power is derived from the language and meaning of the words or phrases, Jumon creates power from the sound and vibration produced by the word. Jumon is part of Usui Reiki Level II as it composes one of the "hidden", or "inner", teachings.

OKUDEN: ATTUNEMENT AND 21-DAY PURIFICATION

Once you have finished learning about Shirushi, Seiheki Chiryo Ho, intuition, Byosen, and Jumon, you will be ready for your next attunement. As with your first attunement for Shoden, you will need to prepare for this process with a detox. You should abstain from harmful chemicals such as nicotine, alcohol, caffeine, and sugar. If possible, try to avoid eating red meat and incorporate as much fresh fruit and vegetables into your diet as you can.

Once again, you will also need to detox spiritually, letting go of harmful thoughts and negative emotions. As with the Shoden attunement, you will also need to visit a Reiki master to receive the Reiju and attunement for Okuden.

During the attunement session, the Reiki master will concentrate on helping your body circulate the universal energy by unblocking the chakras and removing toxins and pathogens. Every attunement session brings about different responses, so you may feel highly sensitive, much lighter, or far more energized. Reactions are both positive and negative—negative because you have begun the process of removing toxins and pathogens. After the attunement session, you will begin the 21-day purification process.

21-Day Purification

Generally, patients are required to go on a 21-day detox after an attunement process. Take a look below at the steps one needs to follow during their detox.

- Perform a self-cleansing on oneself for ten to fifteen minutes every day.
- Keep yourself hydrated by drinking lots of liquids.
- Maintain a diet eating chiefly fresh fruits and vegetables.
- Meditate, practice yoga, or do movement meditation.
- Get enough sleep (about eight to nine hours each day).
- Practice drawing the symbols.
- Repeat the Jumon incantations.
- Practice healing others by using Byosen, drawing the symbols on injured or afflicted areas, and helping others build good habits with Seiheki Chiryo Ho.

MOVING ON TO REIKI LEVEL III

As mentioned already, training courses from different Reiki centers follow unique structures, so you may attend a Reiki institute that covers the symbols in Level I while only going through the five Reiki principles in Level II.

Before you move on to Shinpiden, you will need to study the various sections discussed in this chapter, and you will also need to receive two or three Reiju and at least one attunement —although it is possible to do more than one. There must be a period of 21 days spent on the purification process to prepare you for Shinpiden.

Okuden focuses on "hidden", or "inner", teachings. The art of Byosen, the meditative reflections on Shirushi, and the development of one's intuition all concentrate on hidden or internal knowledge. In this sense, Okuden is essentially intuitive. It forces students to pay attention to sound, vibration, and the signs of toxic manifestations in the body. Once you complete Reiki Level II, you are ready to heal those around you and move on to Usui Reiki Level III.

Shinpiden: Usui Reiki Level III

"Energy and persistence conquer all things." – Benjamin Franklin

SHINPIDEN: USUI REIKI LEVEL III

Shinpiden is the final phase of Reiki training, and upon completion, you will become recognized as a Reiki master. *Shinpiden* is Japanese for "mystery teachings". In Usui Reiki

Level III, the "mystery teachings" assist the prospective Reiki master in attaining enlightenment or discovering their true self (Exploring Mikao Usui's Teachings, 2014).

During this training, you will learn the necessary master healing techniques and will be given the resources to follow the path as a master. Techniques that you learn include Holy Fire or placement attunement, Healing Fire ignition, and master ignition, as well as how to conduct an attunement on yourself and others. Resources also include the Holy Fire symbols necessary to be a Reiki master. At the end of the training, you will look at ethical codes of conduct and practices for a Reiki master.

One thing should be noted before continuing with Shinpiden; while anyone can participate in Shoden, Usui Reiki Level III is reserved for astute students and healers. While this may seem slightly demotivating, you need not feel discouraged. Past Reiki masters include Buddha and Jesus (Bennet). Jesus was famous for his ability to heal. Considering his accomplishment of raising Lazarus from the dead, Jesus was a very skilled Reiki healer.

Thus, with regular practice, meditation, and visualization exercises, you can learn to become adept at Reiki and continue with Shinpiden training.

SHINPIDEN: HOLY FIRE OR PLACEMENT ATTUNEMENT

In Usui Reiki I, you received your first Reiju and experienced your first attunement session with a Reiki master. The moment the Reiki master transferred the Reiju and universe's energy to you, you gained these gifts. You spent Reiki II learning about various techniques to equip you as a Reiki healer, and now you need to integrate what you learned and harness the gifts of Reiju and spiritual cleansing so that you can begin to heal and teach others.

Before offering attunement sessions to others, you need to practice attunement with yourself and setting up the right conditions so you can experience universal energy. Reiki centers such as Balance on Buffalo recommend practicing for about a year before you begin with others (Reiki Master Attunement, para 1).

Setting up an Attunement Session

To set up an attunement session, you need to find a quiet and calm environment (Reiki Master Attunement). If there is too much activity, it will lessen your ability to feel the universe's energy. Try to avoid any movement, music, or conversation being in the room. It is true that conversation and movement all are created from the universe's energy, but what you need is a direct channel with the universe.

- Place a candle in the room, and invite energy into the space with the three steps.
- Attitude of gratitude: "I thank Reiki, all the masters, and myself.
- Use your fingers to draw the Reiki II symbols.
- Invite Reiki into the room: "Reiki, you are kindly invited into the room to do the attunement process for (patient's name).
- Bow to the patient (if you are the patient, bow to yourself so you can channel the universal energy to yourself).
- Take a deep breath.
- Ask the patient to take a deep breath and relax.
- Say thanks to the universe (Reiki 1 Attunement Process, 2020).

Meditation can be an easy way to center yourself and align yourself with the universe's energy. In the beginning, when practicing on yourself or on loved ones, you can meditate for five or ten minutes before the session. On another note, there may be bird or traffic sounds around you. Remember that this is also activity derived from universal energy. If you concentrate on these sounds and this motion while meditating, it allows you to recognize how you are one part of this great whole.

Try to practice attunements on yourself. When you are comfortable, you can offer this healing to your family and loved ones. Furthermore, having more attunement sessions with a Reiki master can aid you in attuning your senses to your ki. If you are interested in becoming a Reiki healer, then familiarizing yourself with the attunement process is vital. With that said, you could also practice this in your own time. Just remember to set up your attunement environment before each session.

HOLY FIRE/MASTER IGNITION

Holy Fire is a type of healing Reiki masters can perform on one's spirit. While the topic of spirit has become controversial, which is discussed more extensively in the introduction, Holy Fire ignition is not affiliated with a religion. However, this healing does concentrate on providing cleansing for spiritual ailments, namely when trying to free the patient of their ego. Reiki Maya explains how a Holy Fire healing is different from attunements.

The Reiki master only has to call upon Holy Fire Reiki, and the energy will come and work with every student, attuning them to Reiki. This is without the need of performing the physical attunement. This process is named "ignition". It is at the forefront of how Reiki is evolving, becoming an "ego-free" process (What is Holy Fire Reiki?, 2019, para 2).

While an attunement tries to connect an individual with the universal energy so that they can be revived from its force, Holy Fire ignition aims to restore a sense of humility in this individual. This is counterintuitive to the overall message media and marketing gives us, yet freedom from the ego and

a sense of humility can be not only liberating, but reju-
venating.

The Ego

Many popular contemporary writers and thinkers such as
Ryan Holiday, Tom Bilyeu, and Alain de Botton are realizing
the benefits of creating a distance from the ego. An interview
with de Botton describes this process: "It's about a surrender
of the ego—a putting aside of one's own needs and assump-
tions—for the sake of close, attentive listening to another,
whose mystery one respects, along with a commitment not to
get offended—not to retaliate—when something 'bad'
emerges, as it often does when one is close to someone, child
or adult" (The School of Life: An Interview With Alain de
Botton, 2019, para 17).

Besides these obvious benefits, liberating ourselves from our
egos is also crucial in bettering our relationships with
ourselves. For example, when you are going through a good
phase in your life, you experience a form of hubris, which is
the arrogance of all arrogances (Hubris, 2020). You have an
elevated level of pride and flatter yourself continuously.

However, at the same time, an internal voice—perhaps, the
voice of your "true self"—warns you that things can change
very suddenly and advises you against being overly confident. Later, when things do eventually go wrong, you berate
yourself, pull your self-esteem to pieces, and say very unkind
words to yourself.

In both situations, it is the ego that is in control. First, the ego seduces you with imagined self-importance, then it pulls you to pieces using the most destructive vocabulary imaginable. What is most important is that your ego stands in the way of you discovering your true self.

Mikao Usui realized how the ego was an obstacle in finding one's true self. In this sense, the Holy Fire ignition is centered around eliminating the ego's hold over the individual. By using the universe's energy, the hold of the ego is diminished, the spirit cleansed of its hubris and destructive nature, and a path to realizing one's true self is illuminated.

A Holy Fire ignition, also known as an "igniting the fire" ceremony, can only be performed by a master. It is fundamental as a Reiki master to first attend a Holy Fire ignition and then perform their own.

SHINPIDEN: ATTUNEMENT

There are two attunements reserved for Level I. The first is the last of your attunements for Reiki training; this is a continuation of your attunements and purification processes of Level I and Level II. The second attunement is an induction into the attunement process, what techniques you need to incorporate, and how to conduct an attunement session to bring healing to others (Dai Ko Myo Reiki Master Symbol And Reiki Level 3 Shinpiden, 2020).

Once you have received your final attunement, next you need to concentrate on how to give attunement to others. Much time is dedicated to practicing attunement with others. You can only pass Reiki Level III if you have mastered this art.

Tips for Mastering Attunement:

- Self-exploration
- Shinpiden focuses on "mystery teachings". While we may believe we know ourselves deeply, we often question our motivations for things we have done in the past. Sometimes, we do not interrogate ourselves enough; we do not ask ourselves why we have certain prejudices, preconceptions, habits, or dislikes. "In the 'true sense', a Reiki master should be a mentor, professor, or trainer—an entity that offers knowledge and wisdom and always seeks the path to enlightenment. You should always seek to work and

improve yourself" (*Dai Ko Myo* Reiki Master Symbol And Reiki Level 3 Shinpiden, 2020). To be able to give someone else the energy of the universe, you need to have a deep connection with this energy. Being your authentic self is essential in acquiring this deep connection.

- Meditation
- The popularity of meditation should not be understated. It is one of the few times when a person is really alone with themselves. During meditation, a person has to confront what their mind is and how it works. While the practice may bring the worst parts of your mind to the surface, it also allows people to see the best of themselves, recognizing their higher beings. Furthermore, being in a still and silent environment helps you in witnessing and experiencing the energy of the universe.

You may be distracted by bird sounds, a hungry mosquito, or traffic sounds. Yet, if you can gently carry your mind back to your breath, you can realize your strength over your mind and thus, your ego. You will also acknowledge how the universe's energy is abundant. It is in everything—the birds, the hungry mosquito, and all the agitated drivers stuck in traffic.

Naval Ravikant sums up the necessity of meditation: "Meditation is intermittent fasting for the mind. Too much sugar leads to a heavy body, and too many distractions lead to a heavy mind. Time spent undistracted and alone, in self-examination, journaling, meditati[ng], resolves the unresolved and takes us from mentally fat to fit" (420 Naval Ravikant Quotes to Make You Happy [and Wealthy]).

- Practice
- This point has already been discussed at the beginning of this section. It needs to be reiterated that practice is essential in acquiring Reiki mastery. Nothing that comes easy is worth it. To become a Reiki master takes a lot of time, work, and determination.
- Review Reiki I and II materials
- The materials provided in Chapters 2 and 3 are the basis of Reiki. Many courses require you to pass tests and write papers to ascend to the next level. For an attunement, you will need to have a good grasp on the locations of the chakras and their functions. Take time to review Shoden and Okuden notes so that you are prepared for conducting a Reiki attunement.

* * *

SHIRUSHI: MASTER SYMBOLS

There are two symbols introduced in Usui Reiki Level III. While one institute may present trainees with both in the program, others may choose to only share the master symbol with those practitioners who become Reiki masters. During

Shinpiden, there is more emphasis on becoming aligned with the energy and vibration generated from each symbol.

- Holy Fire symbol
- The Holy Fire symbol represents the concept of the Holy Fire discussed at the onset of this chapter. It is the surrender of the ego to the quest for enlightenment. When visualizing this symbol, the patient diminishes the ego's grasp over them. The pictogram of the Holy Fire symbol is a burning flame. Reflecting on this process helps to rid the patient's spiritual being of the negativity and toxicity produced by the ego.

- Dai Ko Myo: master symbol
- Dai Ko Myo is the gift of purest light or energy. When you are handed it, a direct channel with the purest

energy is being created. The first pictogram depicts a kind of star with a vertical line being formed at a convergence. The vertical line reveals the channel that is being formed with the purest light. It is then distributed throughout your entire being through Sahasrara, the crown chakra. Thus, when trying to obtain this purest light, you will need to draw this master symbol on your crown chakra. As we mentioned in the previous chapter, visualization and drawing can help you perfect this skill. When you are not using an attunement practice or providing healing to yourself, meditating and reflecting on this symbol is not only beneficial, but necessary as a master. Visualizing and meditating on it reminds you of the purest energy. It brings its power to consciousness.

RESPONSIBILITIES AND ETHICAL CODES OF A REIKI MASTER

Responsibilities

Being a Reiki master brings with it a lot of responsibility. Not only does it require daily practice, regular self-attunement, and leading a spiritually clean life, but you are also responsible for the physical and psychological welfare of others. However, to be a Reiki master, you need to learn many soft skills related to caring for others. The list below includes some of these aptitudes a master must acquire.

- The pursuit of knowledge must be your goal.
- Be kind and compassionate to all sentient beings.
- Be proficient in Reiki skills and obtain a great deal of Reiki knowledge.
- Feed humankind's spiritual hunger.
- Encourage love where it is possible.
- Be a bringer of light.
- Do not lie and motivate others to not lie.
- Heal people honestly and deeply.
- Guide others to live a life of sober habits.
- Always seek self-improvement (Dai Ko Myo Reiki Master Symbol And Reiki Level 3 Shinpiden, 2020, para 7).

Ethical Codes

Like all medical professions such as dentists, doctors, and physiotherapists, you have an ethical code of conduct. These medical professions are in contact with people's bodies, and thus are working with individuals on an intimate level. It is of the utmost importance that you treat all people's bodies with respect.

The following are a list of codes that a Reiki master and healer should follow:

- Do not endorse any form of discrimination, and heal without prejudice.

- Always inform your customer or patient of the details of a healing session so they understand what to expect and make an appropriate decision.
- Maintain professional integrity.
- Do not disclose clients' private information unless asked by the law to do otherwise.
- Respect patients' bodies, and only perform energy healing through touch on areas that the patient consents to.
- Acknowledge all Reiki practitioners and support them as much as possible with their training, but also treat them with dignity.
- Continuously update yourself on new Reiki regulations, and comply with all Reiki ethical codes.
- Strive to build a relationship of trust with all patients.
- Only provide treatment that has been certified by Reiki programs and courses which are offered by centers affiliated with the Reiki Association.
- If you receive criticism or a complaint, reply as soon as possible, and respond in an appropriate and constructive manner
- Recognize the importance of your position and responsibility as a Reiki instructor (Code of Ethics of the Reiki Association, 2020).

Lastly, there are some guidelines provided by the Reiki Association that can encourage transparency and professionalism:

- Display your Reiki certificates and qualifications.

- Offer patients thorough knowledge of their physical and psychological health.
- Try to avoid postponing or canceling appointments.
- Be considerate to all patients and colleagues.

REIKI LEVEL III

As the world of Reiki has become digitized, many organizations promise almost overnight ascension to master level. Unfortunately, this is too optimistic. Genuine graduation to the master level takes about a year after Okuden. Once completing Okuden, usually a student must spend another year or two practicing Reiki healing and reviewing its theory. Not only do you need throughout knowledge of Shoden and Okuden, but you require proficient capability in performing hand positions to master the Reiki techniques to provide healing to yourself and others.

Mastering Reiki is no walk in the park. It takes a lot of mental and physical exertion. Daily practice and meditation are necessary, as well as being an astute example of spiritual cleanliness. This entails maintaining a lifestyle where you avoid harmful chemicals and relinquish the hold negative emotions have over you. Furthermore, it involves a commitment to overcoming one's ego and being a keen-minded student who is always in favor of self-development and gaining new knowledge. These commitments remain constant even after one becomes a qualified Reiki master.

Hand Positions

"Our sorrows and wounds are healed only when we touch them with compassion." –Buddha

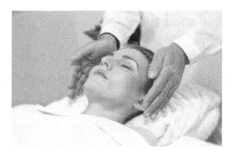

INTRODUCTION

The essence of Reiki is physical touch. The hands are channels through which energy is transferred to unblock tension or to restore one's innate ki. There are many other therapies that use physical touch through the hands to provide healing, such as massages, physiotherapy, and chiropractic work. While it is debatable, Reiki is the only practice that applies this form of healing to assist with psychological and emotional issues. However, if visiting a physiotherapist entails ending chronic pain and, as a result, restoring one's vitality, then one would suffer emotionally as well.

Furthermore, physical touch is not only used by medical professionals, but it is integrated into all cultures. Alex Bennet reveals this innate proclivity for physical touch:

Touching to comfort and relieve pain, or the laying on of hands, is as old as instinct. When humans are hurt, they immediately put their hands on the spot. A mother's touch or kiss provides soothing aid for a child's hurts. A mother's natural instinct with a sick child is to use her hand to feel for a fever. Animals immediately lick injuries and touch and lick their young as they learn. These simple acts form the basis for healing techniques through touch (Bennet).

Hands are the main tools for providing energy healing. They are one of our most valuable assets as humans. The number of functions they provide is limitless. For instance, hands clap to make sound, they wave to greet, the fingers on the hands can point, hands can massage to remove tension, they can balance us to stop us from falling or catch our falls, hands pray, and they are instruments of violence.

Hands are our sources of life and they can be instigators of death; and hands heal. They are some of the most powerful instruments we have. Their energy is immense. Think about how many other functions they perform. We cannot deny the intrinsic aptitude stored in our hands.

More than a hundred years ago, Mikao Usui must have recognized the sheer magnitude of their capabilities; he must have acknowledged the instinct of the hands to heal. Perhaps he noticed that when we suffer from stomachaches, the hands rub the belly to soothe the pain. Or maybe he saw that when people are worried about something, they often use their hands to cup their face. He most likely noticed that hand healing is instinctual and unconscious.

It is now time to revisit hand healing and to bring it into consciousness. In this chapter, we will look at the main and secondary Reiki hand positions to reassert the power of hand healing.

THE MAIN REIKI HAND POSITIONS

Below are the main Reiki hand positions. These are the main positions since energy healing is transferred to vital organs such as the stomach and kidneys, as well as the seven chakras. These hand positions can be utilized in both self-healing and healing to others.

- First position: the crown of the head

Putting both your hands on your crown draws energy to your crown chakra. As the crown chakra relates to your higher being and spiritual connection with the universe, this position optimizes flow to your higher self (What Are The Reiki Hand Positions And How To Use Them, 2020, para 3).

- Second position: the third eye and back of head

Put one hand on the forehand and one directly behind it for this position. As this works with Ajna, it helps to clear the mind, sharpen mental acuity and memory, diminish stress, and revitalize mental endurance (What Are The Reiki Hand Positions And How To Use Them, 2020, para 3).

- Third position: hand over eyes

Allowing your hands to gently cover your eyes helps to give your eyes a visual time-out and returns mental vitality. When you are exhausted or visually overwhelmed, this position can help to reduce the strain on your eyes and face (What Are The Reiki Hand Positions And How To Use Them, 2020, para 3).

- Fourth position: hand over ears

This particular position helps to prevent mental exhaustion by limiting information overload and by cleansing both brain hemispheres of excess information. Think about people who protect themselves from a loud noise; in a similar sense, we protect ourselves from receiving too much information (What Are The Reiki Hand Positions And How To Use Them, 2020, para 3).

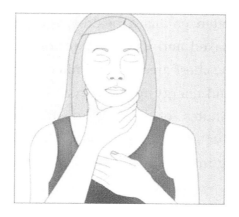

- Fifth position: the neck position

The neck is a very vulnerable area. Like our wrists and ankles, it receives a lot of contact, but is not always sufficiently supported. Furthermore, we tend to overstrain it nowadays with desk jobs. Place your hands around your neck to relieve the pressure. By easing the tension, you are also opening your throat chakra, or Vishuddha, to help you communicate effectively and express yourself more clearly (What Are The Reiki Hand Positions And How To Use Them, 2020, para 3). Wrap both hands around your neck, making sure that every finger has contact with the neck area.

- Sixth position: The center of the chest

This sixth position soothes Anahata, the heart chakra. This is a main Reiki hand position because it provides healing to a much-needed area. Daily interactions with people, both big and small, may cause a build-up of pain and resentment, ultimately creating a reluctance to socialize and love. Moreover, a healthy heart often entails a healthy body, so keeping the heart chakra relaxed and its energy restored results in long-term vitality. The chest area is not limited to the heart; it also supplies light and energy to the curve of our backs and our lungs. Two minutes of healing to this area every day promotes positive social interactions and healthy heart and lungs in the long run.

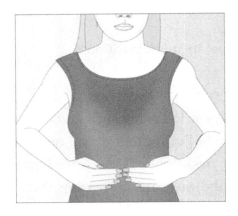

- Seventh position: the solar plexus position

There are many vital organs in this area that use a lot of the body's energy. (What Are The Reiki Hand Positions And How To Use Them, 2020, para 3). According to Reiki Scoop, these organs provide us with protection and essential life force. Spending two minutes doing this hand position can ensure you do not neglect those organs, though on a day-to-day basis, it is easy to forget they are there.

- Eighth position: the navel position

As this hand position works in the region of Svadhishthana, or the sacral chakra, it deals with intimate, sensual, and intense relationships. Using the energy and light from your hands to heal this area aids the patient in having more meaningful relationships. It also can boost creativity. (What Are The Reiki Hand Positions And How To Use Them, 2020, para 3).

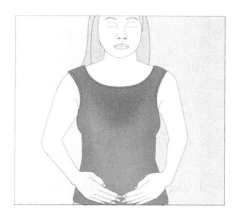

- Ninth position: the kidneys

Most people forget about their kidneys (unless you have kidney stones). On a daily basis, the kidneys work hard to remove toxins from and balance the chemicals in our bodies. They are the undervalued soldiers of our bodies. The eighth main reiki position ensures we spend a bit of time bringing relief to these organs. Reiki Scoop provides more insight into the eighth position: "Not only will healing here enhance the navel area energy center, but it will help you regain your daily energy and vitality as well as sustain and help the

organs" (What Are The Reiki Hand Positions And How To
Use Them, 2020, para 3).

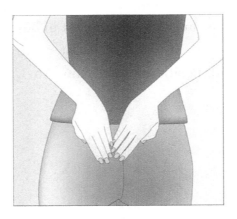

- Tenth position: the sacral area

In Chapter 2, we looked at the functions of Muladhara, the
primary chakra. As this is our root, or primary, chakra, we
need to ensure it is well-balanced and well-supplied with
light and energy. The Muladhara provides us with stability
and a firm platform on which to navigate and experiment
with life. While other chakras, such as Sahasrāra and Ajna,
seek to advance and discover, this is only possible if the individual is well-grounded and humble. Therefore, it is vital that
constant attention is given to the sacral area to provide the
individual with stability and a firm platform from which to
grow (What Are The Reiki Hand Positions And How To Use
Them, 2020, para 3).

* * *

THE SECONDARY REIKI HAND POSITIONS

The next positions are referred to as secondary hand positions. This is because they do not deal with major organs, but mainly limbs and appendages. Despite being secondary, many people struggle with pain in these areas. Though they are not the main positions, including them in a self-treatment or therapy session can help end discomfort.

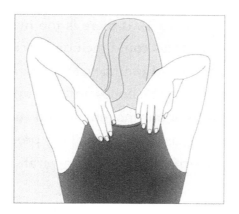

- Shoulders

As many of us have desk jobs or spend much time hunched over a desk, the shoulders tend to tense up, and consequently, light and energy cannot freely travel to them. After a week of tension or this blockage, the shoulders begin to suffer from a lot of discomfort and stiffness, and a person may need to go to a masseuse for assistance at that point. Additionally, Reiki Scoop explains that "when we carry a lot of emotional baggage, these two places tend to be tense and stiff" (What Are The Reiki Hand Positions And How To Use Them, 2020, para 4). Thus, providing daily relief can prevent long-term pain and prevent you from seeking aid from a masseuse, physiotherapist, and chiropractor.

- Hips

Our hips are deeply connected to our sacral chakra. Sexual, intimate, and intense emotional desires are stored here, often unexpressed (What Are The Reiki Hand Positions And How To Use Them, 2020, para 4). If there is too much build-up in this area, long-term issues could include a lack of enthusiasm for sexual intercourse and intimacy. Moreover, since the hips are some of the strongest bones in the human body and responsible for much of our movement and stability, soothing them daily or as often as possible can help promote more flexibility. This can, in turn, initiate more inspiration for intimacy.

- Knees

When you run, the shock of the impact as your foot connects to the ground is absorbed by the knees. This is not only true for running but for walking and movement in general. Many people endure injuries early on because of bad support and a lack of knee protection (Healthwise Staff, 2019). Cleansing and restoring energy to the knees ensures support for the rest of the body as we run, walk, and move.

- Feet and soles

Like our hands, our feet are involved in many activities that are fundamental for movement. This dependence on our feet means that if we experience discomfort in this region, it can incapacitate us. Going for a walk on grass can soothe this area, and so can this hand position. Not only does providing a remedy to this area help us to support our daily movements, but releasing stored up tension can get rid of stress and maintain better emotional balance (Burgess, 2018, para 3).

NOTES FOR HEALING OURSELVES

After Usui Reiki Level I, you are introduced to the main and secondary Reiki hand positions. Shoden training necessitates that you practice on yourself to learn these positions by heart (Reiki Hand Positions, 2014, para 1). This will also form part of your 21-day purification.

Try to set up a daily routine to perform a self-healing session. When starting out, try to spend time learning each of the positions. Also keep in mind that you know your body, so you know where there is tension and discomfort. When you move onto Okuden, you will need to increase the time of your self-healing session so that you can perfect this process.

It should be noted that since your body informs you of where there is pain or a blockage, you should try to search your body for signs of toxins by applying the practice of Byosen. One more thing to remember is this: though your body tells you where there is discomfort, try not to neglect specific hand positions as you will need to be familiar with them during Okuden and when healing others.

NOTES FOR HEALING OTHERS

The Reiki Association has strict codes instructing how to provide healing for others. While during Shoden and Okuden training it is useful to practice on others, the Reiki ethical codes and values should be strictly adhered to. Always give your patient—even if it is a loved one—full knowledge of what the hand positions involve. It could be useful here to show them pictures of the positions so they know what to expect. Although you are now healing another body, you will apply the same hand positions to that person.

For example, the following are examples of hand positions for fifth and sixth positions being performed on others.

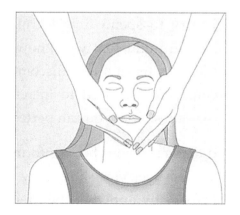

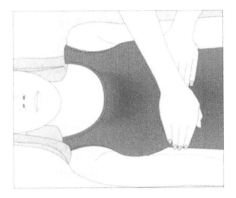

The hand positions are very similar but can be adapted for the patient. The patient will also be lying down to receive the treatment. When providing the treatment, be respectful of the patient's body, and always indicate before the treatment where the various hand positions are located so they know what to expect, once again, even if it is a friend or loved one. If a patient is uncomfortable during the process, energy will not be able to circulate freely, and it will disrupt the abilities of the energy and light to heal.

Lastly, ask the individual receiving the treatment which areas are causing them pain (Code of Ethics of The Reiki Association, 2020, para 1). While it is necessary to rely on intuition and Byosen to know which areas to heal, patients also have a good idea of where they are experiencing tension or discomfort.

CONCLUSION

Our hands are wonderful instruments. Unconsciously, we are aware of their multifaceted nature, but we often forget that one of their intrinsic functions is to heal. On a primordial level, we use them to provide emotional comfort and support and to rub stomachaches or massage our temples. Many therapies rely on physical touch to promote healing, and Reiki is one such therapy.

If you put your hands to your face right now, you will feel their warmth and the energy vibrating through them. They are not simply energy, but light as well. Healing through the hands depends on using the internal energy and light in them to provide healing for a range of issues. Spending some time each day to learn the Reiki hand positions can be useful in providing long-term relief to discomfort, pain, tension, heartache, and loneliness.

This chapter served to discuss the biology of the hands and why they are so crucial to Reiki. The next chapter will briefly explain the main and secondary Reiki hand positions so that you can begin learning them by heart. Finally, it will list important reminders to make a note of before starting self-healing or healing others. Before you begin with self-healing and healing others, you must first master the Reiki techniques.

Mastering Reiki Techniques

"Energy is the essence of life. Every day you decide how you're going to use it by knowing what you want and what it takes to reach that goal, and by maintaining focus." –Oprah Winfrey

INTRODUCTION

Truthfully, this book has not followed a structured format. First, it has explained the theoretical underpinnings of various Reiki practices. In most programs, at the end of each day, you will spend time covering the theory of a practice, then time will be dedicated to its application. For example, in Reiki Level I, you are usually introduced to some hand positions, and later, you will practice them in the training center and when you go home.

For the sake of compartmentalization, this book has taken a nontraditional approach, discussing each concept of Reiki in detail, then later teaching you how to apply Reiki methods. Having said that, in previous chapters, techniques were named for the visualization and drawing of Shirushi, and for preparing for attunements. However, these are primary techniques supporting much more advanced Reiki techniques. For instance, the ability to draw a symbol can be used to initiate a healing practice.

While meditating and visualizing Shirushi is an effective method on its own, it often complements other rituals in Reiki, such as meditation and healing through physical touch. This chapter will not cover those approaches for attunements and the visualizing and drawing of Shirushi; however, they will be referred to for the supplementary functions.

In this chapter, we will cover mastering essential Reiki techniques, namely Reiki meditation, mastering hand positions and Byosen, and Seiheki Chiryo Ho.

REIKI MEDITATION

The goal of Reiki meditation is to connect you with your divine element, to help you discover your true self, and to attune you to the universe's energy.

- Find a peaceful place in which to meditate. Similar to attunements, the external world needs to be as calm as possible so that you can be more sensitive to your internal life force and to the vibrations of the universe.
- Sit or lie down in a relaxed position.
- Take a deep breath, inhaling through your nose and exhaling through your nose.
- For the first two to three minutes, you can concentrate on your breath.
- Pay attention to it entering through your nostrils, sinking down into your lungs, and exiting through your chest.
- Deepen your inhalations so that you enter more deeply into relaxation.
- Try to get your breath to reach the pit of your stomach. (Note: it may be a bit forced now, but breathing into the diaphragm helps to increase the amount of breath you receive.)
- Once you feel relaxed, draw your attention to your mind.
- Send thoughts of loving-kindness and compassion to yourself. You can choose your own words or you can recite the following:

>I would like the very best for myself.

>I would like to make myself proud.

>I send myself love, kindness, strength, and compassion.

>The energy of the universe is in me.

You can also repeat the five Reiki principles during this meditation if you know them by heart.

When you are finished with the thoughts of loving-kindness, dispel any negative thoughts. During the last ten minutes, your mind most likely wandered once or twice to some knee-jerk bitter or angry thoughts; send them out into the universe. Perhaps, you may not have had any negative emotions but brought your mind to other distractions. You could have thought of the chores you needed to do or bills you had to pay. These thoughts can distract us during the mediation and cause anxiety and stress. Send them out into the universe as well.

- Next, place a hand on your seven chakras. Put your palm first on your crown, then your third eye, throat, heart, solar plexus, navel, groin area, and perineum. Remember, all the chakras are aligned, so you need to move the palm vertically down the chakra path.
- Try to spend about 30 seconds to 1 minute on each area. (Note: if a specific area requires more attention, then you can spend longer channeling energy to it.)
- During the meditation, if you experience any discomfort, tingling, or pain, use the appropriate hand position to provide healing to that area.
- Continue to inhale through the nose and exhale through the mouth.
- Count to ten, and every time you count, inhale through the nose and exhale through the mouth.
- When you are ready, open your eyes (Achanta, 2017, para 3).

* * *

HAND POSITION STEPS AND TECHNIQUES

Steps

Whether providing healing through the hand positions to yourself or to others, it is vital to follow the steps provided below. You should follow these steps before, during, and after the healing ritual.

Before:

- Wash your hands first to remove all impurities and toxins.
- Declare to the universe's energy your wish to use light and energy to heal the patient's body (What Are The Reiki Hand Positions And How To Use Them, 2020, para 2).
- Rub your hands to channel light and energy to these regions, or you can use one of the Reiki symbols to open the hands to grant healing (What Are The Reiki Hand Positions And How To Use Them, 2020, para 2).

During:

- If you aim to perform a full cleanse, you can spend two to three minutes on each area. However, if you wish to target some specific areas that require attention, then you can ask the patient which body part is in great discomfort. In this case, you can spend five to ten minutes sending light and energy to the region.

- Place your hand on the area. When the area begins to relax, you can remove your hand. (Note: it is essential to develop one's intuition and knowledge of the chakras and to practice Byosen to fully know when to move on to the next area.)

After:

- Say thanks to the universe's energy.
- Inform Reiki, the universe's energy, that the session will end.

Techniques

There are different approaches to offer healing with the hand positions. They are beaming, cleaning, scanning, tapping, and swiping, which we go over below.

Scanning (Byosen):

We have extensively discussed Byosen in Chapters 1 and 2, so we will not explore scanning in great detail. The process of scanning the body for toxins and negative emotions is the first ritual performed during a Reiki treatment.

Scan the body for signs of toxins:

- Heat
- Extreme heat
- Lack of pulse
- Sweat
- Tingling
- Cold

Alternatively, you can ask the patient if there are pins and needles, sensitivity, or numbness in any area (Petter).

As you conduct your scan, your hands will locate a body part that has an excess of toxins. You can place your hands on the area or just below it. Sometimes, not placing a palm directly on the afflicted area restores its energy. If you do place a hand directly over the injured body part, you have a risk of suffocating the area or obstructing the flow of light or energy.

Beaming:

Rae Jae Reiki explains how beaming works:

A powerful method of channeling Reiki energy is called beaming. It can dramatically increase the amount of Reiki flowing through the practitioner to the client. Beaming also creates a unique healing process of treating the whole aura at once. After treating the aura, the Reiki energy will enter the physical body and treat areas that need it. It is also possible to beam Reiki directly to a specific area (Beaming, 2018, para 1).

Here is the process:

- The patient lies or sits down.

- The Reiki healer channels the universe's energy with sincere intention.
- They stand with their hands raised a couple of meters from the patient, then direct the universe's energy to the individual.
- It is sent to the patient's aura, entering at the crown, then distributed throughout the person.
- The healer needs complete concentration on the patient's healing (Giaser, 2020).

Cleaning:

Cleaning is also known as "combing". This alternate term came about because the practitioner guides their hands over the patient's body in a manner like combing. Direct contact is not applied in this case.

- Imagine your hands removing negative energy, emotions, and toxins.
- Guide your hands like a comb around the patient's head, chest, shoulders, and any other necessary areas. Do this as carefully as possible.
- Imagine the negative energy and toxins falling away and entering the universe (What Are The Reiki Hand Positions And How To Use Them, 2020, para 3).

Tapping:

Cleaning or combing involves a more general approach to healing, while tapping concentrates on a specific area.

- After you have scanned the body, isolate an injured or tense area.
- Place two fingers onto the area.
- Gently tap the area and begin a slow massage.
- Focus on using the universe's energy to unblock the area and remove the tension (What Are The Reiki Hand Positions And How To Use Them, 2020, para 3).

Swiping:

- Swiping restores energy from the left shoulder to the right hip and from the right shoulder to the left hip.
- Begin with your left hand on your right shoulder and, almost like swiping, move your palm diagonally across the body to the right hip.
- Next, start from your left shoulder and move your hand across to your right hip.
- Let the energy from your hands be transferred while you carefully move your hand.
- Repeat this swiping process three times on each side (What Are The Reiki Hand Positions And How To Use Them, 2020, para 3).

Fast Self-Treatment

If you find that you do not have time to conduct a full cleaning and healing ritual on yourself, Reiki Scoop provides a sample of a fast self-treatment you can use:

- Put your palm on the crown and sacral chakras for three to five minutes.
- Next, place a palm on the third eye and navel chakras.
- Then, move your hands to your throat and solar plexus.
- Finally, position both hands on the heart chakra.

Remember to move down and up the vertical alignment of your chakras. Try to keep the vertical alignment intact so a clear path of energy is created (What Are The Reiki Hand Positions And How To Use Them, 2020, para 4).

SEIHEKI CHIRYO HO

If you recall from Okuden, Seiheki Chiryo Ho primarily assists individuals in overcoming negative patterns, namely bad habits and destructive thoughts. Furthermore, it boosts the patient's energy for a clear purpose or target. This is something that can be done alone as part of your self-treatment, or a master can help you with this. Seiheki Chiryo Ho relies on affirmations and repeating mantras to achieve the above.

The website Deborah Reiki provides more insight into the power of Reiki affirmations.

It also provides help with changing mental attitudes (overthinking, planning, controlling, and negative self-talk). Support can be given for stopping smoking, for example. Change happens a step at a time, so the first stage is to decide upon one particular area in your life you want to work on.

The next task is to find an appropriate affirmation. Affirmations need to be both achievable and positive (Working with affirmations: Seiheki Chiryo Ho, 2017).

Self-treatment:

- Name a specific objective you would like to achieve.
- Now specify specific bad habits, patterns of behavior, or destructive thoughts that prevent you from obtaining the above.

- Repeat personalized affirmations that give you power over the specific bad habit. Here are some examples:

>I will stop smoking.

>I will stop drinking alcohol.

>I will pay attention to the words I say to myself.

>I will exercise more regularly.

>I will use more loving-kind words with myself.

Patient treatment:

- Sit before the patient.
- Listen to the patient as they explain their goals and name the patterns of behavior that create obstructions.
- Remind the patient that it takes time to change patterns of behavior and to implement new habits.
- Indicate to the patient that it all begins with will power. Repeating affirmations is therefore central in helping the individual overcome the negative habit or pattern.
- Encourage the patient to repeat motivating affirmations. Here are some affirmations they can use:

>I will treat myself more kindly.

>I will stop overeating.

>I will say more loving words to myself.

>I will take better care of my body.

>I will not hold on to negative emotions.

When implementing Seiheki Chiryo Ho, remember that it takes time for a new habit to become ingrained. Be patient with yourself during this process of change. Make sure to remind yourself and the patient that movement in a positive and healthy direction is a remarkable thing, but it takes courage, patience, and continuous motivation. Thus, encourage yourself and the patient to consistently repeat these affirmations to inspire motivation.

CONCLUSION

In your Reiki training, you will not be introduced to these techniques all at once. This chapter does not intend for you to master these overnight; rather, its purpose is to summarize Reiki meditation, mastering the hand position steps and techniques, and fitting Seiheki Chiryo Ho into a comprehensive list that you can refer to time and time again long after your Reiki training has ended.

For the next few years and beyond, you can return to a section in this book and concentrate on developing a certain technique. Despite the intention to create a summarized list, a devoted Reiki practitioner will spend their lifetime trying to enhance them. Having said that, the steps and techniques mentioned here can accompany your Shoden, Okuden, and Shinpiden and your life-long Reiki training.

Healing Others- Part 1

"You are an aperture through which the universe is looking at and exploring itself." –Alan Watts

SELF-HEALING AND REIKI BACKGROUND

The concept of self-healing is layered. First, on a fundamental level, it is misleading as it is not ourselves, but light and energy which heal us; it is the universal energy which heals us. Yet, since we are composed of light and energy, what are we other than the same thing that composes the universe? Also, what are we other than the thing that heals us? It is circular reasoning at its very best. Yet, that seems to be in line with nature and the universe, which also appear to be circular.

Consider, for example, plants: they create their own food from light and carbon to reproduce themselves. Humans use calories to hunt (or in the present day, work) and, in turn, this gives us more energy. While self-healing may seem like a foreign concept, it happens all the time. When we get sick, our bodies create antibodies to fight off the invaders. We have to do nothing except heal. Unlike our bodies, which first identify the harmful virus or bacteria, we are not aware that we suffer from a spiritual ailment. We do not know that the blockage in our heart chakra is making us unwilling to love or trust people again.

A hundred years ago, Mikao Usui discovered this innate ability of the body to heal itself. It was probably his close encounter with death during the cholera outbreak that assisted Usui in his recovery. "Throughout his education, Dr. Usui had an interest in medicine, psychology, and theology. It was this interest that prompted him to seek a way to heal himself and others using the laying on of hands" (History and Traditions of Reiki, para 2). Therefore, Usui dedicated his education to devise a way of providing self-healing.

* * *

HEALING FOR THE MIND, BODY, AND SOUL

In preparation for your first attunement and during your 21-day purification, you are encouraged to avoid harmful or poisonous chemicals, bad habits, and holding onto negative emotions. Reiki essentially cleanses the Mind, Body, and Soul. It acknowledges that all are corrupted by physical, emotional, and spiritual toxins (although it is not always the case that if one person is corrupted then the others will be too). This is referred to as the "four alignment" (Brenner, 2016, para 2).

The Physical Alignment

Physical alignment concentrates on anatomy. It concentrates on our material form. Biological processes such as digestion, respiration, reproduction, and others compose part of the physical alignment. Self-healing in Reiki aspires to enhance one's physical processes so that chronic pain is eliminated (Brenner, 2016, para 3).

The Mental Alignment

Elise Brenner succinctly describes the problematic nature of mental misalignment: "The mind is sometimes called the 'organ of misery' because it has the capacity to ruin our days, even our lives, with its incessant rambling and ruminating" (Brenner, 2016, para 3). It is necessary for us to learn how our mind works, then to learn how to purify it. This will prove to be the most challenging, but one which Reiki self-healing can help with through mantras, affirmations, and meditation.

The Emotional Alignment

Emotions can be volatile and unreliable in nature. Sadly, it is not so easy to distance ourselves from them. While we may be encouraged to be more rational and reasonable as opposed to emotional, we should instead strive to be emotionally balanced. As this alignment is separated from the mental alignment, you cannot simply reason with your emotions. Self-healing tackles emotional impurities focusing on the core sources of pain: a lack of emotional energy or the heart or sacral chakra being blocked.

The Spiritual Alignment

While Reiki insists on a balance and alignment of the physical, mental, emotional, and spiritual, if there were one that was most important, it would be spiritual alignment. If we do not experience a direct channel with the universe's energy, we become desolate, lost, and uninspired. We do not realize that we have a "higher being" in us which is capable of immense healing and extraordinary accomplishments. Brenner describes how spiritual alignment is vital:

A state of balance facilitates spiritual growth, allowing the individual to connect to an inner peace and serenity, as well as to a sense of oneness and inter-being with all beings. We experience an openness to life, a sense of spaciousness and expansiveness (2016, para 3).

If you cannot find a balance for your mind, body, and soul, everything will be out of sync. We have already seen that it is primarily imbalance that causes sickness. For example, if you are stressed, you lack the capacity or strength to manage a situation. If you have stiffness in your shoulders, you are not receiving enough blood supply and flow to this area. Reiki uses self-healing to achieve the optimum balance between all these areas.

When saying words such as "alignment" and "integrity", there is intrinsic power that resonates from them. This is like the vibration of symbols. The powerful resonance from words like "integrity" not only demonstrate how holistic the four alignments are, but how intense as well.

* * *

SELF-HEALING APPROACHES

Reiki Meditation

Meditation, in fact, is the perfect medium for learning about the mind, which Brenner calls "the organ of misery". When meditating, we have no choice but to contend directly with our brains. There is nothing that can distract us or save us from the mind. It is only through meditation that we can learn how necessary it is to quiet the mind and maintain control over it (Peikon, 2019, para 2).

Reiki meditation not only helps individuals learn how their mind works, but it assists with the four alignments. When you go through the steps of placing a palm on your seven chakras, by vertically moving from one to the next, you are establishing this connection between your mind, body, and soul.

Reiki Bath

You do not need a bathtub for this one. A Reiki bath involves self-cleansing. Like a long soak after a difficult day, the Reiki bath entails a longer Reiki session; it is like a full Reiki treatment. While it is not always practical to give yourself a full treatment, it is advised to do one on yourself once a week or a month.

In the article "How to give yourself a 'reiki bath' for some at-home healing", Fitzmaurice describes how to give yourself a cleansing. The full-treatment begins with choosing a comfortable space, then meditating, going through a chakra alignment process starting with your crown, and repeating the five chakra principles.

Self-Healing With a Master

Finally, if you decide to opt for Reiki training, you can use your sessions with a Reiki master to help you become proficient in self-healing. Learning how to heal yourself is one of the initial aspects of Reiki training. Thus, you will cover this extensively in Shoden. Even if you decide not to do the training, you can visit a master to ask him or her to show you the basics of self-healing. Masters are trained in teaching self-healing, so it is worthwhile to use one of these skilled practitioners for assistance with this.

Healing Others - Part 2

"Carry out a random act of kindness, with no expectation of reward, safe in the knowledge that one day someone might do the same for you." –Princess Diana

HEALING OTHERS AND REIKI BACKGROUND

When one becomes adept in self-healing, they can then heal another individual and teach that person how to heal themselves. This act is not only about healing; it is also about generational transition: the victim becomes healed, and the victim becomes a healer.

A clear illustration of this is seen in Hawayo Takata. Though she is credited with exporting Reiki to the West and being a proficient healer, unlike other great men, she did not learn this ability innately. After her own close experience with death, she attended Chujiro Hayashi's Reiki clinic, receiving treatment for her bladder disease (Hawayo Takata – The Woman Who Brought Reiki To The Western World, 2020, para 1). Takata is a bright example of how healing through Reiki transitions from one generation to the next. In this sense, Reiki is not simply about healing others, but giving them the tools to heal themselves.

Unfortunately, this is not a vocation for all. Some people do not have the concentration to become a Reiki healer nor do they have the intention. Others will also have other commitments, which are equally important, like the production of food and the provision of electrical power. For this reason, learning to heal others will always be a necessary function of Reiki.

PHYSICAL, PSYCHOLOGICAL, AND EMOTIONAL HEALING FOR OTHERS

It is not always easy to know what ailments individuals suffer from. Since Reiki concentrates on a holistic approach, healing others involves treating various symptoms, all belonging to different dimensions. The Reiki Association highlights the importance of listening to the patient intently (Code of Ethics of The Reiki Association, 2020) so that you can provide a holistic approach.

Reiki healer Lisa Brandis explains how listening helps her to make informed decisions as a Reiki healer:

When a client first arrives to have a Reiki session with me, I ask them to take a moment to think about why they have come, and [I] ask them to make a note of what they hope to achieve during their Intuitive Reiki session with me (2013, para 1).

On the other hand, patients will not always know the true cause or nature of their ailments. To assist with this, Reiki training emphasizes the importance of aligning with the universal energy, a healer developing their intuition, and mastering Byosen.

Aligning Oneself With Reiki

Before every cleansing or attunement, the Reiki healer needs to invite Reiki into the environment. They also need to state their intention of using Reiki to heal the individual. Brandis discusses the reasoning behind this: "This is a very important step for me as it also allows me to focus and disengage from my own life and really come into a place of openness and receptivity and most importantly love" (Brandis, 2013, para 1).

Before continuing, it should be noted that if you are not familiar with the universe's energy or do not feel skilled enough to harness and transfer that energy, then inform your patient of this before commencing. Generally, it will require a decent amount of time to practice Reiki.

While it is certainly recommended to practice on loved ones and others to master Reiki healing, if you are not confident, you should also inform your patient or loved one. Being honest and building a relationship based on trust is another ethical code you should adhere to as a Reiki practitioner.

When the Reiki healer invites the universe's energy into the environment, they are trying to channel it into the patient. Though the Reiki healer has the universe's energy in them, they are not to be confused with actually *being* the universe's energy. Naturally, it does flow in beings, but the purpose of Reiki sessions is to direct the universe's energy into the patient. To achieve this, the Reiki practitioner needs constant meditation and attunement sessions—either self-attunement sessions or ones with a master.

Developing Intuition

"Intuition is the wisdom from within from our Divine self" (Brandis, 2013, para 2). The universe will always know what remedy to provide to the patient, so healers need to use Reiki to guide them. It is through intuition that the Reiki practitioner can obtain direction and know what healing to offer.

As a Reiki healer, it is your responsibility to be in touch with the Divine Self. Remember, the "divinity" in you has no prejudice; it does not hate and offers compassion and kindness to all. Thus, before every Reiki session—even with yourself and when practicing on loved ones—you need to meditate and relinquish all prejudice and judgment. As a Reiki healer, it is your responsibility to reach a higher state that is free from all kinds of judgment. Meditation and attending many attunements can assist in strengthening this bond with the higher self.

In Shinpiden, you cover Holy Fire ignition, which is the process of separating oneself from their ego. You may have not reached Usui Reiki Level III, but it is recommended when practicing on patients that you learn to distance yourself from your ego. Once the ego has no grasp over you, you can discover your divine, or true, self.

Once you have obtained this connection with your divine self, then you can focus on your intuition's guidance of the patient's treatment. When performing a scan or Byosen, pay attention to anything that does not seem right. If you sense something is off, do not rationalize but rather use your intuition to provide the necessary healing.

We analyzed this earlier, but if an area is too hot or too cold, do not assume there is no issue. An assumption is generally filtered information. The initial signal is the heat or lack of pulse in the area.

* * *

DISTANCE HEALING

In Okuden, you learned about five different symbols, one of which was Hon Sha Ze Sho Nen. Hon Sha Ze Sho Nen, meaning "no past, no present, no future", reveals that healing does not have any spatial or temporal boundaries (Price, 2019). Thus, it is possible to heal people through online platforms. Meditating and visualizing this symbol will help you to access and harness this kind of healing.

In Portland Helmich's article, the Reiki healer, Libby Barnett, claims that she has moved her Reiki treatment to an online platform (Helmich, 2020). The International Center for Reiki Training seems to verify that distance healing is a new direction for Reiki. (Lipinski).

When offering the Reiki healing, remember to include the Hon Sha Ze Sho Nen symbol in your treatment and cleansing so that you can incorporate this healing over a distance.

HEALING LOVED ONES

Many medical professionals are forbidden from treating their loved ones. Psychologists and doctors must follow these regulations (Treating Self or Family, 2020). Reiki healers do not have the same kinds of regulations (Code of Ethics of the Reiki Association, 2020). This gives you the opportunity to practice on friends, family members, and even pets.

There are two principal reasons for this. First, you as a Reiki healer or master are a channel through which the universe acts. In your quest as a practitioner, your aim is to distance yourself as much as possible from your ego. This separation from the ego allows the universe to act through you. Secondly, Reiki is generally safe (Saleh, 2020, para 6). Nevertheless, as a practitioner, you should do all that you can to carry out Reiki in a safe environment. You should also take your commitment to the patient's well-being seriously, even if they are your friend or pet.

Therefore, when offering to heal a family member, be earnest about their treatment; this will help you to advance as a Reiki healer. Furthermore, similar to providing healing to others, if your loved one feels uncomfortable or reluctant, then do not persist with the treatment as they are averse to that specific cleaning or attunement ritual, or stop with the treatment altogether if they wish it so.

CONCLUSION

While it is genuinely exciting to wish to heal others, it is not easy. Being a Reiki healer is hard work; helping people with their emotional, psychological, physical, and spiritual ailments is not straightforward. This vocation demands separation from the ego, relinquishing all judgment and prejudice, a commitment to self-growth, and the humblest intention of healing others. This is the reason why not everyone is a Reiki master. In the past, "traditionally, the Reiki master level of training was by invitation only" (Can I Learn Reiki Myself?, 2016, para 4). Being a Reiki master and healer is a big responsibility.

If you decide to continue with your Reiki healer, it is vital to acknowledge all the hours you need to spend studying the theory and applying the practices. Besides these duties, it is also important to remember that you need to relinquish your pride and be committed to the emotional, physical, spiritual, and psychological well-being of others.

Faq

In this chapter, we will spend time answering some questions beginners generally propose when learning about Reiki. We hope to clarify any doubts and concerns regarding Reiki in the process. While this section aims to provide as much information as possible, it cannot be as exhaustive as we would like. In this case, it will deal with the most pressing and common questions and concerns in order to provide readers with a little bit more understanding.

- **How much do Reiki sessions cost, and how many sessions do I need?**

First, people typically do not attend one Reiki session. As the 21-day detox indicates, it takes a long time for toxins of all forms to leave your body. Attending one Reiki session might provide immediate relief, but long-term, it is advisable to attend regular Reiki sessions.

One session is usually priced between $60 and $90 (K., n.d.). However, there are many prospective Reiki healers who intend to strengthen their abilities and will charge you less. Try visiting a local Reiki institute and asking them if any students—typically Reiki Level II—healers wish to cement their Reiki practice.

The number of Reiki sessions can vary. Sometimes, patients only seek assistance with a minor ailment and will need just one session, while other patients might wish to find therapy for the mind, body, and soul, necessitating regular sessions with a practitioner (Bedosky, 2020, p. para 9).

- **How much is a Reiki course, and how long are the programs?**

Reiki courses vary in price and length. There are numerous online courses available on Udemy offering Reiki training in Levels I and II over two days. While it is certainly possible, if you are interested in becoming more proficient at Reiki, attending a course that spans six months is probably best.

Keep in mind that the longer the course is, the more expensive it will be. An online course from Udemy is about $130. However, online courses from websites such as Reiki Infinite Healer are priced from as little as $49. If you feel more comfortable training in person, the courses will cost a bit more. In-center, Reiki Level I and II courses start from $300. While it is not always so practical, in-center classes are strongly recommended as they spend a lot of time applying Reiki practices.

Online and in-center courses offer intensive programs that can be completed in two days. Though, when you are finished, you will need to do the 21-day purification process. That means that after Reiki Level II, you can only finish Reiki Level I and II training in about a month. However, more thorough organizations require a 21-day purification after Reiki Level I, adding another month to the training.

- **Is there a Reiki community that can support me during my training?**

If you attend an in-center Reiki course, you will be part of a group. Generally, Reiki training programs require group participation to allow the prospective healers the opportunity to practice on others. As a result, when you begin your training, you are introduced to a group of trainees, and you grow in Reiki together.

This is the same for online training. You do not train alone. While it may be more isolated to train online, you can always join an online forum afterward. You could also go to your local Reiki center and ask about a Reiki community near you.

It is suggested that you try to find a local Reiki clinic. Often, they need healers and trainees, so you can offer your services and further your development in the practice.

- **Where do I find a Reiki healer or master?**

As Reiki has become popular in recent years, clinics devoted to the practice are opening up in various cities worldwide. Try searching for a local clinic for a Reiki healer or master.

Additionally, as with many things these days, Reiki has gone digital. You can also try booking a session with an online Reiki healer. While this is more practical, it is always best during your first few sessions to be in the physical presence of a healer.

- **How long is a Reiki session?**

Reiki sessions are one hour, though there are some that last an hour and a half (Reiki Sessions – What To Expect, 2020). You need to arrive 15 minutes before your Reiki session so that your healer can explain what you can expect from your session.

- **Is there a code of ethics for Reiki?**

Yes. The Reiki Association consistently updates its code of ethics for Reiki healers. It is necessary for Reiki practitioners to remain informed of new regulations. This is one of the ethics of a Reiki practitioner.

You can visit the Reiki Association's site to learn this code of ethics to help you be compliant should you wish to be a Reiki healer (Code of Ethics of the Reiki Association, 2020).

- **How do I prepare for a Reiki session?**

You will be lying on a Reiki stretcher or bed while the healer performs the cleansing, so make sure the clothes that you are in are comfortable. Before your first session, try to also be 15 minutes early as the practitioner will discuss your treatment with you prior to the cleansing (Reiki Sessions – What To Expect, 2020).

If you feel uncomfortable with anything that the Reiki healer explains about your upcoming treatment, mention it to him or her before commencing.

- **Does Reiki really work?**

Many studies conducted have shown positive results suggesting that Reiki is a holistic therapy. While research has extensively shown the effectiveness of Reiki healing, scientists have still not discovered how Reiki works.

In the future, it is possible that scientists will be able to solve this mystery. However, for now, as it remains, Reiki has been proven to help many recover from physical ailments, chronic pain, and mental health issues (Lotus, 2011) (Kisner, 2020) (Newman, 2017).

- **Do I need to attend a Reiki course?**

No, you do not need to attend a Reiki course. If you would like to receive healing for physical discomfort, stress, burnout, regulating your emotions, or increasing your motivation, you can attend Reiki sessions with a healer.

Alternatively, you might find Reiki Level I useful in teaching you about self-healing. Reiki Level II focuses on healing others, so attending Reiki Level I could help you to integrate Reiki practices into your lifestyle. In this case, it is still recommended to see a healer for they will transfer Reiki to you so that you can begin healing on all dimensions.

- **What should I expect from my first Reiki session?**

There is no single answer for this as everyone experiences something different. Some people may become extremely sensitive since toxins have been removed from their bodies, while others may feel lighter and more joyous. After your first Reiki session, it is important to drink a lot of liquids because it can be rather strenuous.

Think of Reiki as a spiritual massage. During your first session, you will remain fully clothed and will lie down on a stretcher or bed. The healer will use various hand positions to channel the universe's energy into your seven chakras, as well as into any other areas experiencing discomfort, such as your shoulders. The healer will explain everything that will happen in the Reiki session before commencing so you will kn0w what to expect.

- **What are the best resources to practice Reiki?**

Reiki has become digital, so you can make use of extensive online tools like podcasts, articles, YouTube videos, and blogs. There are also various institutes and academies providing Reiki training and workshops. However, the best Reiki guidance and mastery can come from Reiki masters themselves. While it may seem daunting to have private lessons with a Reiki master, it is really the most ideal thing you can do.

Furthermore, there are many books written by Reiki healers. Some of these books include Amy Z. Rowland's *The Complete Book of Traditional Reiki*, Bodo J. Baginski and Shalila Sharamon's *Reiki Universal Life Energy*, and Phylameana Lila Desy's *Everything Guide to Reiki*.

Training in person at a Reiki center will also put you in contact with people who can guide you on your Reiki journey and show you the most efficient way to develop your practices.

- **Is Reiki affiliated with any religion, and do I have to join a religion to practice Reiki?**

Many modern individuals are beginning to see Buddhism as a way of life rather than a religion. In this sense, Buddhist philosophy provides moral codes and principles that help one live a more meaningful and happier life. Since Reiki originates from Tendai, Qigong, and Mahayana varieties of Buddhism, the Buddhist way of life and codes certainly influence Reiki.

Nonetheless, the codes and morals Reiki derives from Buddhism do not dictate religious principles nor require practitioners to maintain religious beliefs. With that said, Reiki is a spiritual experience. It aims to provide patients, students, teachers, and healers with a link to their higher self. This is not intrinsically rooted in religious notions, but it does essentially focus on a spiritual experience. Some atheists and secularists do not believe in a soul, so they will find it difficult to accept this Reiki principle and practice.

Afterword

REIKI HEALERS IN HISTORY

In the West, we are raised on tales of Jesus using touch to heal the lives of those afflicted with physical ailments, such as blindness. In the East, people are brought up on Buddhist, Shinto, and Taoist philosophies, repeating how Buddha was able to heal those from their physical illnesses.

Two thousand years later, we still know of these great healers and their remarkable feats. While Jesus and Buddha provided their followers and those who met them with much spiritual guidance and relief from physical agony, they also blessed the world with the knowledge that physical touch can be a source of remedy and revival.

However, as their stories pass from generation to generation, we call their feats miracles, and the capability of offering healing through physical touch becomes more and more questionable, and ultimately, unobtainable. It is believed to be a miracle that can only be performed by spiritual leaders or great men. This is when the religions have a monopoly over this practice and we as humans forget our own capacities to perform these very acts.

Reiki has not allowed us to forget. A hundred years ago, when he had a close encounter with death, Mikao Usui realized it is important that we do not forget that our bodies are made of light and energy. And if we are essentially light and energy, then all we need is light and energy and a channel to these two sources to heal. Always remember the wisdom the great healers of our past have blessed us with.

ANCIENT MEDICINE AND MODERN NECESSITY

Unfortunately, we have quite forgotten our close connection to energy and light. Though religions have not always served us well, belief systems such as Hinduism, Buddhism, Taoism, and even Christianity reminded us how necessary it was to be spiritually healthy and to rid the body of toxins.

For example, Lent in the Christian faith aims to remove an individual's harmful habit for 40 days; it is comparable to the two 21-day detoxes performed after the Shoden and Okuden attunements. These belief systems not only placed an emphasis on spiritual cleanliness but on compassion and kindness to others, as well as emotional and psychological well-being, which lives in our minds yet transcends our physical forms to be of immense utility to others.

In years long past, people turned to ancient medicine as a necessity. Both Mikao Usui and Hawayo Takata had close encounters with death that led them to Reiki. It was their desperation for survival that drew them to the practice. Once healed with it, Takata went on to live until the age of eighty (Bennet, p 4). During her long life, she opened Reiki clinics in the US and spread the power of energy and light healing far and wide.

We have made so much progress in regards to increasing the human lifespan, but we have forgotten that energy and light are essential components to our healing. Not all of us have forgotten, though. For example, light therapy is a New Age treatment that can help lessen the impact of seasonal depression. Yet, despite our progress, people are still sick, continuing to consume harmful chemicals and hold onto anger, draining them of their vitality.

People still lead lives where the consumption of harmful toxins is common practice. People ingest copious amounts of sugar, flooding their bodies with artificial but sought-after energy. It is the same with alcohol; even though it slowly and excruciatingly dehydrates their systems, it provides them with the willingness to party late into the night. The next day is another story, though, as their bodies are completely deprived of all nutrients, electrolytes, and energy. It is a high price to pay.

The currency is energy, and it is the only currency we innately need and are now seeking through artificial but unwholesome sources. Our bodies crave sugar because we desire vitality. Remember, though, that on a purely molecular level, we are energy and light. Our cells are nuclei and mitochondria, and our atoms, protons, and electrons.

Somehow, we think that by supplying our bodies with artificial and unsustainable forms of energy like sugar and caffeine, we will be able to replace pure substances such as light and energy. Yes, go on and try to feed a plant some sugar. Surely, if you gave a plant caffeine, it would grow better and more quickly. I am being sarcastic now, but we have to consider biology deeply. Plants need light just like us, and they also need energy just like us.

The currency is always energy. Redbull, Starbucks, and Nestle all know that deep down, you need a boost. But the more you rely on anything but light and energy to restore your vitality, the more these companies have you chained like a dog.

Our crisis in energy is indicated clearly in the rise in stress, burnout, anxiety, and depression. It is not that life has become too much to handle, but that we are deprived of the necessary stamina to handle it. The sad truth is that the more intense the burnout and stress gets, the more we believe we are weak and destined for sickness.

We have forgotten that our ancestors like Usui and Takata once turned to the universe's energy for their lives. If they could do it a hundred years ago, we can surely do it now, and if Jesus and Buddha used the universe's energy as a remedy for physical ailments and spiritual desolation two thousand years ago, we can definitely do it now.

REIKI AS AN ETERNAL SOURCE OF HEALING

Reiki is an instinctual language that we communicate to provide comfort to others. Consider a hug when you really need comforting. Why do you feel like you need a hug sometimes? The emphasis is on the word "need". Remind yourself of the time you last needed a good embrace. Perhaps you heard really bad news and needed the comfort words could not offer. And when you received that hug, maybe it brought you to tears. It opened a channel in your heart that you didn't know existed. Your sensitivity was frightening at that moment, and so you swallowed your tenderness and spent the next few days or years trying not to look at that sensitivity again.

Yet, that sensitivity was a clue. It showed you an area of tenderness that needed your attention. A hug helped because physical touch can heal that. The problem is that after the hug, you neglected that sensitivity and did not seek a channel to provide it with the necessary healing.

Reiki is that channel. The ancient wisdom of Reiki revived by Usui recognizes how our chakras are tender openings. The essence of spiritual vitality is directed through the chakras, giving us healing to the various dimensions of our being: spiritual, psychological, emotional, and physical. Unblocking one chakra generally entails healing an individual in every dimension.

Consider the heart chakra, Anahata; channeling energy to it through a hand position or drawing Shika Sei Ki over the region can soothe palpitations and decrease chest pain. Meditating and reflecting on Shika Sei Ki or contemplating the power of Anahata can soothe loneliness and prepare an individual to love again after a negative romantic encounter.

Reiki for Beginners serves to be a guide to help newcomers incorporate Reiki practices into their everyday lives and into those of their loved ones. Since Reiki has formally been established for more roughly a century, much has been researched and written about it. Furthermore, it has entered the domain of the internet, where information is limitless.

This guide serves not to be an exhaustive discussion on Reiki, nor does it aim to cover all the various Reiki techniques, but it does intend to go over the main concepts and healing approaches, namely attunements, hand positions, spiritual detox, and meditation.

Many Reiki websites and institutions are constantly updating their knowledge. *Reiki for Beginners* intends to complement them. As Reiki is a necessary practice for personal and communal healing, the utility and benefits of the practice should always be underlined and extended to all. However, this guide aims most of all to inform its readers as to why they should choose Reiki as an alternative and holistic healing approach. It aims to explain the practical value of

Reiki while outlining how physical touch, meditation, spiritual cleanliness, and attunement to divinity are not confined to Reiki healing, but rather highlighted by Reiki.

Healing Hands

Our language does provide us with clues on the power of physical touch. We often refer to "healing hands of love" or the "healing hands of God". Oftentimes, God is represented simply as hands while other religious figures such as Jesus are displayed with an emphasis on his hands. What we have inherited is a tradition that acknowledges how significant hands are. The clue is in the phrase "healing hands". It is ancient wisdom that we derive from the days of Buddha, Jesus, and the reign of the Roman Catholic Church during the days of the Western Roman Empire.

The problem is it is not a mainstream medical treatment. Though many medical breakthroughs have been achieved through science, we often enter the pharmaceutical trap, finding relief from one ailment while being burdened with the next. It is not a mainstream alternative yet, but it is a reliable healing system we have used since the dawn of man.

When we have stomach aches or suffer from nausea, to provide relief, we rub our bellies, or even better, get a loved one to do so. When we suspect an injury may be a broken bone, we check the area to see if our suspicions are confirmed. When we or someone we love feels vulnerable, we put our arms around ourselves or our loved ones to form a circle of protection. When we feel a great spasm of pain in our arms, legs, feet, or hands, our immediate reaction is to clutch on to the area. Once the pain subsides, we rub the area to heal it, subconsciously letting blood flow to it. Lastly, if someone cannot sleep, we caress or massage them. If it is a newborn baby, we rock it gently to help with the restlessness.

Healing through hands has become codified in our nature. Like other mammals, we rely on physical touch to care for our young, protect our loved ones, and heal ourselves. We will not lose this ability because it is innate; it is something given to us by the universe in our genes.

We should welcome medical breakthroughs, because one day, they will incorporate physical touch more extensively in their programs. There are already physiotherapists, masseuses, and chiropractors who are in the medical world providing healing to others through "healing hands".

Reiki Responsibility

On a final note, Reiki masters, healers, and practitioners have much responsibility. Firstly, they are working with an intimate space of people who are from walks of life. As Reiki has been exported to the West, it also has to embrace but work with the diversity of Western societies. Some people may be comfortable with attunements, hand positions, and meditations, but not all people will be. As you are in such close physical proximity, you should be mindful of this and open to a variety of patients. Furthermore, you should always do your best to communicate openly with your patients so that they know what to expect.

Secondly, you are not only dealing with patients on a physical but also on spiritual, psychological, and emotional levels. This is a large burden to carry as individuals suffer from a range of psychological and emotional problems. This includes things like trauma, abuse, nihilism, or a lack of self-esteem. To be part of the process that encourages positive change in people's lives is not easy. That being said, it is immensely rewarding.

As a prospective Reiki healer, you are enriching the lives of others on every level. The responsibility of this duty should not be understated. People need healing in times of spiritual crisis. Reiki is one of the few modern-day approaches that provide holistic healing.

Good luck on your Reiki journey!

References

420 Naval Ravikant Quotes to Make You Happy [and Wealthy]. (n.d.). *Wisdom Quotes.* https://wisdomquotes.com/naval-ravikant-quotes/

5 Signs That A Reiki Cleanse Would Benefit You. (2019, June 3). *Crystal Palace Osteopaths & Natural Therapies.* https://www.crystalpalaceosteopaths.co.uk/5-signs-that-a-reiki-cleanse-would-benefit-you/

Achanta, R. (2017, September 28). Reiki Meditation – How To Do And What Are Its Benefits? *Style Craze.* https://www.stylecraze.com/articles/simple-steps-to-practice-reiki-meditation/

Ankh - Egyptian Symbol of Life. (2015, November 5). *NPS.* https://www.nps.gov/afbg/learn/historyculture/ankh.htm

Beaming. (2018). *Rae Jae.* http://raejae.com/reiki/learn-more/what-is-beaming

Bedosky, L. (2020, May 13). Reiki for Beginners FAQs: Everything You Need to Know to Get Started. *Everyday Health.* https://www.everydayhealth.com/reiki/beginners-faqs-everything-you-need-to-know-to-get-started/

Bennet, A. (n.d.). Reiki: Accessing the Human Energetic System. *Mountain Quest Institute.* https://www.academia.edu/17435888/REIKI_Accessing_the_Human_Energetic_System?auto=download&email_work_card=download-paper

Brandis, L. (2013, May 18). Intuitive Reiki. *International Institute for Complementary Therapies.* https://www.iict.co.uk/articles/15-featured-member/1445-intuitive-reiki

Brenner, E. (2016, August 30). Reiki: A Gateway to Healing Mind, Body and Soul. *Natural Awakenings Boston.* https://www.naturalawakeningsboston.com/2016/08/30/251357/reiki-a-gateway-to-healing-mind-body-and-soul

Burgess, L. (2018, November 23). Foot massage techniques and benefits. *Medical News Today.* https://www.medicalnewstoday.com/articles/323790

Can I Learn Reiki Myself? (2016). *Taking Charge of Your Wellbeing.* https://www.takingcharge.csh.umn.edu/can-i-learn-reiki-myself

Classes. (n.d.). *Reiki by Nataki.* http://www.reikibynataki.com/reiki-magnified-healing-classes.html

Code of Ethics of The Reiki Association. (2020). *Association, The Reiki.* https://www.reikiassociation.net/code-of-ethics.php

Cross. (2020). Britannica. https://www.britannica.com/topic/cross-religious-symbol

Dai Ko Myo Reiki Master Symbol And Reiki Level 3 Shinpiden. (2020). *Reiki Scoop.* https://reikiscoop.com/dai-ko-myo-reiki-master-symbol-and-reiki-level-3-shinpiden/

DiGiulio, S. (2018, August 2). How to spot (and deal with) an energy vampire. *NBCnews.* https://www.nbcnews.com/better/health/how-spot-deal-energy-vampire-ncna896251

Elflein, J. (2016, August 16). Stress and burnout - Statistics & Facts. *Statista.* https://www.statista.com/topics/2099/stress-and-burnout/

Exploring Mikao Usui's Teachings. (2014, May 25). *The International House of Reiki.* https://ihreiki.com/blog/exploring_mikao_usuis_teachings/?v=68caa8201064.

Fleming, D. (2018, February 14). Get Your Life Moving in the Right Direction with Reiki. *Reiki Rays.* https://reikirays.com/40783/life-moving-right-direction-reiki/

Giaser. (2020, May 13). Beaming Reiki Technique. *Holy Reiki Fire.* https://www.holyfirereiki.eu/beaming-reiki-technique/

Hawayo Takata – The Woman Who Brought Reiki To The Western World. (2020). *Reiki Scoop.* https://reikiscoop.-

com/hawayo-takata-the-woman-who-brought-reiki-to-the-western-world/

Healthwise Staff. (2019, June 26). Knee Problems and Injuries. *UOFM Health.* https://www.uofmhealth.org/health-library/kneep

Helmich, P. (2020). Sending Healing Energy Across Space and Time: The Practice of Long-Distance Reiki. *Kripalu.* https://kripalu.org/resources/sending-healing-energy-across-space-and-time-practice-long-distance-reiki

History and Traditions of Reiki. (n.d.). *IARP.* https://iarp.org/history-of-reiki/

How Meditation and Reiki can help you stop smoking. (2020). *Reiki-Meditation.co.uk.* https://www.reiki-meditation.-co.uk/how-meditation-and-reiki-can-help-you-stop-smoking/

How to Tell, Buddist or Taoist or Confucian Qigong? (2017, December 29). *One Energy.*

shorturl.at/cwRV9

Hubris. (2020, December 11). *Wikipedia.* https://en.wikipedia.org/wiki/Hubris

Insomnia Statistics. (2018, December 10). *The Good Body.* https://www.thegoodbody.com/insomnia-statistics/

K., J. (n.d.). How much does a reiki session cost? *Thervo.* https://thervo.com/costs/reiki-session-cost

King, M. L. (1963). *Strength to Love*. New York City: Harper & Row.

Kisner, J. (2020, April). Reiki Can't Possibly Work. So Why Does It? The Atlantic. https://www.theatlantic.com/magazine/archive/2020/04/reiki-cant-possibly-work-so-why-does-it/606808/

Learning Reiki. (n.d.). *The International Centre for Reiki Training*. https://www.reiki.org/faqs/learning-reiki

Lipinski, K. (n.d.). Distant Healing and the Human Energy Field. *The International Training Centre*. https://www.reiki.org/articles/distant-healing-and-human-energy-field

Lottery winners who blew the lot. (2020, April 02). *Lovemoney*. https://www.lovemoney.com/gallerylist/64958/lottery-winners-who-blew-the-lot

Lotus, G. (2011). Reiki Really Works: A Groundbreaking Scientific Study. *UCLAhealth*. https://www.ucla-health.org/rehab/workfiles/urban%20zen/research%20articles/reiki_really_works-a_groundbreaking_scientific_study.pdf

Mitochondria. (2014). *Nature.com*. https://www.nature.com/scitable/topicpage/mitochondria-14053590/

More Concerning Reiju. (2005). *James Deacon's Reiki Pages*. https://www.aetw.org/reiki_reiju2.htm

Newman, T. (2017, 6 September). Everything you need to know about reiki. *Medical News Today.* https://www.medical-newstoday.com/articles/308772

Peikon, M. (2019). How Nature Awakens a Meditative State. *Wanderlust.* https://wanderlust.com/journal/how-nature-awakens-a-meditative-state/

Petter, F. A. (n.d.). Understanding Byosen Scanning, Part II. *The International Centre for Reiki Training.* https://wanderlust.com/journal/how-nature-awakens-a-meditative-state/

Price, N. J. (2019, September 29). Universal Symbols: The Calming Sei Hei Ki. *Kindred Spirit.* https://kindredspirit.co.uk/2019/09/29/universal-symbols-the-calming-sei-he-ki/

Price, N. J. (2019, October 13). Universal Symbols: The Distant Healing Hon Sha Ze Sho Nen. *Kindred Spirit.* https://kindredspirit.co.uk/2019/10/13/universal-symbols-the-distant-healing-hon-sha-ze-sho-nen/

Price, N. J. (September, 19 2019). Universal Symbols: The Power of the Cho Ku Rei. *Kindred Spirit.* https://kindredspirit.co.uk/2019/09/15/universal-symbols-the-power-of-the-cho-ku-rei/

Punjabi, P. (2015, November 29). Reiki Symbols Revealed: Shika So and Shika Sei Ki. *Reiki Rays.* https://reikirays.com/28047/reiki-symbols-shika-so-shika-sei-ki/

Qigong. (2020, December 01). *Wikipedia.* https://en.wikipedia.org/wiki/Qigong

Quest, P. (2003). The Attunement Experience. *The International Centre for Reiki Training.* https://www.reiki.org/articles/attunement-experience .

Reiju and Attunements. (n.d.). *International House of Reiki.* https://ihreiki.com/reiki_info/five_elements_of_reiki/reiju_and_attunements/?v=68caa8201064

Reiki 1 Attunement Process. (2020). *Reiki Store.* https://reiki-store.com/

Reiki. (2019). *Encyclopedia.com.* https://www.encyclopedia.com/medicine/divisions-diagnostics-and-procedures/medicine/reiki

Reiki Attunement - The Process and Purpose. (n.d.). *Centre of Excellence.* https://www.centreofexcellence.com/reiki-attunement-process-purpose/

Reiki Hand Positions. (2014, February 24). *The Thirsty Soul.* https://thethirstysoul.com/tag/reiki-hand-positions/

Reiki Level 2 | OKUDEN – What To Expect From It And Its Symbols. (2020). *Reiki Scoop.* https://reikiscoop.com/reiki-level-2-okuden-what-to-expect-from-it-and-its-symbols/.

Reiki Master Attunement. (n.d.). *Balance on Buffalo.* https://balanceonbuffalo.com/reiki/reiki-master-attunement.

Reiki Master Attunement. (n.d.). *International Spiritual Experience.* http://www.internationalspiritualexperience.-

com/reiki-mikao-usui/reiki-attunements/reiki-level-master-attunement

Reiki popularity growing. (2015, July 17). *ABC Action News.* https://www.youtube.com/watch?v=JU9Au7ILRh4

Reiki Self-Treatment: Procedure Details. (2019, March 20). *Cleveland Clinic.* https://my.clevelandclinic.org/health/treatments/21080-reiki-self-treatment/procedure-details

Reiki Sessions – What To Expect. (2020). *IARP.* https://iarp.org/reiki-sessions-what-to-expect/

Sahasrāra Chakra. (2019). *Chakras.* https://www.chakras.net/energy-centers/sahasrara/about-the-sahasrara-chakra

Saleh, N. (2020, July 30). What Is Reiki? *Very Well Mind.* https://www.verywellmind.com/is-reiki-for-real-1123851

Salguero, C. P. (2016). Paging Dr. Dharma. *Tricycle.* https://tricycle.org/magazine/paging-dr-dharma/

Seiheki Chiryo Ho. (2006, August 29). James Deacon's Reiki Pages. http://www.aetw.org/d_seiheiki.html

Snyder, S. (2017, October 2). Chakra Tune-Up: Intro to the Manipura. *Yoga Journal.* https://www.yogajournal.com/yoga-101/intro-navel-chakra-manipura

Stiene, F. (2012, August 17). The Confusion around Reiju. *The International House of Reiki.* https://ihreiki.com/blog/the_confusion_around_reiju/?v=68caa8201064

Suicide Statistics. (2020, March 20). *Befrienders Worldwide.* https://www.befrienders.org/suicide-statistics

Synder, S. (2017, April 13). Chakra Tune-Up: Intro to the Svadhisthana. *Yoga Journal.* https://www.yogajournal.com/yoga-101/intro-sacral-chakra-svadhisthana

The History of Reiki 1865 - 1926. (2011). *Practical Reiki.* https://www.practicalreiki.com/history-of-reiki.html

The Power of Symbols. (2017, May 01). *Innovative Resources.* https://innovativeresources.org/the-power-of-symbols/

The School of Life: An Interview With Alain de Botton. (2019). *The Daily Stoic.* https://dailystoic.com/alain-de-botton/

Third Eye Chakra - Ajna. (n.d.). *Chakras Anatomy.* https://www.chakra-anatomy.com/third-eye-chakra.html

Treating Self or Family. (2020). AMA Association. https://journalofethics.ama-assn.org/article/ama-code-medical-ethics-opinion-physicians-treating-family-members/2012-05

Vishuddha Chakra: The Throat Center. (2020). *The Yoga Sanctuary.* https://www.theyogasanctuary.biz/vishuddha-chakra/

What Are The Reiki Hand Positions And How To Use Them. (2020). *Reiki Scoop.* https://reikiscoop.com/what-are-the-reiki-hand-positions-and-how-to-use-them/

What Is A Reiki Attunement And Why Is It Necessary To Get One. (2020). *Reiki Scoop.* https://reikiscoop.com/what-is-a-reiki-attunement-and-why-is-it-necessary-to-get-one/

What is Holy Fire Reiki? (2019). *Reiki Maya. https://reikimaya.com/what-is-holy-fire-reiki-2/*

What to Expect During and After a Reiki Attunement. (2020). *Clear Heart Healing Arts.* http://www.clearhearthealingarts.com/what-to-expect/

Who Is Mikao Usui And The 3 Things You Have To Know About Him. (2020). *Reiki Scoop.* https://reikiscoop.com/who-is-mikao-usui-and-the-3-things-you-have-to-know-about-him/

Working with affirmations: Seiheki Chiryo Ho. (2017, August 29). *Deborah Reiki.* https://deborahreiki.com/2017/08/29/working-with-affirmations-seiheki-chiryo-ho/

Image References

(2017). Hand Mom Hold Power Energy (Pixabay) [Photo]. https://pixabay.com/photos/hand-mom-hold-power-energy-2634753/

Altmann, G (2017) Galaxy Space Universe Astronautics (Pixabay) [Photo]. Freiburg, Germany. https://pixabay.com/illustrations/galaxy-space-universe-astronautics-2643089/

Altmann, G (2018) Beyond Death Faith Sky God (Pixabay) [Photo]. Freiburg, Germany. https://pixabay.com/illustrations/galaxy-space-universe-astronautics-2643089/

Chanel, A (2017). Human People Images & Pictures (Unsplash) [Photo]. Boynton Beach, USA. https://unsplash.com/photos/RJCslxmvBcs

Ferreria, M. Dai Ko Myo (Pinterest) [Photo]. https://za.pinterest.com/pin/457467274652963485/

Goldman, M. Instructional pictures demonstrating hand placements for conducting a basic Reiki self treatment. (Pinterest)   [Photo].   https://za.pinterest.com/pin/497155246359434893/

Goldman, M. Instructional pictures demonstrating hand placements for conducting a basic Reiki self treatment. (Pinterest)   [Photo].   https://za.pinterest.com/pin/497155246359434919/

Goldman, M. Instructional pictures demonstrating hand placements for conducting a basic Reiki self treatment. (Pinterest)   [Photo].   https://za.pinterest.com/pin/497155246359434901/.

Hurst, B. Chakra Oils Seven Chakras Set. (Pinterest) [Photo]. https://za.pinterest.com/pin/985231158415577/.

Halacious (2017). A ball of energy with electricity beaming all over the place. [Photo]. https://unsplash.com/photos/OgvqXGL7XO4.

Irina L (2018). Woman Relaxation Portrait. (Pixabay) [Photo]. Los Angeles, USA. https://pixabay.com/photos/woman-relaxation-portrait-3053492/.

Pilney, C (2014). Reiki Symbols (Pinterest) [Photo]. https://za.pinterest.com/pin/684336105858801126/.

Ramiah, B. Twelve Hand Positions Used for Conducting a Reiki Session: Crown and Top of the Head (Pinterest) [Photo]. https://za.pinterest.com/pin/554013191638825263/.

Ramiah, B. How to Position Your Hands for Self-Healing with Reiki: Neck Collarbone and Heart (Pinterest) [Photo].

shorturl.at/mqCN8

Rübig, J (2013). Wellness Massage Reiki. (Pixabay) [Photo]. Haßfurt, Germany. https://pixabay.com/photos/wellness-massage-reiki-285590/.

ScienceFreak (2020). Chakras (Pixabay) [Photo]. Germany. https://unsplash.com/photos/A87rz-MJN_E .

SecondFromTheSun0 (2015). Massage Healing Woman Treatment. [Photo]. https://pixabay.com/photos/massage-healing-woman-treatment-835468/ .

Socha, A (2020). Buddha Statue Thailand Buddhism (Pixabay) [Photo]. Stockholm, Sweden. https://pixabay.com/photos/buddha-statue-thailand-buddhism-5410319/ .

Street, J (2019). Buddha. [Photo]. https://unsplash.com/photos/88IMbX3wZmI .

Wahid, A (2018). Taktsang Monastery (Unsplash) [Photo]. Taktsang, Bhutan. https://unsplash.com/photos/A87rz-MJN_E .

Conclusion

I do hope you enjoyed this book and learned a lot from it, but before you go, I wanted to ask you for one small favor.

If you enjoyed reading this book, could you please consider posting a review on the platform?

Posting a review is the best and easiest way to support the work of independent authors like me.

It would mean a lot to me to hear from you.

>> Leave a review on Amazon US <<

>> Leave a review on Amazon UK <<

Emily Oddo

Made in the USA
Middletown, DE
15 October 2023

40874610R00258